Miracle Collapse

University of Nebraska Press · Lincoln & London

Miracle Collapse

The 1969 Chicago Cubs

DOUG FELDMANN

Foreword by Don Kessinger

Library of Congress
Cataloging-in-Publication Data

Feldmann, Doug, 1970–
Miracle collapse: the 1969
Chicago Cubs / Doug Feldmann;
foreword by Don Kessinger.
p.   cm.
Includes bibliographical references
and index.
ISBN-13: 978-0-8032-2026-3
(cloth: alk. paper)
ISBN-10: 0-8032-2026-X
(cloth: alk. paper)
1. Chicago Cubs (Baseball team)—
History—20th century. I. Title.
GV875.C6F44   2006
796.357′640977311—dc22
2006000129

To my family and friends,
who have given me more
than I deserve.

CONTENTS

ILLUSTRATIONS

In July 1993 I was coaching baseball at my alma mater the University of Mississippi. While on a recruiting trip to the Chicago area, I was sitting alone down the first base line watching some prospective student-athletes play baseball. A very nice lady came up to me and asked, "Are you Don Kessinger?" When I answered in the affirmative, she said, "Happy Birthday." I was amazed that she would know it was indeed my birthday, and I asked her how she knew. Her simple reply was, "I am a Cub fan." It had been eighteen years since my last game with the Cubs, in 1975, but such is the nature of baseball's greatest fans.

Doug Feldmann has written a book on perhaps Chicago's most beloved team, the 1969 Cubs. Even though we did not win the pennant that year, losing to the dreaded New York Mets, it was an unbelievable summer in Chicago. Chapter after chapter and page after page of this book brought back memories, some that had long since retreated in my mind. It is a joy for me to recall those days spent with such great teammates and friends.

If you asked ten players on that team what happened to us late in the 1969 season, you very well might get ten different answers. However, I think each would tell you about the special relationship that existed between the players, and about the special relationship between the players and the Cub fans. I hope as you read this account of that magical season, you will in some small way feel how great it was for those of us who were there.

This book is a personal journey, allowing me to experience all over again the peaks and valleys of 1969. Doug has precisely captured the emotions of leading the National League for most of the year and then watching that lead slip away in a painful September in Chicago. What hurts the most is our failure to finish what we started for the great fans of the Chicago Cubs.

Don Kessinger

ACKNOWLEDGMENTS

The author would like to thank the following writers and newspapers, whose game reports provided wonderful perspectives for this book: George Langford, Richard Dozer, David Condon, Robert Markus, and Edward Prell from the *Chicago Tribune*, and various writers from the *Chicago Sun-Times*, the *Chicago Daily News*, the *New York Times*, the *New York Post*, the *Washington Post*, and *The Sporting News*.

The author would also like to thank the following for their assistance: the campus library of Indiana University, the National Baseball Hall of Fame and Museum, WGN Radio in Chicago, Mr. Mike Korcek, the Society for American Baseball Research, and Mr. Don Kessinger.

INTRODUCTION

> For the first time in a Cubbie gen-
> eration, without fear of ridicule or
> confinement to an asylum, I can
> safely say that I expect a National
> League pennant this year.
>
> —Jay Mariotti, *Chicago Sun-Times*,
> February 18, 2004

Over the last hundred years there has been no shortage of philosophy on the connective metaphor of baseball to "life." In addition to serving all of the emotions that exist within the human
condition, baseball has also long been viewed as an instrument
for bringing subcultures of the United States together in har-
mony. Other institutions have tried to do the same, but few
have been as successful. As one example, educational reformer
Horace Mann claimed in the 1840s that a common elementary
school experience for all citizens would be "the great equalizer
of society; the balance wheel of the social machinery." In relationship to baseball, the idea of a level social playing field has

been described no better than by President Ronald Reagan in a speech he delivered shortly after his final term in office. Addressing a group of aspiring sports broadcasters, he asked the audience to picture a downtown corporate office building late at night, with most of the workers gone for the day. A custodian is emptying the wastebaskets in each of the rooms, while the president of the company is working diligently on some final paperwork inside an office. In the midst of their jobs, however, both individuals are drawn to a radio that is sitting on a cabinet in the hallway. The home team is playing an important baseball game, and the two men stare transfixed at the motionless black box as the sounds of the ballpark pour forth. For a single instant, socioeconomic class is washed away as both men cheer wildly for a big hit, holler with anger at a bad call by the umpire, and question the removal of the starting pitcher by the home team manager. It is a moment in time when race, age, gender, and social class do not matter—the only thing that does is allegiance to the home team.

This scene exemplifies the small, nearly unnoticeable events that draw people together within the great exchange of individuals within the United States of America. More of such lessons were needed in the turbulent American society of the 1960s, a society burdened by growing mistrust between the "Establishment" and the younger generation, as issues of war, poverty, and civil rights dominated the American consciousness.

But once again—as had been the case during the Great Depression, World War II, and the Korean Conflict—baseball helped stabilize American society by providing a diversion from the unpleasant issues that overshadowed everyday living. In 1941, with Joe DiMaggio of the New York Yankees chasing the consecutive-game hitting record, a new phrase entered the nation's "cultural literacy," as former University of Virginia English professor E. D. Hirsch calls changes in social dialect. While stopping at a roadside café in Rolla or Omaha, in Durham or Dallas, the traveler always asked the same question: "Did he get one today?" In 1969—a year that culminated a decade of national unrest—different types of people could walk into the very same cafés and ask, "Did the Cubs win today?" It was a topic on the minds of many, and—in line with Dr. Hirsch's definition of cultural literacy—one needed to know how to "speak the language" to stay in communication with the rest of society.

In writing books about baseball seasons, I have always tried to weave the happenstances of sport into the milieu of society at the given time. Baseball, as much as any other American institution, places our lives in an historical context that enriches our existence and serves to remind us that our lives are divided into increments of time. I pull the stories for the following pages from the events of 1969, a year for which anyone old enough to remember can recall his or her circumstances in one of the most uncertain epochs in the nation's history. Like most annual occasions, the arrival of the baseball playoffs, the Super Bowl, or New Year's Eve prompts us to remember the same event from the previous year and to mark the progress in our lives over the past 365 days. For while we sometimes can't remember the names of all our relatives, we can certainly remember where we were when Vinatieri made the kick or when Bartman and Alou collided.

Miracle Collapse

1

The Lip, the Windy City, and a Society on the Move

> Leo Durocher is a man with an infantile capacity for immediately making a bad thing worse.
>
> —Branch Rickey

The crackle of the voices through the microphone could barely be heard over the airwaves. WDAP was just a tiny radio station on Chicago's North Side, struggling to survive, when on June 1, 1924, a man named Elliott Jenkins from the *Chicago Tribune* newspaper marched in and announced that things were about to change. The station's facilities soon received a complete overhaul—including its call letters. Jenkins spoke to the masses with a few, simple words that would change Chicago broadcasting forever.

"This is WGN, formerly WDAP."

The letters were short for "World's Greatest Newspaper," a moniker that was placed at the top of every edition of the *Tribune*. The paper's venture into radio had actually begun three years earlier, when the city's first station, Westinghouse's KYW, starting receiving many of its stories and market reports from the newsrooms of the *Tribune*. From the time that KYW opened for business until WGN took over, the sale of radio sets in Chicago had increased fivefold, as the Tribune Company had found a great investment opportunity in another—albeit competitive—medium. WGN's first order of business in the summer of 1924 was to cover the Republican National Convention from Cleveland and the Democratic National Convention from New York. In October of that year WGN would broadcast its first professional baseball game, a crosstown match-up between the Chicago Cubs of the North Side and the Chicago White Sox of the South.

Another powerful early station in the city, WMAQ, received the first loosely defined "rights" to broadcast both Cubs and White Sox home games in 1924, although the concept of property law in sports broadcasting had not yet surfaced. It was the work of Hal Totten that secured the "contract" for WMAQ. Totten, a young writer with the *Chicago Daily News*, had personally broadcast almost every Cubs and White Sox home game that season, an amazing feat. Although broadcasting alone, Totten still had plenty of company, as small-scale, "pirated" broadcasts were being heard around Major League parks in addition to the formal broadcasts from radio stations covering the games. One of the more famous pirates in the early days of baseball on the radio was Tom Convey in St. Louis, who sat atop the YMCA building across the street from center field at Sportsman's Park, home of the two local teams, the Cardinals and Browns. Convey was constantly being chased away by Cardinals owner Sam Breadon, who wanted no outside transmission of his team's games whatsoever. Since no station held exclusivity rights for broadcasting the contests, listeners could tune into any number of announcers who seemed appealing. By the end of the 1920s nearly ten stations at any given time were piping the sounds of professional baseball in Chicago through the airwaves.

Radio was a growing, amazing phenomenon that promised to change the nation. The public's fascination began with station KDKA in Pittsburgh when a group of individuals first broadcast the results of the United States presidential election on November 2, 1920, from the top of the Westinghouse building in East Pittsburgh. They used one hundred watts to announce to a handful of listeners the news—received via updates phoned in from the *Pittsburgh Post* newspaper—that Warren Harding had defeated James Cox. Eager to learn their broadcast's geographic radius, the announcers strongly encouraged any listeners to call and reveal their locations. The historic event had its origins four years earlier with the construction of a special transmitter in the garage of a Westinghouse engineer. Soon after the election results were broadcast from atop the building, the novelty of the radio set had spread quickly, soon becoming a veritable family member in most U.S. homes. Historical records indicate that around four hundred thousand sets were in use in private residences and stores in 1922, a figure that exploded to 4 million in 1925 and to 13 million by 1930—comprising nearly two-thirds of American households.

However, baseball broadcasting of the hometown Pirates by KDKA remained quite primitive. A "runner boy" would sit atop the wall at old Forbes Field and scribble the happenings of the game onto a piece of paper. He would then drop the paper to another boy, who would sprint to a nearby telephone to tell the station the "play-by-play." Using a similar method in 1921, WJZ in New York broadcast the World Series over the radio for the first time. The widespread arrival of radio in the 1920s—although still in its infancy—reinforced a long-held fear of Major League Baseball owners who envisioned empty, profitless ballparks, with the masses staying at their comfortable homes while being told about the game through the microphone.

It took a forward-thinking owner of the Cubs named William Wrigley to change attitudes about broadcasts and, in turn, alter the future of sports forever. In contrast to the philosophy of his contemporaries, Wrigley imagined substantially growing the fan base by bringing the ball game into homes. He wanted entire households to become fans of the sport—and, thereafter, paying customers. Wrigley firmly believed in the proliferation of radio broadcasts for baseball, and he passed his aggressive pursuit of airtime on to his son, Phil, who enjoyed a great surge in attendance at the family's Los Angeles park in the Pacific

Coast League (PCL) after putting the PCL games on the radio. The Wrigley family, who had made a fortune in the chewing gum business, now applied their successful business principles to marketing their baseball teams. William never wanted to limit creativity—for example, he was also the first to have a "Ladies' Day" at his ballpark, whereby women would be admitted free of charge (typically on Fridays). Although not receiving any admissions revenue, the club would instead enjoy increased beverage, food, and cigarette sales at the park with the extra customers. Pressure from women's groups ended the practice by the 1980s, but with the idea, William Wrigley had accomplished what he had set out to do: use the radio to make entire families of fans at home and, in doing so, to "invite" all members of the family—not just the lone man of the house—out to the stadium to see a game for themselves. Not long after putting his plan into action, Wrigley became the first owner to have all of his team's games sent over the airwaves. Almost immediately, stations began lining up at his door for the privilege.

Before Walter "Red" Barber took a job as a broadcaster with the Cincinnati Reds in 1934, he rode on a bus all night to Chicago and tried for an interview at WGN but was denied. After two seasons in Cincinnati the twenty-seven-year-old Barber became the announcer in 1935 for the first networked radio broadcast of the World Series between the Cubs and the Detroit Tigers. He remembered the experience well: "Nobody was even thinking about television in 1935. But that [the World Series] was the first sporting event that was ever on the Mutual Broadcasting network. That was a network then of four stations: WGN in Chicago, CKLW in Detroit, WOR in New York and, of course, the mighty, half-million watt transmitter of WLW in Cincinnati." Baseball fans in Chicago regularly heard the voices of Pat Flanagan on WBBM, Bob Elson and Quin Ryan on WGN, and even comedian Joe E. Brown, who made appearances on various stations from time to time. Ryan was a local product, brought into the WGN studios from the campus of Northwestern University, where he had been a drama student. Cubs games were easily heard throughout the Midwest, including the far reaches of rural Iowa—where a young man named Ronald Reagan described the action from Des Moines via Western Union telegraphs.

Elson would serve as the Cubs' primary broadcaster from 1939 to 1942. After his enlistment in the Navy during World War Two, he returned to Chicago to cover the White Sox. Those who heard him would almost invariably speak of his mesmerizing, trademark monotone. Elson would sometimes purposely drift away from the baseball game and regale listeners on, for example, the fabulous session of gin rummy that he had had with his neighbors the other evening. In later years he was likened to Bob Prince of the Pirates, who was said to be able to simultaneously eat an apple, read a book, and broadcast a ball game. During the war years Elson was replaced in the Cubs and White Sox radio booth by an enterprising young reporter from Peoria, Illinois, named Jack Brickhouse. With the exception of spending 1946 with the New York Giants, Brickhouse remained as the chief announcer of the North Siders until passing the sounds of the game over to Harry Caray in 1982, who had just spent eleven seasons with the White Sox. As Brickhouse began to do more work with the television broadcasts of Cubs baseball, it became Vince Lloyd's turn to be the radio play-by-play voice, joining the team in 1965 as WGN established itself as the "voice of the Cubs."

§

Like WGN, another institution in Chicago that had gained national fame through the middle of the century and into the 1960s was the Edgewater Beach Hotel, the premier lodging and entertainment destination in the Windy City. Located on Chicago's grand North Shore along Lake Michigan in the 5300 block of North Sheridan Road, the unmistakable complex with its pink buildings would blare happy music and offer dancing long into the weekend nights. The big bands of Jerry Gray, Frankie Carle, Benny Goodman, and many others would thrill patrons for hours on end. If it was summertime and the weather was right, Gray would open his set with his famous number "Dancing in the Dark" while couples took their foxtrots outside the building to the Beachwalk. An hour-long radio show called *Your Saturday*

Dance Date would join the action live at Edgewater Beach for the last half of the show, after sending listeners tunes from New York in the first half. Indeed, if you were accompanied to the Edgewater, it was a certainly a special date—especially if you were treated to dinner beforehand in the exquisite Marine Dining Room. WGN had done its first primitive broadcasting from the Edgewater in March 1924, only months before it would take over WDAP to firmly establish itself in the city. The Edgewater was also where National League teams stayed when coming to Chicago to play the Cubs. "Club officials enjoyed the location, a five-minute bus ride to Wrigley Field; the players loved the Edgewater Beach nightlife," writer John Theodore noted. Theodore, in his book *Baseball's Natural*, detailed the perilous fate of former Cub Eddie Waitkus. Waitkus was shot on the twelfth floor of the Edgewater in June 1949 by Ruth Ann Steinhagen, a young fan who had become infatuated with the player. Ultimately, Waitkus would recover from his wound and face Steinhagen in court before resuming his baseball career.

Doomed by civic progress, the Edgewater was eventually cut off from its beachfront location with the expansion of Lake Shore Drive. The famous resort hotel shut its doors in 1967. Demolition began in 1969 and was completed the following year.

The demolition of the Edgewater was another symbol of a changing era, of the discarding of the old and subsequent welcoming of the new, particularly in urban America. In the early part of the 1960s, more and more citizens were turning to electronic media for their information on local and world news, athletics, weather, and cultural interests. It was a shift that had been both foreseen and decried by famed syndicated New York sportswriter Grantland Rice half a century earlier. Rice had the privilege of broadcasting that first World Series in 1921, but even as he spoke, he felt as though he were undermining and even dooming his beloved craft of the pen. He passed away in 1954, mercifully before grasping the full weight of the airwave overhaul to come.

As the sixties rolled on, and nightly images of war were seen in American homes for the first time, the new cultural tide of television strengthened. With the help of electronic media, society seemed to change overnight. Mainstream change was everywhere—if change hadn't hit a community or institution yet, it was on its way. A fellow broadcaster of Caray's with the St. Louis Cardinals during the 1960s, Jack Buck, reflected on how even professional baseball players got caught up in the turbulence of the times. Describing a scene during the 1969 season in his autobiography, *That's a Winner!*, Buck wrote: "Once at O'Hare Airport in Chicago, we got off the plane and walked through the terminal. The players were carrying music, wearing sandals and t-shirts. One of the players was wearing Levis without undershorts and had a hole in the seat of his pants. I remember thinking, 'These are the Cardinals?' Almost all of them had long hair, some wore earrings. Other ballclubs were just as motley looking, depending on their leadership and the control the manager and owner had over the players. They were at the age to be rebellious, and they wanted to join in the activities going on around them. They wanted more freedom, and that's when Marvin Miller entered the picture with the players' union and started putting pressure on the owners."

Mr. Buck's point was well-taken. Major League baseball players—who were once mysterious, faceless figures whose activities were known only through newspaper articles—were now Everyday Joes, seen regularly on television and blending in with the other young people who chose to take part in antiwar rallies, marijuana legalization campaigns, and free-love persuasions. The halls of education—at the elementary, high school, and even college levels—were now being invaded with the "Radical Relevant Curriculum," brought by left-wing school reformers seeking to supposedly "free" the student from the "jails" (schools) and "jailers" (teachers) of society. Naturally, the labor front was not immune to the fury of the day, a battleground that was completely new to baseball. After an unprecedented stand by Marvin Miller, players began to push for collective bargaining agreements for their contracts. By the end of 1968 the Major League Baseball Players' Relation Committee and the newly formed "Players' Association" came to what was called an "initial agreement," though it hardly served to prevent future bad tidings. Miller had taken over the players' leadership in 1966, shortly after sharpening his legal teeth on new contracts for the United Steelworkers.

But while the face of the Major League player became more obscure, tangible changes to the game were also taking place in 1969. New to the American League were the Seattle Pilots and the Kansas City Royals, while the National League welcomed the San Diego Padres and the Montreal Expos. Such expansion was seen as a continued, progressive advance for baseball, which was finally stretching to, literally, all four corners of the country (with Florida still enjoying only the stint of spring training, however). And with the expansion, the leagues each split into two six-team divisions for 1969. For the first time ever, two clubs from each league would qualify for the postseason, as a "league championship series" would decide the pennant winner in each circuit. More immediately noticeable would be the shaving of the pitcher's mound to two-thirds of its former size, lowering the crest from fifteen inches high down to ten. Furthermore, the umpires were directed to shrink the strike zone for the 1969 season, with the top of the knee (as opposed to the center of the knee) and the armpit (as opposed to the shoulder) now forming the frame for a pitched strike. In a prelude to the homer-happy days of the late 1990s and beyond, baseball officials feared losing fans to the ever-increasing popularity of televised football games and other shows and thus sought to increase the offensive output—and presumably the excitement—of the games for fans by giving increased advantages to the hitters.

Regardless of the rule changes, social circumstances, or other distractions, the Cubs loved playing for their owner, Phil Wrigley. One team member from 1969 once said, "If all the owners had been as fair to the players as Mr. Wrigley was, we wouldn't need a Players' Association." Wrigley, like his father, had come to grips with the way the game was changing as the 1970s were quickly approaching. "Baseball is too much of a sport to be called a business," he pronounced, "and too much of a business to be called a sport." He wanted an old-school manager to run his club, one who respected the game and fostered respect in his players.

The perfect such candidate was waiting for an opportunity in the middle in the sixties, and he was given one.

Leo "The Lip" Durocher, on October 25, 1965, was finally back running a ball club after being hired by Wrigley as manager of the Cubs and being offered a three-year contract. Some in the Chicago writers' guild were wary about Durocher's employment. "Durocher is in for a savage roasting in the local press," *Tribune* writer Robert Markus would later warn. "A better loser than he is a winner, Durocher has made nothing but enemies on his way back to the top. And every one of them is going to be ready with a verbal knife to stick in Leo's ribs on the agonizing plunge back down."

Born in West Springfield, Massachusetts, in 1905, Durocher had been raised in a strict Catholic home. "The Church played an enormously important part of our lives," he recalled. "My brothers and I were altar boys. You don't ever get away from that kind of upbringing. . . . In all the years I was traveling around playing ball, I very rarely missed a Sunday morning mass. When I was divorced, I lost the right to have my confession heard and receive communion, and that hurt me. I found it very painful to sit there and watch everybody else get up and file up to the altar. And so, while I still feel the urge to go to church from time to time, I always leave without a sense of fulfillment." Years after making this statement, Durocher would return to Mass every Saturday night, lighting candles and taking up the collection as his way of being involved.

A man who had nearly seen it all in professional baseball, Durocher began his big league career in 1925 with the New York Yankees. As roommate of the legendary Babe Ruth for a time, Leo was playfully nicknamed "The All-American Out" by the slugger for his good-field/little-hit skills. After becoming one of the better-fielding shortstops in baseball with the St. Louis Cardinals of the 1930s, Durocher earned his first opportunity to lead a Major League ball club when the Brooklyn Dodgers signed him as their player-manager in 1939. Two seasons later he led the Dodgers to their first pennant in over twenty years. In 1948 he took control of the crosstown Giants and went on to lead them to two pennants and a World Series title. In 1955 Durocher did not receive the contract settlement he sought with the Giants and instead started a brief career in the broadcast booth. He returned to the field as a coach with the Dodgers in 1961.

Leo became an immediate celebrity in Chicago, with his mere presence suggesting to Cub fans that the old days of losing were dead and gone. Brickhouse was one of the many who were initially impressed. He wrote: "When I first knew Durocher, he was one of the sharpest riverboat gamblers I ever saw in my life. You didn't have to tell Leo if a guy had thrown 87 pitches; he knew whether a guy was tired or not." To capitalize on the club's new popularity, Wrigley sent Durocher on a public relations campaign that stretched north to Milwaukee, west to the Quad Cities and Peoria, and south to Joliet, all in an effort to solidify the growing fan base in Cubland. Everyone soon discovered that timidity in making a player transaction was not part of Durocher's makeup. "Back up the truck" became Leo's favorite phrase in Chicago in 1966, as he promised to rid the North Side of whatever vestiges of lethargy remained from the regimes of Bob Kennedy and Lou Klein, his predecessors (Leo's standard phrase to a struggling team member was "You'll play in Podunk before you play here"). No job was safe, as the warning went out to youngsters and veterans alike. As evidence, only five starters from the 1965 club were on the roster for the following season. Why, he was asked, did he even bother to come to an inept club anyway? "That's why I'm here," Durocher answered. "To find out *why* the Cubs are an eighth-place team."

Changes in the club's fortunes would not occur immediately, however. Durocher's first season at the helm—1966—would be the twentieth consecutive year that the Cubs had finished in the lower half of the National League, an infamous record that Durocher would not allow to continue. He also warned the manager of the White Sox, Eddie Stanky, that he had better stay in his part of town. "I've already told Stanky that the North Side of Chicago belongs to me, and me alone," Durocher staunchly announced to the press upon taking the job. "If he dares to step into my territory, I'll have him tossed into the Chicago River wearing a new concrete kimono." Stanky would leave Chicago in the middle of the 1968 season and soon after appear as the head baseball coach at the University of South Alabama.

Durocher was as blunt on the guest-speaker circuit as he was with the media. Once, when talking at an after-dinner affair for a church, he was questioned by a man in the audience about a managerial move that had gone awry in a recent game. He replied, "If you'd come down to the dugout before I did it, and told me that it wasn't going to work, I'd have tried something else. I could win 150 games a year if they'd let me replay the losses." Durocher loved the limelight, and the social opportunities that came with it. Dean Martin was a close personal friend, and Frank Sinatra became a companion as well. As one writer described Leo in 1969, "He's over 60, looks 50, and acts 40."

When describing his competitive demeanor on the field, Durocher was figured by one Chicago observer to be "the kind of fellow who'd stick a knife in your heart while you weren't looking." When it came to his stealing players from other teams in trades, Leo was considered to be a fair man. "Never cheat the other guy," he advised when dealing for players with rival clubs. "Whenever you make a trade, give the other guy a good ballplayer who you think will help him, because you may want to go back and deal again. Branch Rickey's theory was it's better to trade a man a year too soon than a year too late, and I agree with that." And Durocher's search for prospects—especially pitchers—knew no bounds. There was once an eighty-year-old sandlot pitcher in Washington DC by the name of Milton Kronheim who threw the baseball around every Sunday afternoon in a men's league. He received a signed letter from Durocher that read: "Understand that you are one of the brightest prospects around Washington. The next time you are in Chicago, give me a call so I can look at you."

Given his experience as a Major League player, coach, and manager since 1925, many people asked Durocher whom he believed to be the best player he ever saw. "Willie Mays," he replied quickly and convincingly to one such query. "Stan Musial couldn't run or throw with Mays, and didn't have Willie's power. A sound Mickey Mantle may have come close. Joe DiMaggio? Just a thin piece of paper separates Mays and DiMaggio. When I first got Mays with the Giants, we had the Indians as spring training partners. I told Tris Speaker—the Hall-of-Famer who was coaching the Indians—that Mays was the greatest ever." Speaker didn't immediately agree with Durocher, but after twenty games played that spring between the two clubs, Speaker came up to him and said, "Leo, you're right about that Willie Mays."

To get the Cubs to the top, Durocher soon crafted a coaching staff to reflect his baseball values and the type of game he wanted to play. He hired Joe Becker as the pitching coach at the start of the 1967 season, a man who at the time had fourteen years of professional coaching experience, primarily with the Dodgers and Cardinals. Durocher's other assistants for 1969 would be Verlon Walker, Herman Franks, Pete Reiser, and Joey Amalfitano. Reiser had been Durocher's star center fielder on the pennant-winning Dodger team of 1941. The thirty-five-year-old Amalfitano had finished up a ten-year Major League career in 1967 with the Cubs, although he never achieved stardom. Right after one of his greatest moments at the plate, he knew it would not last long enough. "My folks are touring Italy, visiting their folks," he explained. "By the time they get word of my grand slam, I'll probably be back on the bench." Everyone Durocher hired—and everything he did—had a purpose toward winning the pennant. Being of the "old school," Durocher was typically superstitious, seeking an advantage toward winning in even the most inane means. For example, he permitted only one designated player to catch the infield practice ball before each inning started when the first or third baseman threw it toward the dugout. "Yes, Leo was very superstitious," one of his players remembered. "He would chase the batboy out of the dugout if he moved the fungo bats from one end of the rack to the other." To Leo Durocher, baseball was simply one of life's perfect chances to show how gaining an advantage, in any form, was as flavorful as achieving the victory itself.

"I was just a guy who wanted to win," Durocher said in reflection in his later years. "And I would've taken your teeth to do it."

2

Building a Contender

> Some guys are admired for "coming to play," as the saying goes. I prefer those who come to kill.
>
> —Leo Durocher

"Don't fear—this is the year," the Chicago Cubs first baseman had said in his typically smooth meter in previewing 1968. The Cubs had the longest pennant drought of any nonexpansion National League team, going on twenty-three years, and Ernie Banks had been there for sixteen of them. As the 1968 season began, there was some concern about the internal stability of major cities in the United States in the aftermath of the assassination of Martin Luther King Jr. on April 4. With Opening Day for the Major Leagues scheduled for April 10, many were fearing rekindled rioting and looting in city streets. But Brickhouse instead implored the Chicago populace to "forget your worries and come out to Wrigley" as the nation reeled from political and social uncertainty. In a similar tone, newly installed Major League Baseball commissioner Bowie Kuhn kept a positive attitude. "I have a dream about baseball," Kuhn said, paraphrasing King's famous words. "It can build bridges between people of all colors. It can build bridges to countries, as it has built bridges to Canada, Japan, and South America. And I think it can build bridges between ideologies. I'm fascinated by reports of radio listenership in Cuba. And I wonder if this, in some way, can't build a bridge between America and Cuba."

Nonetheless, the hot summer of '68 would still see conflict in the cities and small towns across America, as some people seemed to hardly notice the Cardinals emerging as the National League champions for the second consecutive year. St. Louis pitcher Bob Gibson dominated the league's hitters with a 1.12 earned run average, Don Drysdale of the Los Angeles Dodgers smashed the consecutive scoreless-innings streak with 58 (including six straight shutouts), and Denny McLain of the Detroit Tigers became the first pitcher since Dizzy Dean (Durocher's teammate) with the Cardinals in 1934 to win 30 games in a season. The dominance of these men and others led, in part, to the owners' approval of lowering the pitching mound five inches for the 1969 season. Scoring in the National League also had dropped an aggregate 641 runs from 1967 to 1968, providing yet another prompt for officials to make the move. It didn't matter one way or another to Durocher, however. "If a man can pitch, he can pitch off this table," he asserted at a speaking engagement. "If he can't pitch, it won't do him any good to stand on Pike's Peak."

Finishing in third place in 1968 (a full thirteen games behind the Cardinals) was actually an admirable feat for the Cubs; they had leapt up from ninth place at one point and had crafted the best record in the National League for the second half of the season. But the team certainly had overall weaknesses as well, primarily in the inconsistency of the pitching staff. A writer covering the Cubs for the *Tribune*, Richard Dozer, complained that one particular starting pitcher, Ken Holtzman, was around "only half the time" in 1968, a major reason for the team's fade. But taking the field for the Cubs of '69 would be a veteran-laden club, just as Durocher had always wanted. Going into that year he felt that the Cubs were solid at every position, in the front line of the bullpen, and now in the starting staff as well. What Durocher didn't have—and he knew it—was depth. Still, with their work in 1967 and 1968, the Cubs had pieced together their first back-to-back winning campaigns since 1945 and 1946—the former being the date of their last National League title. It was a team full of seasoned leaders, hungry for a pennant in a city that was starved for a World Series on the North Side.

Behind the plate was as a man as solid as they come, Randy Hundley, the leader of the leaders and a Durocher favorite. Leo did not believe in a platoon system; rather, he relied on putting his best eight position players out in the field—the draining catcher's position included—and then leaving them there for the rest of the summer. "If a man had a slight injury or was just plain tired," Cubs pitcher Fergie Jenkins noted, "Leo didn't want to hear about it. He just rubbed a man's nose in the dirt and sent him back out there. You played until you dropped." To this end Hundley responded in 1968 by setting a Major League record with 160 games caught, 147 of which he played from beginning to end. He was somewhat upstaged by a rookie in Cincinnati named Johnny Bench, however, who set a record that season for first-year players with 154 games behind the plate. By 1969 even Durocher's loyalty to his own man couldn't hide his admiration for Bench. "Bench is the greatest catcher since Gabby Hartnett," Durocher plainly told Arthur Daley of the *New York Times*. "He is a magician with a glove and throws like Hartnett, almost handcuffing infielders with the force of his throws." Bench was from Binger, Oklahoma, population six hundred; when a writer asked him exactly where that was, Bench said, "Two miles from the sign on the highway marked, 'Resume Speed.'"

But as for the Cubs, Durocher had no plans to share the position with anyone else. "Relief for Hundley?" he asked when questioned about potential backups. "He came to catch. You couldn't get his uniform off with a razor." At first the catcher wasn't too ecstatic about all the responsibility being heaped on him, but over time he grew to thrive on it. "My first year, Leo drove me nuts," Hundley remembered. "I thought, 'If this is major league baseball, I don't want it, I don't need it, take this job and shove it.' My second year, he turned it over to me and said, 'Randy, you're my manager on the field, and whatever you say goes.'"

Durocher explained how Hundley grew as a catcher. "When Hundley first came up, he had a reputation for not being able to hit a curve ball. Well, all of a sudden I realized that when he was catching, he'd be calling for an awful lot of curves. He figured that since he couldn't hit curve balls, nobody else could either. But he's learned, and now he calls a great game." The manager continued: "He caught every game but two last year, and those two games he was like a caged animal, walking to the bullpen, back to the dugout, swinging a bat; he didn't know what to do with himself. People keep asking me why I make him catch both games of a doubleheader. What the hell am I supposed to do? He wants to play, so I let him play."

Hundley had been acquired with pitcher Bill Hands from the San Francisco Giants back on December 2, 1965, for Don Landrum, Lindy McDaniel, and Jim Rittwage. It was a deal that at the time seemed to heavily favor the Giants, seemingly yet another in a long line of trades in which the Cubs always got the short end. Both men who came to Chicago soon paid dividends, however. "You get along with certain pitchers in certain ways," Hundley was quoted as saying. "When Hands and I were traded from the Giants to the Cubs, we had been through some tough times in the Giants organization. He was kind of a highstrung, hard-headed mother and so was I, and we used to do battle quite a bit." By 1967 Hundley had earned his first Gold Glove, with only four errors before his iron-man encore in '68. Hundley revolutionized the catcher's position (arguably saving many broken fingers for future catchers) by developing a new style of mitt that allowed for one-handed catching. Up to that time the throwing hand of most catchers hovered freely above the knee, vulnerable to the numerous foul tips over the course of the summer. Thus Hundley may well have been the first catcher to regularly place the open hand *behind* the knee (or behind the back, as would become a trademark of Bench). The new type of catcher's mitt that he used had a hinged design to it that allowed the mitt to close more easily around the ball. This development paralleled advances in fielders' gloves that the Rawlings and Wilson Companies were making at the time, improvements in equipment that would permanently change the way defense was played.

At the plate Hundley could provide respectable power when called upon. In a July 1967 game at Atlanta, he and teammates Billy Williams and Ron Santo, along with Braves players Felipe Alou and Rico Carty, combined for a Major League record of five home runs in the first inning of a ball game.

Despite Leo's confidence, some were concerned that Hundley would wear thin in the heat of a pennant race, as his remarkable omnipresence behind the plate in '68 set a dangerous precedent for his tremendous reliability. In the 1968 season, aside from Hundley, only Randy Bobb (seven games), John Boccabella (four), John Felske (three), and Gene Oliver (one) entered Cubs games as a catcher. Interestingly, that season Bobb, while simultaneously handling his very first pitch in the Major Leagues late in the game on August 18, threw out Cincinnati star Pete Rose trying to steal. More help appeared available for 1969, as joining the twenty-one-year-old Bobb and the thirty-three-year-old Oliver in vying for jobs would be rookie Ken Rudolph and journeyman Bill Heath. It was Rudolph's fourth attempt to stick with the Cubs, as inconsistent showings in the Minor Leagues and at previous spring training stints had him always "on the bubble." Heath was back in the Major Leagues after a one-year hiatus, having previous experience with the White Sox (1965), Houston Astros (1966–67), and Detroit Tigers (1967).

Oliver, also a veteran, was envisioned as the most reliable backup to Hundley as the team headed to spring training. Like Hundley, the six-foot-two-inch, 225-pound warhorse had displayed a penchant in the past for dramatic home runs. The Cubs became Oliver's fifth team, as he joined them from the Boston Red Sox in 1968. He had originally broken in with the Cardinals in 1959 and in the interim had ventured from the Braves to the Phillies in what some might consider rather dubious fashion—he had been traded straight up for fellow catcher Bob Uecker on June 7, 1967. On the last day of the season in 1962, Oliver hit a ninth-inning homer off Johnny Podres of the Dodgers in Los Angeles for the lone run in a 1–0 St. Louis win, a loss for the Dodgers that forced them into a one-game playoff with the Giants for the National League pennant (which the Giants won). A year later Oliver allowed Warren Spahn to become the oldest (age forty-two) 20-game winner in history with a game-deciding blast off Dallas Green in Philadelphia. Oliver also went on to hit three homers in a game on July 30, 1966, as a member of the Braves. After he joined the Cubs, a serious knee injury limited the Moline, Illinois, native to minimal duty—which he was bound to get with Hundley on the roster anyway.

§

No team in baseball could match the quality of the Cubs infield going into the latter years of the 1960s. The left side was iron-clad, with 1968 All-Stars Santo at third and Don Kessinger at short; by 1969 the legendary erstwhile shortstop Banks was seven years removed from his switch over to first base, and the solid, re-liable Glenn Beckert took care of the chores at second. The title of "All-Star infield" began to swell in early 1969, as some fore-casters envisioned all four players headed to the Mid-Summer Classic at Washington in July.

"Nobody ever won a pennant without a star shortstop," Durocher always liked to say. And in Kessinger he had one of the bright young talents in the game at the position. Growing up in Arkansas, Kessinger was nearly equal the basketball player that he was a baseball one. He went on to become an All-American in both sports at the University of Mississippi and made his Major League debut with the Cubs in 1964 at age twenty-one and with only six weeks of Minor League experience, considered by club officials as an able replacement for the light-hitting Andre Rodgers. In his first year of full-time duty in 1965, however, Kessinger hit only .201 himself and had to rely on his defense to keep his spot in Chicago. After he jumped up to .274 in '66, it seemed he had mastered the batting craft. He dropped off again to .231 and .240 the next two years, however, as some suggested that he drop his switch-hitting strategy—which he did not do, as he traced his faith in the technique back to his work a few years prior. "It was late in 1965, my rookie year, and as a natural right-handed hitter I was hitting about .200," Kessinger remembered. "So I said to Alvin Dark, one of our coaches, 'I think I can switch hit.' He said, 'OK, here's what we'll do. You go home this winter, find yourself a gymnasium, and get somebody to throw tennis balls at you all winter. Have them throw them hard, and some of them right at you. You've got to find out whether you can get out of the way of the ball. Sometimes hitters have a tendency to freeze when they switch to the other side, and you've got to find out.'" So Kessinger went home to do the work, seeking to permanently improve his offensive game. Through dedication he became a threat from both sides of the plate. "I believe he is better as a righty," suggested Cubs relief pitcher Ted Abernathy, the man who would become Kessinger's roommate during the 1969 season, to *The Sporting News*. "No—I think maybe he's better lefthanded—Gee, I don't know."

But Kessinger's glove work remained unwavering and led to his first all-league selection in 1968. Kessinger, whose tall, rangy frame reminded many of former Cardinals shortstop Marty Marion, went to his left very adeptly but at first had trouble satisfying his manager in going the other direction, despite almost always providing Banks with accurate throws. "When I first saw Kessinger," Durocher remembered, "I didn't think he could go to his right. I told him he couldn't play short by trying to smell balls hit to his right. I got him to move a couple of feet to the right to compensate. Now I think he's as good as any shortstop in the league. . . . Kessinger makes some plays as well or better than any shortstop who ever lived." Added Atlanta Braves coach Billy Goodman, "Kessinger is as good a shortstop as I've seen. . . . He is a tall guy who just seems to glide to the ball." And Bob Kennedy, who scouted other Major League teams for the Cardinals, said plainly, "Kessinger has all the ingredients to be a superstar."

Kessinger was also a smart base runner who performed all the minute aspects of the game extremely well. An exceptional handler of the bat, he gained favor with Durocher for his ever-improving ability to bunt and execute the hit-and-run. And as with

Hundley, Durocher etched Kessinger's name in the lineup 160 times in 1968; also like Hundley, both Kessinger and Durocher were a bit concerned about the shortstop wearing thin in the heat of the summer. "I know it doesn't show," Kessinger joked as he got ready for 1969 spring training, "but I've gained eight pounds over last year. I'm up to 180, and I feel stronger." His big number "11" had become a fixture on the infield dirt at Wrigley, and like many players of his day, he never turned down a child with an autograph request. His day-to-day dependability in the field reflected his strong personal character.

In Glenn Beckert, the other side of the bag was manned by a player remarkably similar to Kessinger. Both were listed at six feet, one inch tall, with Beckert outweighing Kessinger by 10 pounds, 190 to 180. And like Kessinger, Beckert became a starter for the Cubs in 1965 after graduating from Allegheny College three years earlier, playing in 154 games as a twenty-four-year-old rookie (he had originally received $6,000 to sign with the Boston Red Sox in 1962). Beckert originally proved more of an offensive force than his neighbor, however, as his 98 runs scored topped the National League charts in 1968 and his .294 average was seventh in the circuit and best among league infielders, courtesy of his 189 hits (third in the league). Even with all of the great pitchers in the game in '68, very few of them could get the ball past Beckert; he struck out a mere 20 times in 643 at-bats. No slouch himself around the base, Beckert notched his first Gold Glove in 1968 as well, finally ending the long stranglehold that Pittsburgh's Bill Mazeroski had on the title for Keystoners. His nickname was "Bruno," in honor of pro wrestler Bruno Sammartino, as Beckert had a tendency to plow over his teammates in pursuit of fly balls. To add to the perilous mystique of his double play partner, Kessinger once warned him, "Don't shave next to Beckert—you'll get cut!"

Beckert reflected years later about the good relationship he had with his manager. "Leo just liked me," he remembered. "Somehow, I always got my uniform dirty diving for a ball, and looking back I think I reminded him of him. I really appreciated Leo; he was kind to me."

It was in fact a terrible fluke, however, that Beckert wound up a second baseman. While still in the Minor Leagues, he was moved to the position after the tragic death of Ken Hubbs. Hubbs, who in his childhood was a Little League World Series hero for his team from Colton, California, fatally crashed his private plane outside of Provo, Utah, in February 1964, while returning to Colton. Two years before, he had won the National League Rookie of the Year award while with the Cubs, during which he set the Major League record for consecutive errorless games (78) and consecutive errorless chances (418).

Perhaps no one has bled the green of Wrigley ivy and the blue of the Cubs uniform more than Ron Santo. He was already an eight-year veteran and five-time All-Star by the time spring training of 1969 rolled around, and like most of the other players, he had been excited about Durocher's arrival in 1966. "Leo Durocher has been a tonic for this ballclub," Santo asserted after the fiery skipper took over. "He told us we were good, and we believe him." The year before, Santo had given the National League a 6-5 victory in the All-Star Game with a seventh-inning single. Santo had been introduced to the big leagues as a twenty-year-old rookie in 1960, when Cubs manager Charlie Grimm had him sent to their Houston farm club for half of the season for further experience. After becoming the Cubs' regular third baseman the following year, he missed only nine games in the next eight seasons; this included a stretch of over four hundred consecutive games in the early part of the 1960s, interrupted only by a broken jaw. "If a fellow came up to me tomorrow and said he'd give me one million dollars to quit playing baseball, I'd tell him to get lost," he said in 1966. Santo had been a star quarterback on his high school football team in Seattle—the part of the country that would later produce another great prep quarterback and Cubs infielder, Ryne Sandberg. Santo was the Cubs' captain, and he led the physical and emotional charge of the team onto the field each day. "Nothing succeeds like success," he once said, and the third baseman was as hungry as anyone for a World Championship for the people of Chicago.

As the sixties came to a close, it was the beginning of the end of a long, beautiful run in the blue pinstripes for Banks. Born on

January 31, 1931, in Dallas, Banks did not display much interest in baseball until prodded by his father, himself a legendary amateur player in Texas. Declining an opportunity to play for the Harlem Globetrotters basketball team, Banks instead signed with the Kansas City Monarchs of the Negro Leagues as a shortstop. He was then claimed for $10,000 by the Cubs and so became the first black player for the North Siders as he made his debut on September 17, 1953. It was an uneasy transition for all, but no less for Banks than anyone. "During my half-month stay with the Cubs in September, 1953, I met more white people than I had known in all my twenty-two years," he said.

Banks rose from bed each day with a smile that continued until he returned to his covers at night. It was evident that no one loved to play the game more, for—like Santo—Banks racked up more than 400 consecutive games before a hand infection put him on the bench in 1956. When he returned he played in over 700 more consecutive games. After two Most Valuable Player awards, in 1958 and 1959, he became in 1960 the last National League shortstop until Hubie Brooks in 1985 to have 100 runs batted in for a season. To dispel any doubt about Banks's individual dominance through the late 1950s, consider that he had more home runs from 1955 to 1960 than any player in the game—including Mickey Mantle, Willie Mays, and other superstars who were enjoying the prime years of their careers. After a brief 25-game interlude in left field in 1961 (a misguided idea of a member of the "College of Coaches," an experiment by Phil Wrigley in the early sixties to use multiple managers), Banks had been settled in comfortably at first base since 1962, a move necessitated by repeated leg injuries from playing an aggressive style at shortstop. Despite his legendary status, newcomers were arriving each year to try and knock him off the post. Dick Nen, Clarence Jones, and several others had been anointed the "First Baseman of the Future" for the Cubs throughout the sixties, but none could supplant the man who came to be called "Mr. Cub" by all Chicago fans. As Durocher himself admitted early in 1969, "I've retired Banks for three years and he always comes back."

There seemed to be, at least to the Chicago newspaper writers, an immediate clash between Banks and Durocher when Leo took over the club for the 1966 season. Durocher once had told the Chicago sportswriters, "Mr. Wrigley is the owner of the club, and *he's* Mr. Cub. Banks is no more Mr. Cub than I am." Banks, however, credited Durocher with inspiring him to reach within himself to finish his career in strong fashion. "Leo made me work harder to get that little extra you need for success," Ernie said. "I wish there had been someone around like him early in my career. You might resent his efforts in the beginning, but all of a sudden you realize he has made you a better ballplayer—no, not only a better ball player, but a better man. He's made me go for that little extra you need to win."

Banks continued: "Mr. Durocher is always saying, 'Give me a little bit more.' That's what has made me a better man—just being around him. I kind of marvel at people who have this knack of leading. The young guys on this team respect Mr. Durocher. They do what he wants them to do, and they feel like they are going to benefit by it." The 1968 season had been only the fourth time since 1954 that Banks had not made the All-Star team, however, and he challenged himself before going to spring workouts in Arizona in February 1969 to return to the league's elite.

Banks was perhaps best described by late Chicago mayor Richard J. Daley as an "incurable optimist." Added Durocher, "I don't know where Ernie Banks gets those pep pills to stay so young, but I'm going to check out his pharmaceutical house and get a double order for myself." And the person who perhaps knew Ernie best—his wife, Eloyce—agreed. "I marvel at how well Ernie combines his careers of celebrity and husband and father," she said proudly. "I couldn't combine a public and private life as perfectly as he does." Banks took time out from his precious resting month of November in 1968 to visit U.S. troops fighting the war in Vietnam. He was so popular, in fact, that Illinois governor Richard Ogilvie gladly appointed him to the board of directors for the Chicago Transit Authority, the massive bureaucracy that oversaw the city's buses and elevated trains (known as the "El"). "You lose the blues in Chicago," Banks once said of his adopted hometown. "Ah, the friendly confines of beautiful, ivy-covered Wrigley Field, where you play ball under the world's best lights—the solar system. And hear me when I say—the Cubs will be fine in '69."

The infielders drew very close to one another, and as good ballplayer-friends do, they began to play jokes on one another, with Beckert usually the main culprit. Beckert told a writer of a time that he and the others played one particularly haunting trick on Santo. "The funniest was when his life was threatened," the second baseman remembered of a certain stressful stretch of time for Santo in the past. "It went on for two months. We don't know who was sending the letters and making the calls. And this went on, and the Cubs finally called in the FBI." Beckert continued:

> They sent two or three agents with us. I was rooming with him, and I said, "I can't take this." So in New York we were staying at the Waldorf; of course, there are four of us now, including Ron and myself and the two FBI guys. But everyone is asking me questions about how I feel about this whole thing. So I decide, "Hey, let's have some fun." So I put a big sign over his bed—Santo Sleeps Here.
>
> After we came off a road trip, I went to the ballpark. When we get back from a road trip, you get a big pack of fan mail. Our lockers were, in order, Billy [Williams], Ernie, myself, and Santo. Billy was there when I arrived. Billy said, "Let's have some more fun with Santo. He's playing tight. We need to loosen him up."
>
> People sent you balls to autograph in those little boxes. Billy and I cut one of those boxes addressed to Santo with a razor blade, and took out the ball. We got a minute timer, which ticked louder than hell, and we put that in there and taped it back up and threw the box underneath the mail.
>
> Santo came in. He was hyper. We were just sitting there, and Billy said, "You know, Beck, do you hear something ticking?" I said, "Yeah, I heard that ever since I got here this morning."
>
> Santo rooted through his pile, and he found the box.

"It's a freaking bomb!!!" he screamed.

We lockered in the left field area, and he took it out and threw it onto Waveland Avenue. A few minutes later Al Schoonmeir, our trainer, came out and said, "What the hell happened to my timer?" I said, "Doc, Santo just threw it onto Waveland Avenue."

The four men on the infield dirt soon became as reliable at Wrigley as the sun in the right fielder's eyes. Cub fans had come to know Durocher's managerial style well since he took the job in 1966. His lineup was so regular that the names were often typed onto the lines on the scorecard, which was placed on the left-hand side of the famous cardboard programs sold at Wrigley Field amid ads for French's Mustard, Borden's Frosty Malt, Oscar Meyer Hot Dogs, and Old Style Beer. Fans cringed at the thought of the typed-out "Santo" or "Kessinger" being deleted at some point, however, because the bench was thin. The reserve jobs for the infield were wide open, with only Lee Elia and Jimmy Qualls being known commodities heading into training camp, and with Elia possessing the sole big league experience, as he had batted .173 in seventeen at-bats with the Cubs in '68. Despite being only twenty-two years old, Qualls had already spent five years in the Cubs' Minor League system by the time 1969 had rolled around. He had grown up a Yankee fan and dreamed of playing pro ball in the Bronx, but an adult friend advised him at age seventeen, "Why sign with a winner? Sign with a downtrodden club, and make it to the big leagues quicker." The Cubs had been giving Qualls his first try in the outfield after primarily playing him at second base for most of his professional career, but with the lack of depth in the infield, Durocher wanted him to spend practice time at second as well. Leo envisioned the speedy, switch-hitting, 155-pound Qualls as a quality defensive man in the late innings at several positions.

Qualls was one of many players in the 1960s who had military obligations to fulfill. The Cubs' traveling secretary Blake Cullen told a humorous story about one of Qualls's departures for service: "He was headed off for two weeks of military duty, and we had to send the obligatory telegram to National League president Warren Giles telling him to put Jimmy on the military list. Well, it just so happened that Dean Martin's daughter was getting married that same day in Beverly Hills, and Leo wanted to send her a telegram, too. Somehow, we got the two wires switched. So here is Dean Martin at a party opening this telegram, and he says, 'I didn't even know we had a military list.' Meanwhile, Warren Giles was getting a wire that said, 'Love and Kisses—Leo Durocher.'"

While some uncertainty existed about the Cubs' infield and outfield depth heading into 1969, the team had yet another superstar among the regulars in left fielder Billy Williams. Williams had established himself as one of the most productive hitters in the game, leading the National League in 1968 in total bases (321) and extra-base hits (68). Williams had originally been signed by the Cubs in 1956 and had spent his first Minor League year at Ponca City in the Sooner State League. For what the Cubs paid, it was one of the all-time greatest investments in a player. "I hate to say it, but the Cubs got me for a cigar and a bus ticket to Ponca City," Williams would reveal in 1972. "At the time, the highest bonuses were about $4,000 to $10,000. But I was so anxious to play baseball that I just put my name on the dotted line. There was no money involved. My father got a cigar and I got a bus ticket to Ponca City."

Making his big league debut in Banks's last MVP season in 1959, Williams went on the fast track to Chicago when Rogers Hornsby, considered the greatest right-handed hitter ever and then working as a Minor League instructor for the Cubs in Houston, saw the graceful swing that Williams possessed and informed the Chicago brass about his merits. As the story goes, Santo and Williams were later sitting in the stands at spring training with eighteen other Cubs prospects. Hornsby pointed to the two of them and said, "You can hit in the Major Leagues right now." Hornsby then told the other eighteen that they would never make it.

After brief auditions in '59 and '60, Williams became the Cubs' left fielder the following year and took home the Rookie of the

Year award. Once given his chance, Williams never let go of the job; coming into 1969—after four All-Star appearances—he was on schedule to break Cardinals legend Stan Musial's National League record of 896 consecutive games by late June. He had not missed a contest since September 21, 1963.

Williams was overly quiet with reporters when he first came up, a stance that some writers took as antisocial. His teammates, however, said that he was just misunderstood. "He loves the game as much as any of us; he just has a different way of expressing it," Banks explained. "Some guys like me go around hollering, but he quietly does it all. It's too bad that a lot of the things Billy does are overlooked. He is a tremendous asset to this team. He gets so many big hits, makes so many great plays, and yet he is the most underestimated player in the game."

"Ernie deserves all the fanfare he gets," Williams said of his teammate in return. "Just remember all the thrilling moments Ernie has given Cub fans since he came up in 1953. . . . When I go to bat, the fans respond well. I feel it. However, they're certainly not going to respond to me or Ron Santo the way they react to Banks. We wouldn't expect that."

"The enduring Williams is modest, with a keen, subtle sense of humor," added David Condon in the *Tribune*. "He is obliging. His eyes flicker with admiration around Ernie Banks, and he doesn't begrudge anything that Ernie gets . . . but Williams frankly feels that there should be more public interest in Billy Williams. How about all you Cubbies and Cubbie fans getting together for a 'Billy Williams Day?'"

Or, as Bill Gleason of the *Chicago Sun-Times* put it, "The leader of the Cubs is, of all people, the quiet man of the clubhouse, Billy Williams. Billy Williams, who seldom speaks in a voice that can be heard beyond his own cubicle, who wouldn't say 'Rah! Rah!' if Phil Wrigley promised him a $10,000 bonus for each 'rah.'"

In further transgressing its general history of bad trades, the Cubs (in addition to the Hundley-Hands deal) had also concocted two others in early 1968 that would improve the team's fortunes for the next several years. On April 23 Chicago had dealt pitcher Jim Ellis and reserve outfielder Ted Savage—both of whom had contributed little to the club to that point—to the Dodgers for relief pitcher Phil Regan and outfielder Jim Hickman. Regan's stock had dropped with the Dodgers because of a statistical collapse from 1967 as well as a string of mysterious injuries (ultimately diagnosed as rheumatoid arthritis). The Dodgers thought he was damaged goods, but upon Regan's arrival in Chicago, the Cubs' team physician couldn't find anything wrong with him. Then, in May 1968, the pain left his body as quickly as it had come. "If Regan's assertion that he feels as sound as he did in 1966 is true," one writer for the *Tribune* reasoned after the soreness went away, "the Cubs must be accepted now as a solid contender." Regan's delivery was unorthodox, and most players in the league (as well as most umpires) believed that Regan was throwing a spitball, a pitch that had been outlawed since 1921.

Then, in June of '68, the Cubs improved themselves further by flipping Lou Johnson to the Cleveland Indians for fellow outfielder Willie Smith. It would have been addition by subtraction for the Cubs anyway, as the bitter Johnson was becoming more and more of a problem in the clubhouse. Both attitudinally and athletically, Johnson had been a big disappointment. A former starter with the Dodgers during their championship years of the mid-sixties, Johnson had figured to become the Cubs' permanent right fielder. He tended to blame others for his personal difficulties, however, and when asked to leave those things behind when he took the field, he seemed to develop new excuses for his diminishing play. The other players had wearied of his poor demeanor, and Durocher knew he had to dispose of him. Bad feelings between Johnson and some of the other players had accelerated when Martin Luther King Jr. was assassinated. While riding in an elevator with Hundley and a couple of other players shortly after the shooting, Johnson (who was black) got the idea that Hundley was being indifferent about King's death—when in fact he was not. From that point until he was traded in June, Johnson barely spoke to any of the players, and most of the other players (Hundley especially, and understandably) wanted nothing to do with him. Johnson claimed that Durocher had it in for him as well. "The man never talked to me," Johnson said. "He relayed his orders through messengers." Before the 1969 season even began, Johnson would be traded once again—this time to the California Angels.

Smith was the personal opposite of his counterpart Johnson. Unlike Johnson, Smith was easygoing and everyone liked him—leading to his nickname of "Wonderful Willie." He could always be heard humming a song or even making up his own lyrics to well-established tunes. Interestingly, he had come to the majors as a pitcher with the Detroit Tigers in 1963, despite hitting .380 in his final year of Minor League ball—a career that had begun with the Duluth, Minnesota, team in the Northern League in 1960. His bat soon became too much to ignore, however, and he spent several years in the Detroit and California outfields before landing in Cleveland. He could never regain the stroke of his career-high average of .301 with the Los Angeles Angels in 1964 (the year before the club moved to Anaheim) and thus became a left-handed specialist off the bench. Despite hitting only .261 with the Angels in '65, he did manage to place fourth in the American League with nine triples. A gifted athlete, the Anniston, Alabama, native proved that he could hit, run, throw—and punch, for he also had been a formidable amateur boxer. Always making himself available for relief roles, Smith in 1968 made his final appearance as a pitcher in the big leagues, hurling two and two-thirds scoreless innings for the Cubs, which included two strikeouts—but it would be the only time he would ever take the hill in a Chicago uniform. This would come after he had thrown three scoreless innings for the Indians on June 24, prior to his trade to the Cubs, a game that Cleveland lost 14-3 to McLain and the Tigers, part of McLain's historic 30-win season. Smith was ready to go, and was in the shape to prove it. "I figured I was going to get to play a little more this year," he reasoned, "so last winter I took this weightlifting course and built my weight up from 178 to 190 pounds."

Right field would become a battle among Smith, Hickman, and impressive rookie Jim Dunegan. Hickman had been one of the infamous original New York Mets from 1962, leading the club in strikeouts as a rookie that season with 96, as well as the next season with 120. Mets manager Casey Stengel saw talent in him—especially some impressive power potential—and the young slugger remained in the lineup. He hit the last homer ever struck in the old Polo Grounds in New York (on September 18, 1963, as only 1,752 fans bothered to show up to watch the hapless Mets in the stadium's final act). A month earlier Hickman had become the first Met to ever hit for the cycle. But as Wes Westrum took over the New York club in the middle of the '65 season, Hickman saw that his favor was beginning to run out, even though he produced a three-homer game against the Cardinals in September of that year. He would wind up his days in Flushing as the Mets' all-time home run leader, with 60. Two seasons later Hickman found himself in Los Angeles for a year before arriving in Chicago with Regan in the April 1968 trade. He reminded Durocher of one of his personal favorites, Joe Medwick—a strongly built, power-hitting outfielder with physical "tools" but an inconsistent display on defense. Medwick had been a Gas House Gang teammate of Durocher's on the Cardinals of the 1930s, and Leo thought that he now might have a clone of "Ol' Ducky." Westrum had relegated Hickman to the bench in '65 and '66—and Hickman had gotten more of the same with the Dodgers in 1967—but he arrived in Chicago with Durocher planning on his eventually becoming an everyday player in right field. In his first foray as a Cub, however, Hickman was lackluster. After batting just .223 with only five home runs in 1968, he was sent back to the Cubs' triple-A Minor League team in Tacoma. However, for 1969, both he and Durocher expected a breakout year for the farmer from Henning, Tennessee.

Jim Dunegan was much to Hickman's likeness—big, strong, and powerful from the right-handed batter's box but somewhat clumsy on defense. Durocher was hoping that the rookie could display enough talent in spring training to earn significant playing time either in right or center.

Back in March 1968 Durocher had been positive about his prospects for the center-field position for the coming season. "People sometimes wonder about our center field situation, but I'm not one of them," he told reporters at the time. "We have three of the hardest-hitting prospects you could ever hope to see in Oscar Gamble, Jim McMath, and Jim Dunegan." In center field for 1969 Durocher had a threesome of promising but erratic possibilities in Gamble, Adolfo Phillips, and Don Young.

It was Phillips who turned out to be the biggest disappointment for Leo, who originally had described the Panamanian as "one of the most physically-gifted players I have ever seen. . . . He just might be another Willie Mays." It was a phrase that would haunt Phillips for the rest of his career. Phillips had debuted with the Philadelphia Phillies in September 1964, when the Phils were trying unsuccessfully to hang on to their pennant hopes against the rampaging Cardinals. In April 1966 the Cubs acquired Phillips, Fergie Jenkins, and outfielder John Herrnstein. At the time, Jenkins and Herrnstein were considered the "throw-ins" in the deal and Phillips was the prized recruit. Almost immediately, Durocher wanted Phillips to be a lead-off hitter, but Adolfo had two things working against him: he was afraid of being hit by pitches, and he was beginning to strike out far too often (in June of '66 Phillips tied a big league record by striking out nine times in two back-to-back games, leading to a grand total of 135 strikeouts for the year). "Adolfo Phillips was Leo's pet project," recalls Northern Illinois University sports information director Mike Korcek, who in 1969 was covering the Cubs for the campus newspaper, the *Northern Star*. "The Lip made him a very aggressive player."

Durocher thought he might be able to overlook Phillips's shortcomings, as the talented youngster wound up the 1966 season with 32 stolen bases and 16 home runs. In spring 1967 Santo got into a fight with Phillips in spring training because he felt the young outfielder wasn't trying hard enough, and during the season Phillips was dropped from the lead-off spot in the batting order to eighth, which seemed to help him relax and make better contact at the plate. His average dipped to .241 in '68, however, prompting Durocher to throw the center-field job wide open in advance of the 1969 campaign. The last straw for Leo had come in June 1968, when he fined Phillips $200 for "loafing on the bases," perhaps the greatest sin of all to the former player known for his hustle. "Adolfo can hit, has the power, and can run, field, and throw," Durocher said plainly. "He lacks desire. He has to show me he wants to play." With Phillips perpetually in the Durocher doghouse, nineteen-year-old, 155-pound Oscar Gamble appeared to be on the fast track for the starting job in center field despite his inexperience. He would be invited to spring training as a nonroster rookie, but while Durocher was high on Gamble's talents, it appeared more likely that this was intended to give Gamble experience preceding a trip to the Minor Leagues for more playing time once the season began.

Durocher was cautiously optimistic about Don Young. "He could have a great future, but it's up to him," Durocher commented. "I don't care what he hits. I want to see more enthusiasm from him. He's got to be more aggressive." Young had shown some promise in arriving with the Cubs in 1965 as a nineteen-year-old, although he and teammate Byron Browne became the first players in Major League history to make their debuts on the losing side of a no-hitter—which was in fact a perfect game fired by Sandy Koufax of the Dodgers that year on September 9. After acquiring thirty-five at-bats in September 1965, Young had not seen the majors for four years, as he attempted to make the Cubs roster once again. Some baseball veterans around Chicago had likened him defensively to Jim Landis, the fly-chasing center fielder for the "Go-Go" White Sox of the late 1950s. Over the winter Young could have been acquired by any club for the small price of $12,500—the cost of taking a player in the Minor League draft, of which Young was a part. All the clubs passed on him, however, and he wound up back with the Cubs.

Competing for the final outfield spots were Qualls, Manny Jimenez, and thirty-five-year-old Al Spangler, the latter a graduate of Duke University who had hit a solid .271 in part-time duty in 1968. That season the veteran Spangler was one of several Cubs thrown out of a game on August 8 against the Braves, as umpire Chris Pelekoudas accused Regan of throwing illegal pitches and thus reversed two outs that had been recorded. This event would indirectly lead to the appearance of the first female umpire in professional baseball a few years later. As Pelekoudas thought that Regan was throwing a spitter, Durocher advanced out to the mound.

"Did you find anything on the ball?" Durocher asked.

"No," Pelekoudas answered.

"Then leave him alone," Leo retorted.

Durocher, Regan, and Hundley were also later ejected, but league president Giles later came down hard on Pelekoudas as well, suggesting that he arbitrarily singled Regan out because of his spitball reputation. After the game Durocher pulled Regan aside and said, "Don't talk to the press about this. Let the umpires do the talking." But Durocher soon after did a radio conversation himself with Bernice Gera, a woman who was trying to make it to the majors as an umpire. "You probably wouldn't do any worse than some of the guys who are umpiring right now," Leo offered. With this public boost, three years later—and after several court fights—Gera would debut as the first female umpire in professional baseball as she took a job in the New York-Pennsylvania League. She would umpire only one game–the first game of a doubleheader on June 24, 1972—and would resign before the start of the second game because her lone contest had been filled with arguments, controversial plays, and even alleged abuse from her fellow umpires.

Jimenez had not been a starter in the big leagues since his rookie season with the Kansas City A's in 1962, when he had finished ninth in the American League batting race with a .301 average.

It was imagined that the Chicago outfit, on a day-to-day basis over the long haul of the summer, could place as much talent on the field as anyone. "The Cubs, indeed, may have the best or nearly the best eight-man ball club in the league," offered Jerome Holtzman of the *Chicago Sun-Times* in viewing the upcoming 1969 campaign. The pitching staff also looked solid, and its foundation could be traced back to a single year—1966—when the three mainstays made their marks as rookies. The three men had thrown a collective total of just twenty-two innings in 1965, as they had barely touched the mound in the Major Leagues. But for Ferguson Jenkins, Bill Hands, and Ken Holtzman, the upcoming season of '69 was a chance to prove that they, like their teammates in the field, were seasoned veterans, ready to take a pennant-contending ball club onto their backs.

3

"Sociable Scottsdale"

Having [Randy] Hundley catch for
you was like sitting down to a steak
dinner with a steak knife. Without
Hundley, all you had was a fork.

—Fergie Jenkins

There is an old saying in baseball that claims "statistics don't lie."
That may be true, but they don't always give the whole account,
either. In 1968 Fergie Jenkins was indeed the game's hard-luck
story. He won twenty times as a pitcher for the Cubs, the second
year in a row he had accomplished that feat. But he also lost
fifteen, and the amazing story behind that figure is that nine of
those losses came with his team being shut out, the most by any
pitcher winning 20 games in the past one hundred years. This
string of misfortune included a six-day stretch in late June when
the Cubs were shut out five straight times with Jenkins allowing
a lone run over eighteen innings of work in his two starts during
that week. Furthermore, his five 1-0 losses in 1968 tied a Major
League record.

But Jenkins had endured the adversity and was now the head of the staff, a budding superstar, a son of a Canadian chef who looked forward to hunting and fishing with Billy Williams and others near Jenkins's Chatham, Ontario, home at the end of each season. "Chatham is in southern Ontario, 53 miles east of Detroit," Jenkins mentioned as he chatted with William Wallace from the *New York Times*. "It's flat farm country. My family has been there for three generations. My father's family came from the Bahamas. My father would drive that 50-or-so miles to Detroit to watch the Tigers play and to watch Jim Bunning pitch." (Banks enjoyed fishing along with Jenkins and Williams, too. Once, while fishing with the guys off Lake Michigan, he dropped his expensive sunglasses in the lake. Ernie vowed to sit there all day until he caught the fish that stole his sunglasses.) Williams was always a willing partner to get in the Jenkins boat. "When I fish, I can think about things, such as how some of those pitchers got me out," the outfielder said. "While I wait for some fish to bite, I figure out how some of those pitchers got me on the hook."

At the time Jenkins arrived to the Cubs with Phillips in April 1966, he had exclusively been a reliever in his eight appearances in the big leagues for Philadelphia, who had given him a $6,500 bonus and $400 a month to pitch for Miami in the Florida State League when he was first signed professionally. With his strong six-foot-five-inch frame, however, Jenkins was envisioned by Durocher—and, more adamantly, by pitching coach Becker—as an innings-eating starter who would flourish as the heat of the Wrigley Field sun started taking its toll on more brittle players toward August and September. Jenkins had already impressed Banks long before the pitcher wore the blue pinstripes for Chicago. "We [the Cubs players] agreed that Fergie had the equipment to become a big leaguer," Banks noted, reflecting on the battles already waged with Jenkins when Fergie was a member of the Phillies. "We were impressed with his size, his speed, his control, and most of all, his poise. He looked like a winner. . . . He was like Victor Borge—a one-man show."

Forty-eight hours after joining the Cubs, Jenkins had shut out heralded rookie Don Sutton and the Dodgers while homering himself in a 2-0 win. But after remaining mostly in the bullpen for that first season in Chicago (he started only 12 of 60 games in which he appeared in '66), Jenkins (at age twenty-four) had already started a total of 90 games for the Cubs by the end of '68, completing nearly half of them and becoming the first Cub 20-game winner since Larry Jackson in 1964. Earlier, in July 1967, the Cubs had risen to first place for the first time since 1945. Jenkins recounted the surreal scene to a writer.

> The Cubs had been a second-division team since 1947. That's twenty years of losing baseball. I beat the Reds to put the Cubs in first place. It was the first time the Cubs had been in first place in so long [since 1945]. Wrigley Field was packed, and after the game was over, the fans all stayed there to see what would happen on the East Coast, whether the Cardinals would lose, to see if our pennant would fly on the top of that pole in Wrigley Field. See, we had pennant flags to show the standings of the teams, and I can recall that when they announced we went into first place—the Mets had beaten St. Louis—there was a cheer for, man, ten minutes.

> A lot of us were in the dressing room, and when this cheer came up, we knew with all the excitement that something was happening. We said to each other, "Hey, the fans are still in the ballpark." And we were happy to hear we were in first place for the first time.

> We all rushed outside to see what the heck was going on. We stood in the doorway and we watched them put that Cubs flag up at the top of the pole.

Durocher planned on giving Jenkins the ball as much as possible in 1969, as his forty starts the season before had matched the club record set nearly fifty years earlier by Grover Cleveland Alexander. His "stuff" was becoming all too apparent to National League hitters, as he finished second in strikeouts in the league in 1967 with 236 (behind Bunning) and in 1968 with 260 (behind

Gibson)—both times, he established new Cub records. Jenkins went into 1969 training camp at 208 pounds, determined to be down to 205 when the season started. He had grayed a few of Leo's hairs in spring training of '68, however, as he ignored repeated warnings about his beloved horseback riding. He slipped off one of his stallions and was out of action for nearly two weeks with injuries.

Also new to the Cubs pitching staff in 1966 had been another promising young right-hander in Bill Hands, who in arriving with Hundley in the Giants trade the previous December had given more hope for the future. The son of a New Jersey baker and club musician ("My dad did a lot of weddings—in multiple ways," Hands noted), Hands allowed a league-high 26 home runs in 1968, but it was because he was mostly around the plate; he issued only 36 walks in 259 innings of work. He was discovered by a Giants scout after pitching on the college campuses of Ohio Wesleyan and Farleigh Dickinson.

Despite establishing himself as a force off the mound, Hands—nicknamed "Froggy" because his style resembled Yankee great Don Larsen, who had previously held the nickname—also set a dubious record as a batter in 1968 as he struck out in fourteen straight plate appearances.

Ken Holtzman was a nineteen-year-old left-hander from the University of Illinois when, after one year of school, he arrived at the -Cubs' winter camp in 1965 with a $25,000 bonus in his pocket. It was Durocher's plan to get the southpaw in the starting rotation as soon as possible. "I owe Leo a lot for getting me into the major leagues quick," Holtzman remembered. "He gave me a chance right away at age 20." Because of his Jewish background and graceful motion from the left side, Holtzman drew immediate comparisons to Koufax, who was in the midst of his brief-but-complete dominance of the National League. As it would turn out, Holtzman and Koufax would face each other only once in their careers, with Holtzman seizing a 2-1 triumph on September 25, 1966. After that game Holtzman sheepishly asked Koufax—in the Dodger locker room—whether Koufax could sign a baseball for him. "My mother," Holtzman laughed, "wouldn't have let me in the house if I hadn't gotten Sandy's autograph that afternoon. She is his greatest fan—she doesn't care what I do, as long as I stay up-to-date on him" (four days earlier Holtzman had defeated the Reds in front of only 440 fans at Wrigley Field, one of the smallest "crowds" ever at the ballpark).

"I batted against Sandy a few times," Holtzman would also recall about that match-up in Dodger Stadium, "and what impressed me was that everybody talked about how fast he was, but he had the best curve ball in baseball—it dropped right off the table. And that fastball started down, and then rose. And when he put it where he wanted it, low and outside and with all he had on it, there was no way you could hit it." It was Becker, the Cubs' pitching coach, who gave perhaps the most valid opinion; he had worked with Koufax for nearly ten years with the Dodgers, and he couldn't contain his excitement about his new left-hander's possibilities. "I think Holtzman can be just as good as Koufax," Becker said plainly. "I told him he has a better opportunity [for quick success] than Koufax, because Koufax broke in during 1955 with a Dodger team that was winning and already had an established pitching staff."

The 1967 season was indeed an unusual one for Holtzman, as he had to balance baseball time with his commitment to the Army Reserves. "After my duty was finished on Friday," he recalled about that year, "I'd fly to wherever the Cubs were playing. And whatever I did was right. Whatever runs I needed, the guys got for me. Whatever help I needed in the field, I got. All I can say is that it was a most fantastic, once-in-a-lifetime thing." Holtzman was speaking of the perfect 9-0 record he had accumulated that season as a self-proclaimed "weekend pitcher." He fell to 11-14 in 1968 (even though he said "We're still about two Cadillacs apart" in talking about his contract negotiations with the Cubs before the season), as military commitments interrupted his year once again. Holtzman served proudly, however, as his unit stood guard for a one-week stint during the tumultuous Democratic National Convention in Chicago in August.

Holtzman's service was an example of the frequent comings-and-goings of players to their duties during the era. Since the beginning of the Vietnam War—as well as with most wars of the twentieth century with American involvement—such absences had been a regular occurrence, and such stories were not exclusive to baseball. In the stretch run of the 1968 baseball season, for example, Robert "Rocky" Bleier was enjoying his rookie year with the Pittsburgh Steelers in the National Football League after a stellar career at the University of Notre Dame. Bleier was drafted into the United States Army in December 1968, and the next May his unit was sent to Chu Lai in southeast Asia. On August 20, 1969, Bleier's leg was shattered in the Heip Duc region as his area came under grenade attack. Instrumental in assisting seventeen soldiers of his thirty-three-member platoon to survive the ordeal, Bleier was awarded the Bronze Star and the Purple Heart. He underwent surgery a week after his injury at a hospital in Tokyo, but the damage to his leg was such that doctors gave him little hope of ever walking again—let alone returning to the gridiron. Amazingly, Bleier convalesced, and after more than two years of painful rehabilitation—and with the unconditional faith of team owner Art Rooney—he returned to the Steelers backfield, ultimately becoming a thousand-yard rusher in 1976 and part of four Super Bowl championships in Pittsburgh.

Holtzman did his best to minimize the impact his absence had on the smooth flow of the starting rotation. In terms of stability and depth, the Cubs' starting pitchers followed suit with the rest of the positional segments on the club; after the first three individuals, there were a few question marks. One was third-year man Rich Nye, who after winning 13 games as rookie in 1967 had slipped to a 7-12 record in '68. Nye had played with Phillips in the Venezuelan league over the winter, however, and according to both had regained his form as they led their La Guaira team to the league championship. "The whole thing last year was confidence," Nye admitted. "I just wasn't putting the ball where I wanted it. And mentally I would have to say that my pitching in Venezuela this winter did me a lot of good." One of the more cerebral Cubs, Nye was working on a master's degree and making plans to go to veterinary school when his baseball days were through.

Another possibility for the rotation was Joe Niekro, who had gone 14-10 for the Cubs in '68 but whose ERA was 4.32, almost a run and a half over the league average. Durocher had become disgusted with Niekro's reliance on the knuckleball. "I threw one in a game once to Mike Shannon of the Cardinals, and he hit it out of the ballpark," Niekro remembered later. "Leo came out and told me to save that pitch for Toledo," in an obvious reference to the Minor Leagues. Thus it appeared that Durocher was always looking for reasons to get Niekro off the roster. "Leo told Niekro to 'take his knuckleball and shove it,' and threatened Hundley never to give the sign for it," Nye once revealed.

To this end Durocher promised rookies Jim Colborn, Joe Decker, Archie Reynolds, Alec Distaso, and Dave Lemonds long looks in Arizona in March. And to help bolster the bullpen, the Cubs reacquired Ted Abernathy from Cincinnati for Bill Plummer, Clarence Jones, and a Minor Leaguer. Abernathy was an accomplished Major League pitcher whom Durocher regretted originally letting go back in 1967. Abernathy threw side-arm, the result of a shoulder injury from high school that prevented him from throwing over the top. He had found success with the "submarine" technique upon entering the big leagues as a twenty-two-year-old with the Washington Senators in 1955; in the two years he spent in Cincinnati in 1967 and 1968, Abernathy amassed 16 wins and 41 saves, was named the top reliever in the National League, and now looked to be a strong complement to Regan in the late innings for the Cubs.

Just as spring training was set to get under way, Cubs general manager John Holland announced that the team had added Hank Aguirre, a thirty-seven-year-old, fourteen-year veteran who threw from the left side, to the bullpen as well. Aguirre, a native of southern California and an alumnus of East Los Angeles Junior College, had spent the 1968 season with the Dodgers but was released when the season came to a close. He had originally broken into professional baseball with the Indians organization in 1951 as a nineteen-year-old, signing a contract worth $200 a month. Aguirre was certainly a welcome addition to the club, for at the time he and Nye were the only left-handed relievers on the roster—and furthermore, it was quite possible that Nye would again be used in a starting role by Durocher (as Durocher had regularly done for the past two seasons, during which Nye started 50 games for the Cubs), leaving Aguirre as the lone southpaw in the bullpen. Suddenly, the Cubs had bolstered the experience level in their relief corps, as Regan and the thirty-six-year-old Abernathy were seen as solid right-handed complements to Aguirre; soon, fans would be calling the bullpen trio the "Three-Headed Monster." *Tribune* writer Robert Markus was particularly impressed. "The Cubs, apparently convinced that if one relief ace is good and two is terrific, then three must be supercolossal," he wrote. "They are going after a pennant fight armed with a trio of top flight firemen."

"John Holland has traded the Cubs into a pennant this time," Markus added. "With the exception of the [Lou] Brock trade, Holland's maneuvers have been worthy of a Machiavelli."

§

As the Cubs got ready to begin spring training workouts at their preseason home of Scottsdale, Arizona ("Sociable Scottsdale," as Banks liked to call it), there was tremendous collective sentiment that they could overtake St. Louis in the National League. "The Cubs are two players away from being a pennant winner," Jenkins tantalized the fans and the media as he arrived. "All we need is another good outfielder and a starting pitcher who can win about fifteen games." The Cardinals were having a bit of trouble re-signing some of their stars but finally inked pitchers Gibson, Nelson Briles, and Ray Washburn, as well as position players Mike Shannon, Lou Brock, and Curt Flood, in the early days of spring camp. Overall, the deals were reported to have cost Cardinals owner August A. Busch Jr. close to half a million dollars. Gibson, the overpowering force off the mound in '68, got the top deal, at $125,000 per year. The work was hardly done, however; remaining unsigned was the Cardinals' double play combination of shortstop Dal Maxvill and second baseman Julian Javier. The newest Redbird was Vada Pinson, as the former all-star was coming over from the Reds to take Roger Maris's place in right field.

The Cubs were among the first teams to begin spring exercises, with initial reportees—mostly pitchers and catchers—scheduled to arrive on February 19 and the rest of the squad to follow on the 23rd.

Money was indeed changing the game, and some of the widespread social ills of the day were starting to spill over into the industry of baseball. "Reconciliation for the nation" had been the theme of Richard M. Nixon's candidacy for U.S. president, for which he had been elected the previous November, defeating sitting vice president Hubert H. Humphrey from the Democratic Party and third-party runner George C. Wallace. Nixon, who had lost one of the closest presidential elections in history eight years earlier to John F. Kennedy, had just finished serving his first month in office by the time the Major League clubs headed to spring training in 1969. Labor troubles had been on the horizon for some time, however, and by the end of February, the Major League Baseball Players' Association (MLBPA)—headed by Miller—had reached an impasse with the owners over the issue of salary arbitration.

In addition, another concern had been stoked in midsummer 1968 when the players demanded a permanent percentage share of the new television revenue that was beginning to pour in; instead, the owners had offered a "flat total," which had been rebuffed by the players' association. The players had figured that proceeds from television and arbitration would bolster their pension fund, a plan that the owners in turn dismissed. "I was hoping they would accept it, since it would provide the opportunity for the most rapid means of attaining a settlement," Miller commented afterward. "We believe their refusal to submit the matter to arbitration indicates they have a real lack of confidence in their position." In lieu of going to arbitration, the owners offered to contribute an extra $200,000 to the pension fund, an idea that Miller instructed the players to refuse. Miller had certainly been through the wars before; in addition to the United Steelworkers, his client list had previously included the Machinists' Union and the United Auto Workers. When he took charge of the MLBPA in 1966 at age forty-nine, the players' association had $5,400 in the bank. Within two years he had successfully gotten the owners to raise the minimum Major League salary from $6,000 to $10,000, the first time any such similar increase had been seen since the 1940s.

It was thought that the pension issue would delay the opening of the training camps, as many veterans skipped the voluntary workouts that had already taken place in the third week of February; even a player boycott of all of spring training seemed possible. "You can't perpetrate a fraud on the fans," Kuhn stated, as some vacationers complained about not finding their superstar heroes in Florida and Arizona. "But as long as the fans know who you're fielding, I think you should go ahead and play the games." Kuhn, a lawyer, had previously served as a general counsel to the National League, and the 1948 Princeton grad held a commanding presence in most rooms when he entered with his six-foot-five-inch frame. In his younger days he had been a "scoreboard boy" for Washington Senators owner Clark Griffith, keeping the patrons up-to-date on the out-of-town scores during the Senators' games.

Almost all of the clubs made public statements that assured spectators of *some* type of games at training sites, even if more Minor League players had to be called into the fray. Other officials added their optimism to the situation. "The American League will be open for business on April 7th [Opening Day], no matter what," Junior Circuit boss Joe Cronin assured fans about his corner of the baseball world. The bitterness of Griffith—now the president of the Minnesota Twins—toward the players was apparent, however. He stated: "I'm going to be a hard-nosed guy because they're hurting us, they're hurting themselves, and they're hurting the American public when they do a thing like this. Anytime you can get a pension at 45, I'd like to be in on it. I have to wait until I'm 65 before I can get a pension."

All of the nonrookies were due in the Cubs' camp in Scottsdale by the evening of February 24, and several stragglers were coming in at the very end. Hickman, Elia, and Willie Smith were three among those who arrived from flights that got in just under the deadline. Meanwhile, a few pitchers who had already been there a week were working two-hour sessions with Durocher, who cautioned them not to labor too quickly and injure themselves in the unusually cool temperatures.

Over at the spring home of the White Sox in Sarasota, Florida, visitors may have thought they were at the infamous neighbor of Comiskey Park—the stockyards of Chicago—when seeing a restrictive sign regarding employment that hung over the clubhouse door: "Under no circumstances will players who are not signed be afforded the facilities of the clubhouse or be permitted to work out with the signed players. These players may work on their own, but not while the signed players are on the field." This sentiment was held firm by all owners and general managers. "When you see them on the field, you can assume they are signed," Holland said of the veterans who reported for the Cubs, "because they can't be there until they're under contract."

As the night of February 24 fell, more and more Cubs began to check into the team hotel, the Ramada in Scottsdale. Some had been in town for as long as a week—including Glenn Beckert, who was taking care of personal matters, which included hammering out the final details of his contract with Holland—but a player wasn't deemed to be officially "in camp" until he had moved into the hotel (in addition, players who weren't yet signed had to pay for each night they stayed until their contracts were inked). The fact that players from most teams were near their spring training towns offered more hope, as if they were awaiting word of a pension settlement with the owners at any moment. Strolling into the Ramada lobby came Billy Williams, and with each additional player passing by, the idea of the spring training boycott appeared to disintegrate. No one had seen Santo yet, but he was expected to arrive shortly. And all of the players had agreed to deals except for Jenkins, Kessinger, and Phillips, each of whom it was believed would be under contract soon.

Meanwhile, Miller and the player representatives from each of the clubs (who, for the Cubs, was Hundley—although he would soon pass the job on to a teammate) met with the owners back in New York without achieving an agreement during negotiations that went on until two o'clock in the morning.

More directly related to the fans' interest, the most curious of eyes were on Fort Lauderdale, Florida, where the New York Yankees were hoping to soon open camp. But whether that would be done with or without legendary outfielder Mickey Mantle remained to be seen, as Mantle was thinking of leaving the game. His current deal with New York had him being paid $100,000. If he chose not to retire, as he hinted that he might do at any minute, it would be his nineteenth season in the big leagues.

February 1969 was also a professional crossroads for another legend of the game, as former slugger Ted Williams donned a Washington Senators uniform for the first time (with his familiar old number "9" on the back of his jersey from his Red Sox days) in his rookie season as a big league manager. "A sort of revival center," Don Pierson of the *Tribune* called Washington DC at the close of the decade with Williams leading the Senators, President Nixon taking over the White House, and legendary Green Bay Packers football coach Vince Lombardi being lured out of retirement by the NFL's Redskins. "Vince Lombardi is everything I heard and more," star Washington quarterback Sonny Jurgensen proclaimed as football fans looked toward the fall. "Everything is different with us now—the atmosphere, the attitudes. We're not going to resemble the old Redskins in any way." The "old Redskins" had not seen a winning season since 1955, and everyone knew what had happened the last time Lombardi inherited a perennially losing club.

Everyone stopped and stood transfixed whenever Williams began to talk hitting, as the baseball kingdom was still looking for someone to match his season mark of .406, still the best since Williams had performed the feat in 1941. As his practices began in Pompano Beach, Florida, he was without his big slugger Frank Howard, who had yet to reach contract terms with the club. In discussing other managers around the league, Williams was impressed with his counterpart on the North Side of Chicago. "He is a great leader," Williams said. "Did you ever see a guy who didn't want to play for Durocher?"

The owners' negotiations with the players' union remained stagnant into the night of the 25th, with little hope apparently in sight. Then, in an eleventh-hour deal (at least as far as the timely opening of spring training was concerned), a compromise was struck. Described as the "7-Point Plan," it listed the following stipulations (as presented in the February 26, 1969, issue of the *Chicago Tribune*):

1. Reduction of minimum qualification for retirement benefits from five to four years;

2. Retirement benefits at age fifty increased from $500 to $600 a month for ten-year players;

3. Early retirement permitted at age 45;

4. Establishment of a dental program;

5. Life insurance increased to $50,000 for each active player and $25,000 for each presently inactive player;

6. Improved widows' benefits, disability benefits, maternity benefits, and other health care benefits; and

7. Lump-sum payments of a portion of benefits to retired players.

Kuhn exulted the agreement and boldly predicted that Major League Baseball would shatter all of its attendance records in 1969. "I am immensely pleased with the settlement which I feel is fair to the players and the clubs alike," he enthused. However, who were the real winners and losers on the scorecard? Phil Wrigley wasn't sure. "It was a tie, called by darkness or something," the gum heir proclaimed. "I think it ended with both sides saving face. But I thought it was a foregone conclusion from the start of all the fussing that there would be no delay in our spring plans."

So as practice began for the Chicagoans, the momentary no-shows among the "regulars" were Holtzman, Kessinger, Hands, Niekro, Nye, Regan, and Spangler, with the former two finishing up their obligatory military duty for the weekend and Regan driving down after completing some personal business in Michigan.

Hands was due any minute, having been held up by a snowstorm that had socked his native New Jersey as he left there by car, trying to catch a flight out of Chicago to Arizona. Niekro and Nye had driven from Chicago to Scottsdale and were among the last ones to arrive on the first day, just ahead of Spangler, who had driven in from Houston. Spangler had a home in Houston, and he had played in the very first game in the Houston Astrodome in 1965 as a member of the Astros ("Before I knew it, though, I was traded to the Angels," he reflected later on his short stay in the new indoor arena). On the afternoon before the players' association and owners came together, Jenkins agreed to a contract deal, leaving Kessinger and Phillips as the only outstanding negotiations. The Cubs were ahead of the game in this area; none of the other teams had all of its players signed at this point. There would ultimately be a total of forty-four players in the Cubs' Major League camp, consisting of the allotted thirty-five roster players and nine nonroster invitees.

Santo arrived in Scottsdale in impressive form, while Williams was a few pounds underweight from a lingering sickness over the winter. Santo was looking to bounce back from a subpar year in 1968, during which—despite smacking 26 home runs and driving in 98—he had batted only .246, the second-lowest figure of his career. He credited a vigorous training regimen over the colder months for his finely tuned physique. "I played basketball all winter," Santo revealed, "and I feel like I'm in great shape." On March 1, however, Santo injured his elbow during practice and needed to have fluid drained from the inflamed joint. Santo was afraid he had reaggravated a similar problem that had surfaced the previous August. "Luckily, last year when I had it, there was a day off the next day and I got the elbow drained and it was okay," he reminded worriers. "I didn't miss a game because of it. Glenn [Beckert] had the same thing later that month and he missed two days with it. We thought maybe it had something to do with the way we were throwing."

The very next day both Kessinger and Phillips came to terms on their contracts. For the first time since Durocher took over the team in 1966, he would enjoy almost an entire spring training with all of his players in the fold. It was the young outfielder Dunegan who impressed in the early intrasquad games, as the rookie was beginning to make a case for a starting job. "Dunegan will have to win the right field job permanently now, or we won't keep him around just sitting on the bench," Durocher pointed out. "I would rather he went to the minors where he could play regularly and get the experience."

On March 1 Mantle answered the question that folks had been asking all spring: he would indeed hang up his cleats and leave behind the game that he loved. "I'm not going to play baseball anymore—that's all I know," Mantle told the press as he emotionally glanced up and down behind a microphone at the Yankees' spring training hotel. "I can't play anymore. I can't hit the ball when I need to. I can't score from second base when I need to." In Ruthian fashion the comet from Commerce, Oklahoma, had lived New York life in the fast lane, and the hard living had finally caught up with him. While much was made of his nighttime frolicking, however, Mantle had painted a brilliant, gutsy, eighteen-year career. "I hate to see him go," observed fellow American League star Al Kaline of the Detroit Tigers. "I thought he was the greatest player I ever played with [on All-Star teams] or against." The adored Mick left the Major Leagues as a sixteen-time All-Star and a three-time MVP, and with more home runs than any switch-hitter in history. "Mantle is one of the last of a breed," Markus wrote of Number Seven's ability to dominate all facets of the game. "The super-player in baseball is dying out. . . . Perhaps there can be no more superstars when players are a symptom of our time, a time when mediocrity seems to be the goal, when to stand out, to be different, is to be avoided. Perhaps there can be no more superstars when players are more concerned with their pensions than they are with playing the game."

Nearly a week after Mantle made his announcement, reigning National League batting champ Pete Rose ended his holdout and agreed to a contract with the Reds. The deal, which was believed to be paying Rose between $85,000 and $90,000, was the most ever given to a Cincinnati ballplayer. As with Holtzman and Kessinger, part of Rose's delay in getting to training camp had been due to military obligations. Soon after, on March 8, it was announced that Don Drysdale had agreed to a $120,000 salary to remain with Los Angeles. For the past several months Drysdale, Santo, and eight other major stars had been courted by a proposed maverick new league to be called the "Global League," with Al "Happy" Chandler as its first commissioner. The league, wishing to establish teams from Tokyo to the Dominican Republic and at several American sites in between, dangled large sums of money in front of the players to entice them to jump from their current contracts. Santo wasn't interested, however, and nor were most of those contacted. One of the American cities being considered for a team was Milwaukee, who had lost the Braves to Atlanta three years earlier. The *Washington Post* reported on March 3 that the proposed league had failed to reach a television agreement with any network and that the concept was thus doomed. Two days later the Cubs gave their four pillars—Santo, Williams, Banks, and Jenkins—new two-year contract extensions.

For some of the exhibition games in the spring of 1969, Major League Baseball had decided to try an "experimental pinch-hitter rule," with a batter designated to hit for the pitcher. Durocher, for one, did not care for the idea. "It takes the managership away from me," he complained. "It ties my hands. . . . These rules are going in my wastebasket." In a similar tone American League chief Cronin added, "The battle of wits between managers, which I'm sure the spectators enjoy, would be virtually eliminated if these rules were permanently adopted." Leo had not been in a particularly good mood recently anyway, because it was an unusually cold and damp March for Arizona, and he had spent much of the first week holed up in his hotel room with Franks. (Incidentally, it had been while managing the Giants that Franks, in part, had gotten Leo back into baseball in 1966, as he placed a phone call to Holland and suggested that the Cubs hire Durocher.) The two passed the time by chatting about the upcoming season and by playing gin rummy with themselves and any two partners they could grab out of the hallway. "I've been here since February 20," Durocher had muttered on one occasion as he viewed his hand, "and I haven't seen a really good day yet. I don't think the Cubs have had three games rained out in the 16 years they've been coming to Arizona. Well, we got one today, and we might have more."

"Worst weather I've ever seen out here," added Franks, as he whipped a sequence of hearts onto the table, much to Leo's further dismay.

"What are you two yappin' about?" asked Reiser, coming down the corridor. When he played for Durocher in Brooklyn, Reiser became famous for running into outfield walls in pursuit of fly balls (in addition to being known as a gifted player). "We play in Montreal in April, right?" he continued, referring to the upcoming games with the expansion Expos. "If they get a day like this up there, they go on picnics."

But it was Becker, the pitching coach, who really had reason to moan. He was forced to continuously reshuffle his rotation for the exhibition games as the weather had altered his plan for his main men to get the work they needed. The lefty Holtzman was causing him further chagrin by insisting on throwing only fastballs for his first ten days in camp; Becker refused, wanting instead for Holtzman to start working on his curve. Commented Becker: "I went along with it for two years and finally this spring I said to him: 'All right, we've done it your way and it hasn't worked; now start working on all three of your pitches on the first day.'"

Reiser continued his diatribe in a team meeting later that week when he took over the club (on his fiftieth birthday) with Leo back in Chicago making a public appearance. The club had lost eight of the first nine games to its Cactus League opponents. Reiser had seen enough of the lax attitude that had been going around camp, and he stated in no uncertain terms that things would change—especially with the players' children, who had been running rampant all over the grounds. "I've been serious all along, but apparently some people haven't," he mentioned in reference to the poor start for the team in the preseason schedule. "We had a meeting, and we didn't chew anybody out; we just told them that we're going to enforce some clubhouse rules.

We're not running a country club around here. We told them they couldn't bring their kids on the field anymore, or in the dugout. They're down here to play ball, not to be nursemaids." In addition, morning practice was moved up from 10:00 to 9:30 as an extra wake-up call to the lethargic players.

In the second week the Cubs brightened things up for themselves by welcoming a special guest from Chicago to join their workouts in Scottsdale. Gale Sayers, who had stormed onto the NFL scene as an amazing rookie running back with the Chicago Bears in 1965, would train with the Cubs in an effort to strengthen his repaired right knee. The knee had been shattered nine games into the Bears' 1968 season against the San Francisco 49ers, as Sayers headed toward the sidelines on a sweep and was ferociously struck by 49ers defensive back Kermit Alexander. Later in the year Sayers would sign a three-year contract with the Bears for $25,000 a year, making him the highest-paid player in team history under tight-fisted owner George Halas, founder of the league who finally gave up the coaching reins of the team after 1967.

But Sayers's presence couldn't help Durocher sort out certain problems on his team, such as the situation in the outfield. Part of Leo's frustration with Phillips had been Adolfo's continuing unwillingness to bat in the lead-off position, an attitude that stemmed from his unrelenting fear of getting hit by the ball. Those fears had not been allayed on March 11, when he had been nailed twice in an exhibition game against the Angels and driven to the ground on two other close pitches. One pitch that struck Phillips caused more than just psychological damage, as it was revealed the next day that a small bone in his right hand had been fractured. At the time he had been off to the fastest start of any of the players, leading the team in early exhibition play with a .444 average and two stolen bases. He was flown back to Chicago immediately for further treatment, and the center-field pasture in Scottsdale temporarily belonged to Oscar Gamble. It was expected by Dr. Jacob Suker expected that Phillips would miss up to four weeks, approaching the start of the regular season. Phillips was to be in a cast until the first week of April, when the team would return to Chicago. The season would begin for the Cubs on April 8, and Phillips's healing speed in the five-day interim would determine his availability.

In the meantime the flashy Gamble showed off the power and speed that had Durocher excited about the teenager. "He's got it all," the skipper said of Oscar. "All he needs is experience." In his first day on the job on March 12, Gamble socked two hits, drove in three runs, and threw out a runner at home plate in the very first inning of a game in which the Cubs posted an 8-6 win over the Giants. Before the game Banks introduced the young Gamble to Willie Mays, and the rookie was obviously awe-struck. "It was the first time I've seen him so excited," Banks chuckled. "He was so nervous he was shaking. I told him, 'I've got somebody I want you to meet.' I didn't tell him who until we got over to Willie." The Giants' other big Willie—imposing first baseman Willie "Stretch" McCovey—would end his hold-out that afternoon, agreeing to a contract of $160,000 over two years. And a few days later the Giants' front office had deals with all their key components, as star pitcher Juan Marichal got a $15,000 raise to put his yearly rate at a nifty $115,000. He promptly celebrated by throwing four hitless innings at the Cubs on March 16. He retired the twelve straight batters on forty-one pitches, allowing only three fair balls to be hit out of the infield. Meanwhile, the immortal Mays was looking more like a rookie with something to prove. "He has tossed himself around more recklessly than a 38-year-old should," reported James McGee for the *San Francisco Examiner*.

The other promising young outfielder, Dunegan, had begun to cool off considerably. "I've got to get Hickman in right field," Leo observed, as Dunegan's lack of big league experience was starting to show. The Burlington, Iowa, native was only twenty-one years old, however, and displayed physical capabilities that boded well for the future. Don Young had performed well, and Durocher was beginning to think about a Gamble-Young platoon in center field to start the season if Phillips wasn't ready.

On March 16 Elia became the first roster casualty of the spring as he was dismissed from big league camp. Elia, who had played in 15 games during the '68 season for Chicago, was soon joined by twelve other players who were released. Elia, the only Major League veteran out of the thirteen players to get an early pink slip, had won a game for the Cubs with an extra-inning single against the Cardinals on August 4 of the previous year. As the Cubs were announcing the placement of Elia on waivers, St. Louis was also causing a stir over the transaction wires: in a one-for-one, star-for-star deal, they sent first baseman Orlando Cepeda to the Braves for catcher Joe Torre, who would join Pinson as the new big names in the St. Louis lineup. Relations had become strained between Torre and the Braves' general manager, Paul Richards, because Torre had been holding out for more money—a move that didn't impress Richards. "He can hold out until Thanksgiving if he wants to," Richards had answered.

By the third week of March, Qualls had not given up on the center-field job either, as he had gone 9 for his last 14 at the plate (.643) and had played sparkling defense. His hot streak was thus a prelude to the reassignment of Gamble (along with eight other players) to the Minor League camp on March 23. Durocher and Holland had now changed their minds, deciding that if Phillips was not ready to go on Opening Day, Qualls or Young would start in center field. Gamble, who was hitting .316 at the time and was third on the team with 12 hits, was disappointed in the move. "It is a certain bet, however, that the little speedster will return before too long," George Langford predicted in his *Tribune* column, "as soon as he attains the required experience." Dunegan had not completely played himself out of the right-field position, as Durocher and others continued to marvel at his strong power and the long home runs that he stroked in batting practice each day. "Sure, he's going to strike out a lot," Leo reasoned, "but so did Reggie Jackson of the A's last year, and in between he hit 29 home runs. I've got to look a long time at Dunegan. It will be a difficult decision." The Cubs' biggest concern was about Dunegan's awkwardness on defense. He spent an extra half-hour each day with Reiser on tracking fly balls off the coach's machine-like fungo bat.

Despite the games being only exhibition contests, on March

25 Leo proved that his forensic fire still burned as he argued balls and strikes with umpire Mel Steiner in a game against one of the new expansion teams, the San Diego Padres. Durocher was most upset at Steiner's stance, which was basically a sitting position that, while probably more comfortable, did not afford a very good view of the pitches—at least in Leo's opinion.

The manager finally announced the next day that the center-field job belonged to Young, who was enjoying the finest spring of his career in his long jump from class-A ball. But Qualls (who was seeing time in the infield as well) and fellow rookie John Lung were not satisfying Durocher as backups to Kessinger at short, so quickly signed was Charley Smith, a thirty-one-year-old journeyman infielder who had most recently been with the Yankees as a starter and in the Giants' Minor League system after a trade between those two clubs the past winter. "I was surprised I came here," Smith admitted, "but I think I can help the Cubs. They've got a good chance to win the division."

Smith was a choice almost by default, however, as quality reserve infielders were becoming hard to locate. "Finding a shortstop who can play seems like pulling teeth," a frustrated Holland said while looking for someone to give Kessinger a rest. Holland hoped that Smith was the answer. Lung, who had starred at UCLA, was sent to the Cubs' triple-A team at Tacoma, as was reserve catcher Randy Bobb. Also ordered to Tacoma was Dunegan, as Durocher set himself on Hickman as his right fielder. While the skipper liked Dunegan, Durocher repeated his desire for him to get regular at-bats in the minors instead of sitting on the bench at Wrigley Field. "The trip to the minors will do him good," Leo pointed out, "and he may be back with us in a couple of months." The veterans were impressed with Dunegan and the other youngsters as well. "I've been a Cub for 17 years," Banks reflected. "Kessinger's in his fifth year, and Hundley his fourth. But the young kids are proof that baseball's not suffering from the new crop. Great ones are coming up every year."

The spring crowds got smaller and smaller, and the players took notice—especially of the paltry 1,800 that showed to watch the Cubs play the A's in Oakland on March 29. Part of the reasoning for the trip was to allow Oakland fans a chance to see the Cubs in their local stadium, but, apparently, not too many were interested in the opportunity. "It would have been cheaper to fly the crowd to Arizona than bring both teams here," Beckert opined. Perhaps most people were instead tuned into the news as, the day before, former President Dwight D. Eisenhower had passed away at age seventy-nine.

Nearing the end of March, the bats were popping. Five out of the eight Cubs position starters were hitting over .300 for the spring: Kessinger (.431), Hundley (.393), Beckert (.318), Santo (.309), and Banks (.305). The team's winning percentage, however, was hovering around the .500 mark, with their not having won half of their twenty-one games by March 30. But Leo was none too concerned. "I like for our spring training record to be right around .500," he said. "Two above or two below .500. What were we at the beginning? One and eight. Now we're 10-11. That's about what I wanted." The team batting average was also very healthy at .302 but was tempered in the pitching department by a lofty staff ERA of 5.12. Perhaps the new mound was having its effect after all, and fans everywhere wondered about the pennant race in the National League with all of the good pitching that still abounded. "I know it's going to be tough, especially with the Cardinals and Mets," Kessinger ominously predicted as training camp drew to a close. "The Mets are going to surprise a lot of people."

Indeed, everyone and *everything* had their thoughts on the upcoming season. As mainframe computers started to enter more facets of society, the monstrous machines were fed data in order to make their predictions on the pennant races—and their result was the Cubs finishing third behind the Cardinals and the Pirates. "Last year the computer hit a home run," reminded Bud Goode of the *Washington Post.* "On the opening day of the season, 'Computer Corner' [the program developed by the paper] tabbed the Detroit Tigers as the walkaway winners in the American League and the St. Louis Cardinals in the National League. Both won."

But, as usual, those in Chicago were undaunted by preseason forecasts, even those calculated by the impressive new machines.

It was obvious to those wearing the Cubs uniform that a sense of family had developed among the players. "We got a chance to know one another," Jenkins would reflect years later. "It was a very small clubhouse [at Wrigley Field]. An integral part of that was having closeness. I don't think anyone was bitter about this guy's ability or that guy's ability. And by far, we didn't make any money, so nobody was jealous of our salaries. We didn't make squat back in those days. It was terrible."

"But we were definitely close," he continued. "A lot of times, we used to all go out. I can recall the first time I ever got caught after curfew. There were a bunch of us out in St. Louis. We were staying at the Park Plaza Hotel. Leo was not one to check on everybody, but he gave the night elevator operator a ball. 'Hey, would you sign this ball for my kid?' And it was like signing your death warrant."

It was time to head north, the majestic beginning of all things in late March, as the weather warmed and thoughts of outdoor activity perennially took hold. The pens of the writers had warmed up too, and like the computers, they began their own baseball soothsaying. "It is conceded that St. Louis will dominate the division and that the Chicago Cubs ought to finish second," Leonard Koppett of the *New York Times* claimed. "That leaves Philadelphia and Pittsburgh as the teams the Mets must beat for third or fourth. . . . If some key Cubs have a bad year, the club could easily drop back into the Pirates-Phillies-Mets pack." Added his colleague at the *Times* Arthur Daley: "The East is the personal property of the St. Louis Cardinals, perhaps the best and deepest ball club to be seen in the preseason tournament. It is impossible to pick against them. Under the driving lash of Leo Durocher, the Chicago Cubs have become a genuine threat. They finished third a year ago and conceivably could be a winner this season if geographers had placed them in the Western Division. Unfortunately for them, however, they are in the East."

But ironically, it was the ever-cautious Durocher, he of the "driving lash" and usual self-deprecation of his clubs, who seemed to have the most enthusiasm about his team going into the season. "These guys have shown me they want to pick up all the marbles," he commented. "We finally reached the spirit and desire on this club that we've been trying for three years to get."

"He'll do anything to win; he's one in a million," Santo said of Durocher. "You don't have to love a man to respect him, but I know that everybody on this club respects him. Other clubs respect him, too."

"He doesn't even have to tell you he's the boss," added Ernie Banks about his manager. "You know that when he comes onto the scene."

§

The Cubs finished the exhibition schedule with a 13-15 record, ending things by losing three out of four to the White Sox in a barnstorming road show that stopped in Memphis, Indianapolis, Milwaukee, and finally Wrigley Field. The temperature at Milwaukee was in the low forties, and Durocher chose to skip the event and stay in his Chicago apartment, nursing a cold. It was the first of fourteen Major League games that were to be played in Milwaukee in 1969, a city that had been abandoned by the Braves three years earlier—although, to local fans, it seemed like only yesterday. The Badger State was thankful to entertain the two clubs from down the road as a substitute. "The White Sox have come up with some good ones," Jenkins noticed about the impressive youngsters in the South Siders' lineup. "They say that pitching is eighty percent of this game, and the Sox have the people to pitch."

The Cubs and Sox were not too pleased with the condition of the ballpark in Indy, as just over four thousand people entered to watch. Langford noted that "there was painters' scaffolding in the third base stands, the sideline pitching mounds were plowed like a vegetable patch, and there were broken whiskey bottles in the outfield. . . . Indianapolis' Bush Stadium had been caught in the middle of spring cleaning, obviously not expecting company." Durocher was so mad at the state of the grounds that he started mostly reserve players in the game, in fear of his stars getting hurt.

As the clubs made their way north, they arrived in Chicago to find Bears owner George Halas making his own pleas regarding stadiums—specifically, to the city council and the state legislature—for a domed arena for his team, similar to the astounding new $31 million Astrodome in Houston. Many in Chicago, including Condon, agreed. "The impossible dream should become a dream fulfilled," he wrote in painting the vision of a massive structure to sit on the city's lakefront. "If any city requires a domed, all-weather sports stadium to seat 80,000, that city is Chicago. . . . Too many minor league cities are already ahead of us. With an all-weather stadium, Chicago could bid for both the Super Bowl and the National Football League's playoff bowl." Such a venue was seen as a possibility for baseball, too. Added Ted Williams, "Chicago is the one city where a domed stadium would really pay off." Executives in Houston were playing the fabulous new building to the hilt, offering Astros fans free circus tickets and tours of the structure in addition to baseball tickets. Some, however, didn't see the move toward such architecture as progress. "I think domed stadiums will take something away from sports, whether it's baseball or football," one Major League coach suggested. "It reminds me of chickens being raised in heated coops and never being exposed to the ground."

An even more grand facility was being planned for New Orleans. Talks had begun in 1967 on the construction of a climate-controlled domed stadium for the hot, steamy region of southeastern Louisiana. The "Louisiana Superdome" would surpass Houston's venue in every regard, including football capacity (eighty-three thousand in Louisiana compared to Houston's fifty-two thousand), height (280 feet to 208), concession stands (sixty-eight to forty-nine), and even restrooms (sixty-four to forty). The seats at the Superdome would be an average of 65 feet closer to the field than those of the Astrodome, and for seats at the level of 75 feet off the ground, the seats at the Superdome would be 100 feet closer to the field than those at the same height at the existing home of the NFL's Saints, Tulane Stadium. New Orleans high schools were told that they could use the dome for football games on Friday nights—if they could pay the negotiable cost of rent and the $800-per-game air-conditioning bill, smirked an editorial in the local newspaper, the *New Orleans Times-Picayune.*

But despite the skeptics, the Bears envisioned the same type of facility for Chicago, and the head man was convinced he was going to get it. "Halas told the [Illinois] House executive committee that such a facility is necessary to maintain the city's standing as one of the sports capitals of the world," the *Tribune* reported on April 2. The original plan was for the massive arena to seat the eighty thousand people that Condon suggested, and to be adjustable to occasionally accommodate any of the city's five major sports teams (in addition to the Bears, Cubs, and White Sox, it would also be made ready on demand for the Blackhawks of the National Hockey League and the Bulls of the National Basketball Association). Moral and political debate on the issue heated up, however, when Halas suggested that horse racing could take place inside the venue as well. The Bears were looking to move out of Wrigley Field, their home for the first fifty years of the team's existence. And increased revenue had certainly been on Halas's mind anyway, as he was struggling to sign one of the team's top draft picks, left-handed quarterback Bobby Douglass out of the University of Kansas.

Ernie Banks had his own humble thoughts to offer on the subject. "Maybe I'm showing my age, but I still think baseball is best when it's played with that sun shining down and the wind blowing—especially if it's towards left field which makes those Wrigley Field seats easier to reach," Mr. Cub countered in reference to the possibility of the sport going indoors in Chicago. "What would I have done all these years without some occasional help from the breezes?" The possibility of a domed stadium for Chicago's sports teams would be decided later in the summer.

In getting the roster to the mandatory twenty-five players, the Cubs ordered pitchers Decker and Reynolds, as well as catcher Bill Heath and infielder Francisco Libran, to the minors. Three other catchers made the squad, as Ken Rudolph reaped the benefits of a strong spring to find himself on the roster with Hundley and Oliver. The other position players included Beckert, Kessinger, Santo, Banks, Willie Smith, Charley Smith, Qualls,

Spangler, Hickman, Phillips, Williams, and Young; also, pitchers Abernathy, Aguirre, Distaso, Hands, Holtzman, Jenkins, Niekro, Nye, Regan, and Gary Ross made the team. The tenures of Ross and Distaso were expected to be brief, however, for while the required number had been crafted, Holland warned that there may be a trade or two occurring before Opening Day (April 8). Specifically, he was still trying to find someone besides Kessinger who could play shortstop, as neither Qualls nor Smith had yet demonstrated any proficiency at the position.

While the Cubs were making their way to Milwaukee, Holtzman's National Guard unit was called to active duty to quell an uprising on Chicago's West Side, and the left-hander quickly traded his glove for a rifle. Civil unrest was still touching American cities in early 1969, and Chicago was seeing its share. The *Tribune* reported on April 5 that "the city counted 90 injured and 271 arrested in the hours of fighting, rock throwing, gunfire, and looting which began about noon Thursday [April 3] and lasted through the late afternoon [of Friday]."

But most of the city's residents tried to ignore the madness going on in the streets and instead settle in behind the sports reports in the newspapers and on television; the information they truly wanted to hear was the conjecture for the upcoming pennant races. The Mets indeed thought they had positioned themselves for a run at the National League flag, even though most experts didn't give them much hope of taking the crown. "I've got so many young people who have great ability," warned manager Gil Hodges, "that we've got to be better." Hodges was boldly predicting that his Mets would win at least eighty-five games on the year, which would amount to twelve more victories than the club had attained in 1968, in his first year at the helm. "There are only two kinds of managers," Hodges had said when he took his first skipper's job back in 1963 with the Washington Senators, "winning managers and ex-managers." He had spent five years in Washington before becoming the Mets' top man, returning to New York, where he had been a star first baseman for the Dodgers in the 1950s and, later, one of the original Met players in 1962 and 1963. Hodges had broken into the big leagues as a nineteen-year-old rookie in 1943, appearing twice at the plate that season with Durocher as his manager in Brooklyn.

The predominance of the prognosticators had the Cubs and New Yorkers following the Cardinals, as St. Louis was generally expected to repeat as the National League winner. "There is, however, hope for the Cubs," Langford pointed out. "There is the theory that the champion Cardinals, with the highest payroll in baseball and three pennant checks in the last five seasons, may lack the hunger, the motivation for another title. A writer for a national magazine remarked after a visit to the Cardinal camp this spring: 'Something is rotten there.'"

With the Major Leagues expanding to twenty-four teams, it was deemed reasonable by the league offices and owners to divide each league into two six-team divisions, which would also provide an expansion of the playoff system—even if one's glance at a map would not correspond with the set-up. The Cubs wound up in the National League's "Eastern Division," while the crosstown White Sox, ironically, found themselves in the American League West. "The immediate reaction is that the National Leaguers must have flunked geography," wrote Arthur Daley in the *New York Times*. "They have placed St. Louis and Chicago in the East, although each is situated on the sun-setting side of Cincinnati and Atlanta, which were dropped with quaint arbitrariness into the West."

On the South Side of Chicago, a strange scene was unfolding at the corner of 35th Street and Shields Avenue. At Comiskey Park, the home of the White Sox, the grass sod had been removed. In its place went the newly designed "Astroturf," which was already in use at the Astrodome in Houston. The artificial surface took some getting used to by the players, but many—especially Yankees manager Ralph Houk—thought it would ultimately benefit the Sox. "With the turf, the White Sox will possess a definite advantage in their home park," Houk said. "I'll tell you one thing—it's a good bit faster than regular grass." In addition, the outfield wall at Comiskey was shortened five feet toward home plate at center field and the power alleys, as well as seventeen feet down the foul lines, in an effort to increase home runs at the stadium. The Sox appeared committed to providing a good product for their customers and at what they thought to be a convenient, comfortable venue. "Getting to Wrigley Field is like getting to Havana by train," Condon complained, although biased as a self-proclaimed "South Sider" of years gone by. He insisted that it was time for the Cubs front office to consider sweeping changes. "The Cubs have been outhustled by White Sox promoters. . . . For more years than most of us care to remember, the Cub owner [Phil Wrigley] has resisted all pressures to install lights and give fans a percentage of night games. We've heard a score of baseball executives declare: 'If I could buy the Cubs, I'd install lights and set an all-time major league attendance record.'"

The White Sox were expected to mildly compete with the Minnesota Twins and the Oakland A's for loop honors in the American League West, which also included two expansion franchises in the Seattle Pilots and the Kansas City Royals, as well as the California Angels. In the East a close race was forecasted between the defending world champion Tigers and the talent-laden Baltimore Orioles, both expected to leave the Yankees, Red Sox, Senators, and Indians far behind. The Orioles were rejuvenated when Earl Weaver took over the manager's position in mid-1968, leading to a 91-71 finish and second place. Despite the lowering of the mound, great pitching duels were still anticipated between the Tigers' McLain and Mickey Lolich (the latter of whom was the actual World Series hero in 1968 against the Cardinals, winning three\ games) and the imposing staff of the Orioles, including Jim Palmer, Mike Cuellar, and Dave McNally.

Durocher figured that front runners in these new "divisions" who gained sizable leads by midsummer would be hard to overtake. "It's going to be much harder in this divisional play for a club to catch up," he warned. "You only have to worry about five clubs. The others don't bother me. My only worry about the Western teams is when I play them, and we only play each other twelve times."

Joining the Cubs, Cardinals, and Mets in the National League East would be the Pittsburgh Pirates, the Philadelphia Phillies, and the Montreal Expos, the latter bringing Major League Baseball to Canada for the first time. "The Mets, who have finished tenth in the National League five times and ninth twice, can do no worse than sixth this year," Joseph Durso of the *New York Times* encouraged his readers with the new set-up, "and are even gunning for third or fourth place." Soon, the NFL would follow suit, as a merger would take place with the American Football League to form divisional play for the 1970 season.

The Pirates— with all-league right fielder Roberto Clemente— were thought to be a factor in the race, while the Phillies were imagined to be rebuilding around rookies Don Money and Larry Hisle. Over in the National League West, a three-team race was figured among the veteran-laden teams of the Reds, Giants, and Dodgers, followed by the Braves, Astros, and Padres to round out the division. The Padres were playing for the first time as a Major League unit, with the seaside city long hosting a team in the Pacific Coast League. There was indeed much that was new to the majors in 1969, with fledgling teams in San Diego, Seattle, Kansas City, and Montreal; the new pitching mound height; a new commissioner in Kuhn; and eight new managers who would be guiding different clubs.

Taking over the managerial duties of the new Montreal team was Gene Mauch, who had been relieved as manager of the Phillies not quite halfway into the 1968 season. "An expansion team figures to lose, granted," Mauch offered about his club's fortunes in their inaugural year of 1969. "Yet, an expansion team doesn't lose as much as it gives away. I don't think we'll be giving away lots of games—not as solid as we figure to be at catcher, second, and short. The ball is handled too much by those three men, and we have the men to handle it. These guys can play, and what's more important, they know it."

In addition, Mauch had the good feeling of falling back on the leadership of established players Rusty Staub and Maury Wills. Staub almost was not an Expo, for Kuhn had threatened to veto the January 22nd trade that was to send him from Houston to Montreal for Donn Clendenon and Jesus Alou. A month after the trade, Clendenon announced that he was going on the "voluntarily retired" list, and Kuhn ordered the trade to stand—despite the protests of the Astros organization, which viewed the move as infringing on the reserve clause. They wanted Staub back and were threatening to sue everyone—Kuhn, the Expos, and Major League Baseball itself—to get that accomplished and thereby rectify what they viewed as a crime. "We are pledged to try and overthrow the decision," Houston owner Roy Hofheinz stated on March 22. "Unless it is changed, no trade in the future will be final until the commissioner decides how he wants to shuffle the deck." Hofheinz didn't think that Kuhn had the authority to make such judgments—even if his interim job title was about to be made permanent. "It is regrettable that this decision was made by a pro-tempore commissioner," he added. Kuhn suggested that the Expos send another player to the Astros as compensation for Clendenon's retirement, but Montreal didn't think that idea was fair either. Ultimately, Kuhn threatened to choose a player himself from the Montreal roster for shipment to Houston if the two clubs could not reach an agreement. Finally, in an ironic twist, Clendenon signed with the Expos on April 2, while Montreal sent pitchers Jack Billingham, Skip Guinn, and cash to the Astros as a peace offering.

"I needed two years to take the club apart," Mauch bemoaned about assuming the manager's job with the beleaguered Phillies back in 1960. "With Montreal, I don't have to disassemble a team—just assemble one. One of the beautiful things about baseball is that every day is a brand new day."

Durocher, however, wasn't a fan of Mauch's. "If the Expos stick with that little genius long enough," Leo said, "they'll continue to stay in last place."

4

Opening Day

> I believe in the Rip Van Winkle
> Theory: that a man from 1910
> must be able to wake up after be-
> ing asleep for sixty years, walk into
> a ballpark, and understand base-
> ball perfectly.
>
> —Bowie Kuhn

Things were right on schedule for the Cubs as Dolf Phillips had the cast removed from his hand, as planned, on April 4. "The x-rays of his hand showed good healing," Dr. Suker informed the press about the outfielder, "but it will probably be a week to ten days before he can return. It is a matter of strength return-ing to his hand. . . . You can't make a hard-and-fast statement on just when he'll be ready. It's an individual matter." Young, Phillips's replacement, had been working with Reiser every day to develop his arm strength; both men had noticed that Young's arm would stiffen if he did not keep a throwing regimen each day. Meanwhile, Durocher announced that it would be Jenkins,

Hands, and Holtzman (as expected), in that order, to start the season for the Cubs against the Phillies.

On April 8 the Cubs enjoyed their largest Opening Day crowd in forty years, as nearly 41,000 spectators crammed into the ballpark (43,824 had seen the opener in 1929). Out of those, 27,000 had purchased tickets on the day of the game starting at 8:00 a.m. (5,000 of which were bleacher seats), as all of the reserve seats had long been sold out. (The previous year Wrigley Field had cleared 1 million customers for the first time in sixteen seasons.) The weather was better than expected in Chicago, as temperatures rose to the upper sixties, but with threatening skies, as the Cubs sought to increase their National League record with their fortieth Opening Day victory. On April 7 four games had already launched the one hundredth year of professional baseball, as the Dodgers beat the Reds behind Drysdale, 3–2, and the Braves beat the Giants on Mike Lum's ninth-inning single, 5–4, in the only National League contests. Over in the American League a city record for an opener (45,113 fans)—including President Nixon, who threw out the first ball—came out in Washington to see Williams lose his debut as a manager, 8–4, to the Yankees. Part of the Yankee output had come from the bat of Bobby Murcer, a promising young center fielder who had been given Mantle's locker in Yankee Stadium. The only bright spot for the home folks had been when Howard shot a home run to straightaway center field in the ninth, at which the president sprang to his feet in enjoyment.

"It's only a game," manager Williams said stoically in review of the much-ballyhooed event.

In other senior circuit inaugurals on the 8th, Steve Blass would be taking the hill for the Pirates against Gibson and the Cardinals in St. Louis, the Expos would play their first game ever in New York against pitching phenom Tom Seaver and the Mets, and the Padres would start writing their history at home against the Astros behind Dick Selma, Seaver's companion from high school in Fresno.

Ernie Banks's father attended the Chicago opener, there to support his son, whom Langford described in the *Tribune* that day as "the inspiration and symbol of optimism to a large cult of north side baseball devotees." Preparing for the start of the season, Banks was his usual positive self. "This is my biggest chance to be on a winner," he said in anticipation. "I feel like this year we really do have the talent to do it and I want to be able to do everything I can to make it happen." Helping to usher in the new season was an appearance by entertainer Jimmy Durante, a special guest of the Cubs for the occasion. He was given a Cubs jacket by Santo in a pregame ceremony.

"The Cubs are ready to go for all the marbles," Durocher had told the *Chicago American* earlier in the week. "We have sound hitting, the best defense in the league, and pitching that is constantly improving."

The ex-Phillie Jenkins walked to the hill for Chicago, making his third straight Opening Day start for the Cubs, while the ten-year veteran Chris Short would fire for Philadelphia. The Loyola Academy band tooted out the national anthem, marking the first time in many years that "Colonel" Armin Hand's orchestra had not performed the ceremony on Opening Day. The crowd roared as Banks emerged from the dugout and made the short jog to his first base position. Beckert was right behind him, and the second baseman turned and wished the TV men in the camera area next to the dugout a good season. After the first ball was thrown out to Hundley by *Chicago Sun-Times* writer Edgar Munzel (who was the dean of baseball scribes, supposedly logging the longest record of service to the game by 1969), the Phillies started things by getting a run off Jenkins in the first. But Ernie responded to the audience in the bottom half with a long three-run homer to left, scoring Beckert and Williams and giving the Cubs a 3–1 advantage. Among the loudest cheers were those from seventy-three-year-old Eddie Banks, who flagged down his son with both arms after Junior had crossed home plate. Ernie meekly nodded to his father and quickly tipped his helmet to the rest of the fans.

The crowd buzzed with anticipation when Banks sauntered into the batter's box again in the third, and once again Banks rose to the occasion. He destroyed another pitch from Short, landing it in the bleachers for the 476th round-tripper of his career, jumping him ahead of Stan Musial and into the top ten for all time. The Cubs held a 5–1 lead and appeared to be cruising. But then came the Don Money show. The twenty-one-year-old rookie shortstop, whom the Phillies had acquired from the Pirates organization for veteran star pitcher Jim Bunning, launched a home run in his first Major League game to make the score 5–2. Jenkins sailed through the Philadelphia order until the ninth, when he gave up bloop hits to Johnny Callison and Cookie Rojas. The right-hander then made a crucial mistake to the eager youngster Money, and the rookie had his second big league homer, a long drive onto Waveland Avenue and good for a 5–5 tie. The contest then went into the eleventh, when Money—who had only four games of Major League experience under his belt from the 1968 season—drove home his fifth run of the game by scoring Callison again, this time on a double off of Regan. The Phillies had a 6–5 lead and looked to finish off the Cubs in the bottom half behind another rookie, pitcher Barry Lersch.

After retiring Banks, Lersch allowed a single to Hundley. Hickman (who to that point was 0 for 4 on the day) was due next, and Durocher—sensing an opportunity—summoned Willie Smith from the bench. Smith nervously took his place on the left-handed hitter's side of the plate, stretching out a strained muscle he had just suffered from a hard swing in the on-deck circle. "Just a dying quail over third, that's all I want," Durocher muttered to himself in the dugout as Lersch got set. Hands, standing next to his manager, had another idea. "The hell with that, Skip— he'll hit it out." Lersch let fly, and Smith cut loose with a furious swing, releasing that nervous energy into a violent wallop like the right hooks he used to throw in the boxing ring. "Look out, wall!" Smith said to himself as he left the batter's box, which had become his customary utterance immediately after a long drive off his bat, usually taking place during batting practice. The ball screamed on a line into the right-field bleachers before anyone knew what happened, and Smith was rounding the bases within seconds, bringing home a 7–6 Opening Day win for the Cubs.

In addition to all of his teammates, Smith was also greeted at the plate by five or six fans who had eluded the "Andy Frain" ush-ers to sprint to the victory circle. In the process Smith received a heel spike from one of his teammates onto his big toe, but in the ecstasy of the moment he didn't mind too much. The players were so excited by the victory that nobody even wanted to take a hot shower in the locker room; even after being out in the cool temperatures all day, it took a half-hour before the first faucet was turned on by the jubilant mob.

Elsewhere around the majors on the second day of openers, McLain picked up where he left off in 1968, as he and the Tigers beat the Indians in Detroit, 6–2; Gibson went nine strong innings in St. Louis, but the Cardinals couldn't push across enough runs for him as the Pirates won in fourteen innings, 6–2; and ironi-cally, all four expansion teams were in first place, having won their maiden voyages as big league clubs (over in the American League, the White Sox were embarrassed by the Pilots, 7–0, as the Pale Hose were shut out by the Pilots in the first game ever for the Seattle ball club). Commissioner Kuhn was perhaps the most excited person about the new clubs. "With 24 major league teams, we are utilizing the available manpower," he proudly an-nounced. "We can't put on a second-class show. Of course, there are chances for expansion to dramatic new areas. Not now, but someday; like Tokyo and Mexico City. And I'd be disappointed if it didn't happen in my lifetime."

In the Cubs' second contest of the year, a stiff breeze blew straight out to center field, causing the flags at the ballpark to resemble "frozen wash on a clothes line," according to the *Tri-bune*. Even cooler temperatures and the lack of Opening Day novelty caused the attendance to drop all the way to 6,297. The fans saw an offensive outburst by Williams, as the Cub left fielder nailed four doubles—becoming the first National Leaguer to ac-complish the feat in fifteen years—as part of sixteen Chicago hits in an 11–3 drubbing of the Phillies. Williams was trying to ditch his reputation as a pull hitter, as his opposite-field work in spring training paid off with two of the doubles going the "other way." Banks followed up his grand beginning with three hits, as did Beckert, while Kessinger and Spangler added two safeties apiece.

Hands went the distance for the win, although he complained of stiffness in his arm as he labored through long innings in the seventh, eighth, and ninth. "I thought I had worked the stiffness out in the eighth by taking a few extra warmup pitches," he reasoned after the game. "I didn't feel tired then, but I sure do now." Williams's four doubles, in addition to one each by Beckert and Kessinger, had the Philadelphia outfielders retreating to the wall seemingly all day—much the chagrin of left fielder Ron Stone, who later complained that he was "pelted with two eggs, a salt shaker, pins, and cups of ice" from certain overly zealous fans in the bleachers.

Such spectators soon became known as the "Bleacher Bums," patrolling mostly the left-field stands and recognizable by the bright yellow construction helmets they chose to wear. "They are mostly college boys and night workers," an observer from the *New York Times* revealed, "who can spend their afternoons in the only park in the major leagues without lights." They were led by twenty-four-year-old Ron Grousl, an employee of a bar in Wrigleyville. (Grousl would allegedly catch Henry Aaron's 521st home run ball, which tied Aaron with Ted Williams, and then offer it back to Aaron. Aaron, apparently so disgusted with the Bleacher Bums, refused to take it. When this occurred, it was reported that Aaron had beer dumped all over his head the next time he went back to the wall to retrieve a Cub hit.) The Bums' headquarters was Ray's Bleachers, a bar across the street from the ballpark at 3655 Sheffield. Ray's wife, Marge, described the scene when the Cubs were out of town: "They [the Bleacher Bums] come in here to sing and holler and shout and to watch the game on TV—on our plain, old, black-and-white TV. Ninety percent of these kids have color TV in their homes, but they want to come here." Before, after, and even during the home games, a row of yellow-helmeted Bums could be seen lining the seats in front of the cold tap at the bar. "The beer cans are stacked against the walls at Rays," described Condon on his venture into the establishment. "The linoleum is worn. The hamburger grill serves outsiders thru a large window when the Cubs are at home. There's one pay telephone, but it's almost nonsensical to try to use it because the adjacent jukebox continually is blaring those songs dear to the foot-stompin' young in heart." He also noted that just about every other selection made on the jukebox was the tune "Hey Hey, Holy Mackerel," recorded on an album called *Cub Power.* The song included the voices of Willie Smith, Gene Oliver, and Nate Oliver humming in the background, which would ring throughout Chicagoland for the rest of the summer:

Hey hey, holy mackerel
No doubt about it
The Cubs are on their way
They've got the hustle
They've got the muscle
The Chicago Cubs are on their way . . . HEY HEY!

After receiving a load of initial complaints from opposing outfielders who had been pelted with an assortment of missiles, the Bums threatened to take their act to the south side of town at Comiskey Park. Banks tried to mediate with an open letter to the fans, which appeared in the sports section of the *Tribune:*

I only hope no one gets hurt in Wrigley Field this season from the fans going too far. I know when a large group of people have that feeling, it's hard to keep control. "The Friendly Confines of Wrigley Field" has become a wonderful slogan for a fine, old ball park. . . . I know this: the only way we want to harass those guys from the other 11 teams is with our bats and our gloves. We want to beat 'em fair and square.

The victory wouldn't be so sweet if a rival player would say his team lost because of a barrage of firecrackers, cracked ice, a tomato, a rubber ball, deviled egg, or something else thrown to distract the outfielders.

So, how about a little kindness for the players on the other teams? After all, some of them may be Cubs some day!

But Condon, in his own *Tribune* article, was less apologetic. "The bleachers have been the base of the true fan since Abner

Doubleday was in the Three-I League," he claimed. "The bleacherites are the game's greatest hero-worshippers, and the greatest hero-haters. A home town athlete needn't have talent to become an idol of the bleacher gang. He does need color."

It was Santo's day in the series finale, as the third big gun in Durocher's lineup slammed two home runs in a 6–2, complete-game win for Holtzman, who scattered ten Philly hits. Endurance was a new goal for the left hander in 1969—in the previous season Holtzman had finished only one-sixth of his starts. Leo was back to his usual spritzy self as he bolted out of the dugout on a called third strike of Richie Allen from Holtzman—a pitch that plate umpire Paul Pryor had indeed called a strike but which Leo didn't realize. Durocher went over to an usher and told him to relay his message to the press box that he was protesting the game. Pryor and the other umpires ultimately calmed Durocher down, and the Cubs wound up victorious anyway. Vintage Leo, for sure—making a protest on a call that actually went his way. Frankie Frisch would have been proud.

The defending champion Cardinals were off to a slow start, losing three in a row in St. Louis to the Pirates, as Pittsburgh was tied atop the early standings with the Cubs.

Both Beckert and Hundley survived scary collisions in the game, incidents threatening two gears in the machine that the Cubs could not afford to lose. "It scared me to death when I first saw Randy on the ground," Santo admitted, describing the scene after Hundley applied a tag at the plate and had his foot turned unnaturally. About an hour after the game the catcher described the ankle as "awful stiff," but he planned to ice it all night in hopes of being ready for the next day's game. Beckert, while fielding a ground ball, had been plowed bull-like by the bulky Allen, a crash that folded Beckert like a lawn chair and crashed his right side into the infield dirt. Holtzman had allowed twelve base runners over his nine innings of work—despite being nailed in the ankle by a line drive in the very first inning.

The team with the funny name, odd uniforms, and foreign country next came to Wrigley, making its first appearance on the shores of Lake Michigan. "Many a Montreal team has lost 1–0 decisions in overtime on frosty April days in other years," recalled Langford in his column on Saturday, April 12, "but the activity was always confined indoors until yesterday. The sport in the past was always ice hockey and the tradition was the long and proud one of the Montreal Canadiens. Yesterday, the activity was baseball in Wrigley Field." The Expos club, in its fourth official day of existence, did take the Cubs and Joe Niekro into extra innings, only to be stymied by a single off the bat of Williams that scored Kessinger from second base in the twelfth for the lone run of the game. The victory went to Abernathy, splendid in three innings of relief, who triumphed in front of a freezing collection of 7,281 fans, "most of whom had migrated into a corner of the right field grandstands by the end of the game to get the only available sunlight," Langford continued. The Expos were nearly as "green" as their starting pitcher, twenty-five-year-old Carl Morton, who in making his Major League debut matched outs with Niekro through the ninth before giving way to his bullpen as well (in their first three games, no Montreal starting pitcher had produced more than three innings of work). After his poor performance in spring training (allowing 13 runs in the same number of innings), Niekro wasn't sure whether he would even see the ball again from Durocher; with only the first three spots settled in the starting rotation, however, Leo was forced to give him the opportunity. Niekro proved stronger as the game went on and did not permit an Expo hit over his last six innings of work.

The clubs split the final two games of the series as Jenkins was knocked out in the third inning of the third contest in losing to Jim "Mudcat" Grant, who readily admitted that he would not have a Major League job if two new teams hadn't been added for the season. "There is nothing like the opportunity I've been given by expansion," the veteran said. The Cubs beat their former teammate Bill Stoneman in the finale, 7–6, as the Chicagoans scored three runs in the ninth inning to prevail. One of the runs in the rally was scored by Phillips, who made his first appearance of the season by pinch running for Willie Smith, who had reached on a fielder's choice. The crushing blow came off the bat of Banks, as the veteran simply blooped a fly ball into short left field for a hit, scoring Kessinger. At that point part of the twenty-seven-thousand-plus fans stormed the field in a frenzy, similar to a World Series victory. It was a raucous display that Cub observers had not seen, it was believed, since Don Cardwell threw his no-hitter for the North Siders in 1960. Perhaps the city was sensing something special about this team. "The Cubs are not playing superior baseball—but they are winning," Langford pointed out, "which is the sign of a champion, they say."

Even the infamous "Curse of the Billy Goat" appeared to be dashed. Sam Sianis, the owner of a local tavern, had been booted out of a World Series game at Wrigley Field in 1945 because he had brought his pet goat with him to the ballpark. He was so angered by this perceived mistreatment that he put a hex on the Cubs as he was cast out into the intersection of Clark and Addison, announcing to one and all that a World Series would never be played at Wrigley Field again—and to date, he had been correct. The team's recent success had apparently put Sianis in a reconciling mood, however, as he said that all was forgiven here and now in 1969. He even rescheduled an autumn trip to Ireland because he was so confident that the Cubs would be playing come October. "Most of the Irish are White Sox fans anyway," Sianis was quoted in the papers, a statement that didn't make sense to some local historians. It was pointed out to him that Al Capone's Italians had mostly dominated the South Side of town (with Capone himself being an avid White Sox fan), while the Irish of Bugs Moran established the North Side as their turf. "Oh, I had it backwards," Sianis corrected himself.

Durocher, Hundley, and Verlon Walker missed the celebration, however; the former was home with a cold, and the latter two were ejected in the sixth inning for arguing balls and strikes (it was the first time in nine years that the normally reserved Walker had been dismissed from a game). The officers were certainly thin in the ranks, as Reiser was also absent, having gone to Los Angeles for treatment for what was believed to be a heart ailment (it would later be diagnosed as hypertension, and as a result Reiser would be mostly sidelined for the next five weeks). Regan, replacing Hands in the eighth inning, got another win in relief.

The Expos were headed home, and people up in Montreal were hopeful that the ice on the field at Jarry Park would melt by Monday the 14th—the first time that a Major League regular-season baseball game was scheduled to be played outside the United States. The frozen playing surface was a boon for baseball purists, some of whom had scoffed at the perversion of the game being played at its highest level north of the border. Jarry Park, a virtual sandlot of a field and five miles from downtown Montreal up St. Laurent Boulevard, was hurriedly enlarged from just 3,000 permanent seats (originally constructed in 1948) to 28,456 in time for the '69 season. It was to be only a temporary home for the club, as plans were being made for a new domed stadium closer to the city's business district, scheduled to be open by 1972. (The city mayor, Jean Drapeau, had almost precluded the possibility of Major League Baseball in Montreal, as he had to be thoroughly convinced that Jarry Park was an acceptable place to play, even temporarily.) The St. Louis Cardinals would be the first visitors, playing before a sellout crowd that included people who had ordered tickets from as far away as seven hundred miles north of Montreal. The Expos franchise had taken its name from the "Expo of 1967," the World's Fair that drew 50 million visitors for six months from April through October, primarily taking place on the banks of the St. Lawrence River adjacent to the city.

The Expos transmitted their radio broadcasts in both English and French, yet another first for big league baseball. In a troubling sign for some, no English-format Montreal station would carry the games (strangely similar to the scene now unfolding in the twenty-first century); therefore, broadcast rights were given to an American station, WEAV in Plattsburgh, New York, just over the border from the province of Quebec. Twenty-one games would also be provided over French-language television, with fifteen of those being shown with English-speaking commentators as well. In charge of all the Expos' broadcast operations was Gene Kirby, a man who had most recently worked with Dizzy Dean on the Game of the Week productions and with sporadic telecasts of Atlanta Braves games. The popular but extremely casual Dean had been released back in 1966, which would have been his twenty-fifth year on the radio. "For the first time since he started broadcasting for the old St. Louis Browns in 1941, Ol' Diz is out of the racket," Kirby had said three years earlier in a disappointed tone. "I consider my association with Diz the highlight of all my years." "Ol' Diz" was a nickname that Dean had actually developed for himself years back, speaking of himself in the third person; it was ultimately picked up by everyone in a friendly, endearing manner. Kirby was confident that he could use the creativity he had learned from Dean to create a marketable product for the baseball fans of Canada.

Things were so scrambled in getting Jarry Park ready for the opener, in fact, that the Expos' general manager, Jim Fanning, was seen putting folding chairs in place for fans just minutes before the first pitch was to be thrown. He also had to worry about the public swimming pool behind right field, as its unsuspecting patrons could potentially have home run balls landing on their heads. There were problems in the field too, as the grass was in poor shape and the infield dirt was soggy, which slowed down the vaunted running game of the Cardinals. "It was unbelievable," Curt Flood said of the condition of the playing surface. "A stolen base is going to be unheard of here until something is done about it. You just can't get the proper footing. I've played on some bad diamonds, but this is the worst. I pray I don't get killed out there tomorrow." Ironically, as Flood was worrying about the conditions, the umpires were still out on the field—huddled around fellow umpire Mel Steiner, who was nervously measuring the distance from the pitching rubber to home plate to make sure it was the correct distance before play began.

The Pirates came to Wrigley Field tied with the Cubs for first place, with each team sporting a 5-1 record. The weather stayed its typical inclement April self in Chicago. Holtzman, pitching on a wet mound that Langford likened more to a "California mud slide," lifted the Cubs to the top spot in the division with his second victory of the year, a 4–0 shutout. ("The mound was so bad," Holtzman said afterward, "I was slipping on every pitch.") Young upped his early average to .333 (7 for 21), trying to make a case for his remaining in center field, with Phillips ever closer to being ready for the lineup. The bullpen—traditionally a sore point for the Cubs—came through again the following day, as Abernathy and Aguirre combined for nearly five shutout innings to help Niekro beat Pittsburgh once more, 7–4, finishing a great home stand for the Cubs, who had won seven out of their first eight to start the season. Aguirre attained his first victory in a Chicago uniform in the finale (and Abernathy the team's first save of the year), as Niekro was lifted in the fifth with the Pirates scoring three runs in closing the gap to 6–4. Durocher, who was at home suffering from a bad cold, had turned the club over to Becker and Amalfitano for all three wins. The two stand-ins received a phone call from Leo after the game in the locker room. "Tell Aguirre he's beautiful," the Lip said on the other end of line. Becker told the press that, in all his time with the Cubs, the bullpen was now at its strongest.

The Cubs were off to St. Louis (with Leo feeling better from his cold and making the team flight—he had originally planned to meet the club in St. Louis later) and then on to Montreal and Pittsburgh for their first road trip of the year. Meanwhile, across town, the White Sox were preparing for "Baseball on a Billiards Table." This is what the *Tribune* labeled the newly installed Astroturf at Comiskey Park. The Sox opened the home portion of their schedule against a team almost as new as the turf, the Kansas City Royals. "I've got to get used to this," veteran shortstop Luis Aparicio said as he took some pregame grounders on what he and the other Sox were calling the "$100,000 infield." "It's not too bad. The ball bounces very true, and the only thing that seems to need work is the skin part of the infield. . . . I'm sure you'll see a big jump in our double plays this season."

"The park is freshly decorated," contributed Markus in his report from 35th Street and Shields Avenue. "The parking lots, completely illuminated for night games, have been paved and extended. . . . For South Siders, the White Sox opener is as gala as Election Day or St. Patrick's Day. The fire stations close in Canaryville. Merchants in the Back of the Yards neighborhood shut up shop." Before the opener Chicago fans saw the return of two members of the infamous 1919 "Black Sox" team, eight members of which were accused of conspiring to throw that year's World Series against the Cincinnati Reds. As a result those individuals—though found innocent in a court of law—were banned from baseball for life by Commissioner Kennesaw Mountain Landis. However, two players from that team who were not among those in on the suspected "take," pitcher Red Faber and catcher Ray Schalk, were welcomed back to Comiskey by the fans as the old battery took care of the ceremonial first-pitch duties, assisted by Mayor Daley. "Mayor Daley is Number One," Durocher had said proudly during an interview earlier in the week. "At least the people of Chicago aren't up to their fannies in garbage."

The ancient players Faber and Schalk, both Hall of Famers, kicked curiously at the strange synthetic surface as they took their old positions. A notorious spitballer, Faber playfully licked his first two fingers as Schalk pounded his fist into his raggedy old mitt. Faber fired one in there, and the festivities were under way.

Less than a month later, one of the last surviving members of the infamous eight, Eddie Cicotte—the main pitcher for that 1919 White Sox team and the main hand in the ruse—died in Detroit at age eight-four. When Cicotte hit the first Cincinnati batter of the first game of the World Series, Morrie Rath, he later admitted that it was the prearranged signal to let gamblers know that the fix was in. "Cicotte undoubtedly took several secrets to the grave," wrote Condon, "because the complete truth of the Black Sox never can be known." In attendance at Cicotte's funeral was Dan Cassidy, the lawyer who had helped acquit Cicotte and the other seven players of criminal charges fifty years earlier.

The home club did not disappoint, as two home runs off the bat of twenty-year-old Carlos May helped the White Sox beat Kansas City, 5–2. The Royals had been brought into the league, in part, because of the efforts of U.S. senator Stuart Symington (D-MO), who had claimed on the Senate floor that the city of Kansas City had been "done wrong" when the A's and owner Charles Finley left town for Oakland before the 1968 season.

The Opening Day crowd numbered just over eleven thousand

fans, a meager amount that in part prompted Markus to ask, "Is Chicago really a great sports town?"

§

While Holtzman had lowered his ERA to an even 1.00 with his recent shutout of the Pirates, Jenkins brought a beefy 9.00 mark into Busch Stadium to face the Cardinals. Pitching was not a problem in St. Louis, as the starting rotation of Gibson, Steve Carlton, Nelson Briles, and Ray Washburn, which had dominated National League lineups in '68, was intact. Manager Albert "Red" Schoendienst had built a team reminiscent of the outfit that preceded him as a player in St. Louis—the gritty Gas House Gang—as Red's boys were using high spikes and fast legs for consistent winning baseball. They had it all, including the thing they were missing at the end of 1968: hunger for another championship. The Tigers had surprised them in the last Fall Classic, and the Cards were focused on recapturing the title they had wrestled from the Red Sox in 1967. It was the third full season at beautiful Busch, the circular castle of St. Louis baseball, which had risen simultaneously along with the Gateway Arch when constructed in the mid-1960s. The two structures were intended to signal a commercial and cultural renaissance of a downtrodden downtown area. Playing in St. Louis had always been an imposing visit for any club, and the Cubs knew that they wanted to make a statement early in the 1969 season as the teams took the field along the Mississippi River. The Cub-Cardinal rivalry had been defined by most as a relatively "friendly" one, but the sparks flew as the proud clubs got into their battle.

The Cubs were donning slightly new road uniforms in 1969. The small differences were the absence of red piping around the neck and the presence of "CHICAGO" lettering on the jersey. Underneath the lettering the club included what some started to call "TV numbers"—small versions of the players' jersey numbers, which previously had been shown only on the back in most cases. They were able to scratch a run across in the third against Carlton, as he and Jenkins held the bats in check until the seventh. In that frame Shannon, the fiery St. Louis third baseman, hit a shot off of umpire Dave Davidson on the third base line, and the ball rebounded straight into Santo's glove. Shannon raced around first, as Santo was very late in a throw to Banks. Ernie subsequently turned and threw to Beckert at second, but he and Shannon imploded in a spectacular collision that left both temporarily senseless, with Shannon being called out. The home crowd cheered as Shannon was the first to draw himself to his feet and stagger toward the Cardinals dugout. "I was so damned surprised," Shannon said afterward in the locker room. "I don't know what happened. All I know is that I've got a bump on my head." Shannon would complain of a little blurred vision, but nothing further. Beckert, however, lay motionless for a while on the field and was then carted out of the stadium to a local hospital for X-rays on his head. The results were negative, however, and Glenn later rejoined his teammates at the hotel with some unsightly facial bruises and a slight concussion.

Jenkins held on for a 5-hit, 1–0 shutout, propelling the Cubs to an 8-1 mark, their best start in thirty-five years. Schoendienst, on the other hand, decried his team's poor execution of fundamentals, as the Redbirds fell below the .500 mark to 4-5. It was another shutout for the Cubs the next night as Hands—dealing his twentieth straight inning without an earned run, before yielding to Regan in the ninth—knocked the bats out of the Cardinals' hands to the tune of a 3–0 final. After losing their fifth straight in Busch Stadium, Shannon suggested that "maybe we should wear our road uniforms here tomorrow night."

The doctors had advised Beckert to be inactive for at least forty-eight hours, and with Qualls having to go to California for training with his National Guard unit, Durocher was suddenly without a second baseman save the rusty Charley Smith. Not wanting to make a roster move, however, the executives back in Chicago asked Leo over the phone to "make do" until Beckert was ready to play.

That same evening Stoneman brought some attention to the new club north of the border as he fired a no-hitter for the Expos against the Phillies in winning, 7–0, in Philadelphia. Stoneman, who had previously never even thrown a complete game in the

Major Leagues, had actually been drafted by Montreal out of the Cubs organization. The Oak Park, Illinois, native had appeared in forty-six games over the past two seasons for Chicago, starting only twice, and was never considered to be a top prospect by those in the Cubs front office (Durocher wanted him banished to the bullpen permanently, a desire that the five-foot-ten-inch Stoneman claimed was a result of his smaller stature). Condon, in his *Tribune* article, wasn't terribly impressed. "Stoneman's no-hitter has to be considered one of baseball's accidents," he wrote of the accomplishment of the previously unsung pitcher, "because he was a most unlikely candidate to come up with such a performance." The very next day, as the Cubs were making their way from St. Louis for their first visit to Jarry Park, Expos executives took Stoneman's contract out of the main office desk, tore it up, and immediately produced a new one that paid him $2,000 more. He followed up the feat with another shutout in his very next start, a 2–0 blanking of Carlton and the Cardinals in St. Louis. After the game a reporter came up to him and said jokingly, "I'm Leo. . . ." Stoneman, however, wasn't amused. "I ain't talking to anyone named Leo," he shot back. "Here [with Montreal] I can pitch my own game. Leo [Durocher] wouldn't let me. That's the big difference playing for the Expos."

To be sure, Leo had some interesting personal differences with some of his players. About this time he had gotten wind of the apartment Holtzman and Niekro had rented in Schiller Park outside Chicago, near O'Hare Airport, and he was none too pleased about the social surroundings that his players would have to "endure."

"There must have been 750 airline stewardesses living in our apartment building," Holtzman recalled later, in telling the story to Rick Talley. "It was paradise.

"But one day, Leo calls a clubhouse meeting and says in front of everybody, 'We've got a guy on this team living in a whorehouse.'

"Now, we're all looking around—what is he talking about? But he's looking right at me and yelling, 'How in the hell are you gonna get through the season living in that place with all those stewardesses??? Can't you find a damned apartment in Evanston or somewhere???'

"Afterwards, half the guys came up to me and said, 'How come you never invite us up there?'"

§

As the baseball season was getting warmed up, so was the spring practice schedule for football on the nation's college campuses. Spring practice in football usually passes by as inconspicuously as strangers on a sidewalk; coaches use it to order the depth chart for the fall, keep the players active as school draws to a close, and perhaps insert a new strategy or two. Down the road from Chicago in Iowa City, however, spring practice at the University of Iowa took on more attention than ever before. As workouts began, sixteen of the twenty black players on the team—including four starters from the 1968 squad—refused to show; as a result, the players were expelled from the team. "Those who stayed away without permission dismissed themselves," explained Iowa's head coach, Ray Nagel, who announced that his team consisted of those individuals who showed up ready to work. For several days thereafter the reasons behind the "boycott" (as it was characterized) remained a mystery. While the protesting members had been practicing on their own in the hopes of later rejoining the team, Nagel stood clear in his stance that they would not be welcomed back. Finally, a few days later, the boycotting players listed their grievances, which requested that adequate counselors be provided for athletes to help them in their studies and lead them toward graduation in a positive and progressive way; that financial aid be provided until graduation; that five-year scholarships be provided for those athletes requiring five years or more to graduate; that some autonomy be left to the athletes to control their social and personal lives, such as not having expressions of political beliefs held against them; and that the National Collegiate Athletic Association's allowance of $15 a month for athletes be adopted by the Big Ten.

When asked why they had waited until this moment to release their displeasure, the athletes stated that, the previous spring, one of them had been misquoted about a grievance in a campus newspaper and thus they had waited until their collective union was strong enough to launch an actual boycott. After meeting with the players, university officials admitted shortcomings in each of the stipulated areas and provided a covenant for improvements to be made, but they also supported any disciplinary measures imposed on the players by the coaching staff as a result of their skipping the practices.

Meanwhile, very little seemed able to stop the rampaging Cubs, but they met their match atmospherically by flying into a thick snowstorm in Montreal on April 18. The inclement conditions as the charter flight wobbled into the airport only added to the mysterious, haunted nature of the city for some of the players. Many players had been wearing light summer clothing on the plane, having just left toasty St. Louis, with its temperatures in the mid-eighties. Chicago's weather conditions had not been much better than Montreal's, however, as nearly three-fourths of the high school baseball schedule in the city had been canceled to date. "We're tired of trying to beat the elements," said Ed Mitchell of Taft High School on the city's far northwest side, which was the current holder of the Public League championship. "We're ready to try and beat a baseball team."

Even though it had been an off day, Durocher was disappointed in the Montreal weather because, upon arrival, he had wanted to send Phillips through some physical drills to test his sore hand. Santo was looking forward to some extra batting practice too, as he was only 1 for 21 at the plate in recent days, one of the few Cubs to not contribute to the recent winning streak. His performance had prompted a letter to the press box at Wrigley Field:

> Dear Jack Brickhouse,
>
> I have a parakeet one-and-a-half years old. He watches your telecasts, and every time Ron Santo is batting he says, "Strike Three." Why he picks on poor Ron, I'll never know.

To bolster their strength in the middle infield after Beckert's injury, the Cubs signed Nate Oliver away from the Yankees. Oliver had only gotten one at-bat in New York by the time the Cubs picked him up, and he had been a journeyman in all of his six Major League seasons with the Dodgers and Giants. But Durocher and Holland liked what they saw in Oliver, as their paper-thin depth in the middle of the diamond had recently become all too apparent. This meant that Qualls, who was still in Stockton, California, with his Guard unit, would be sent from there to Tacoma to open the roster spot. This was not seen as a demotion by anyone except Qualls, as Durocher and others with the Cubs foresaw the speedy young man having a future in the outfield and they wanted him to continue honing his skills in the minors for the interim.

In conditions that Langford described as perfect for "a robust drinking bout, but not a baseball game," an eleventh-inning single by Hickman, who had come off the bench to pinch-hit for Spangler, gave Chicago a 6–5 victory in its first regular season game in Canada. Spangler had been hitting .370, good for seventh in the league, but was pitted against lefty Don Shaw in this situation—and Durocher thus sought the right-handed bat of Hickman. In what would become a frequent occurrence throughout the year, Hickman stayed in the game as a defensive replacement for Spangler—and in what would also become customary, Gene Oliver suddenly pulled out a fishing pole from the Cubs bullpen and flung a good cast in Spangler's direction when he was removed for Hickman. Having Spangler be "hooked" by Durocher greatly amused the fans, the rest of the Cubs, and even Leo himself. All five Expo runs had been allowed by Holtzman, who leaned on five flawless innings by Abernathy and Regan to finish the job. And a healed Adolfo Phillips helped seal the deal too as he was sent into center field by Durocher in the bottom of the eleventh, seeing his first action of the year.

Like the Cardinals, the Cubs had their own issues with the strange ballpark in the strange land. The seats behind home plate had been inexplicably painted white. Durocher spotted this before the game and asked Fanning that they be painted a different color before the contest started. Fanning supposedly later sent word to Leo that his wish would be granted, but come the first pitch, the white seats remained. As a result the Cub infielders complained of not being able to see the ball off the Montreal bats. "The infield was soft and lumpy," added Langford after his own pregame tour of the diamond. "The crust of the infield was puffed up and gave the sensation of walking on balloons."

That same day, back in Chicago, the football Bears had come to contract terms with first-round pick Douglass, the strong-armed, fast-running Kansas quarterback. He was envisioned by fans to be the final piece to the puzzle—along with established stars Sayers and linebacker Dick Butkus—to bring the "Monsters of the Midway" back among pro football's elite, as the mediocre quarterback play of Jack Concannon, Rudy Bukich, and Virgil Carter appeared to be only a memory. The Bears had just completed their first season under new head coach Jim Dooley with a 7-7 mark. Dooley had taken over the sidelines for Halas—the only coach the organization had known since the league's inception in 1920.

After splitting a doubleheader to finish the Montreal series on April 20, the Cubs departed for Pittsburgh with a solid grip on first place and with ten different players having delivered the game-winning hits in their eleven triumphs so far:

National League East	W	L	Pct.	GB
Chicago	11	2	.846	—
Pittsburgh	8	4	.667	2.5
New York	5	7	.417	5.5
Montreal	5	7	.417	5.5
St. Louis	4	8	.333	6.5
Philadelphia	3	8	.273	7

As the team arrived in Pittsburgh, Kessinger became the latest "casualty" of interruption with his military service. He had to hop a quick flight back to Chicago to join his unit, which had been called to order in a surprisingly quick manner. The rest of the team would soon follow him back home, as this trip to the Steel City would last only one day, just long enough for one doubleheader.

It was the last full season in Pittsburgh for venerable Forbes Field, the long-standing home of the Pirates, which was nestled snugly in among Schenley Park and the University of Pittsburgh campus. A new circular stadium was being built downtown and would become the Pirates' home in June 1970 (the last game at Forbes would be played on June 28, 1970, almost sixty-one years to the day after its first game in 1909). Forbes Field had been named after British general John Forbes, whose troops captured Fort Duquesne (an area that later comprised Pittsburgh) in 1758 during the French and Indian War and who subsequently renamed it "Fort Pitt." The park had not seen many improvements since the capacity had been expanded to thirty-five thousand in 1938. As in Sportsman's Park in St. Louis, a screen covered the face of the right-field grandstand to prevent cheap home runs (since another renovation in 1925, the screen was a mere three hundred feet from home plate). Over time the screen had been left to rot, for the only thought of replacing it had occurred during World War II, when metal was at a premium, but had not been acted upon. Also as in Sportsman's Park, a flagpole stood in the field of play in center field, but—unlike at Sportsman's—a batting cage also stood in play at Forbes just to the left of the flagpole. The first ballpark to have an elevator and the first to have "crash pads" on the wall to protect outfielders, the park was grandly imperfect—as evidenced by the seats at the top of the left-field bleachers, whose occupants could not see home plate past the obstruction of the upper deck grandstand. But the park was, more than anything, the beloved possession of the Pittsburgh people.

Both Hands and Ross would make quick exits as the Cub starters in the twin bill, dropping both contests, 7–5 and 6–5, under drizzling skies. Durocher entertained himself by being ejected in the second game by rookie umpire Andy Olsen. The Pirate bats were assisted by the extra work of Elroy Face, their forty-one-year-old batting practice hurler and currently unemployed Major League pitcher, whose career had encountered an abrupt shift in only the past eight months. Beginning in 1953 Face had spent fifteen years with the Pirates, amassing 188 saves out of the bullpen. All that came to an end on August 31, 1968, when Face tied the Major League record for appearances with one team (held jointly by Walter Johnson of the Washington Senators) as he took the hill for the 802nd time for the Pirates against the Braves. Late in the game Face came in to pitch in replacing Blass, but Blass remained in the game in left field. After Face retired Felix Millan to tie the record, he was removed and Blass resumed pitching. The Pirates went on to win, 8–0, but before the final out was made, an announcement came forth that Face had been sold to the Detroit Tigers. The Tigers released him in spring training of 1969, and now Face found himself back in Pittsburgh in an unusual role, propositioning each of the visiting teams that came to Forbes Field about their need for a relief pitcher.

April 23 marked the homecoming for one of Boston's sons, a wayward and often misunderstood soul whose contributions to the city made the negative folks set aside any hard feelings for the day. Ted Williams was back in Fenway Park. When he emerged from the dugout before the day's game to take his Senators line-up card to home plate, the old house erupted with glee—which got louder when he shook hands with Red Sox coach and former teammate Bobby Doerr. "It feels good, and it's nice to be back," Williams admitted, though feeling strange wearing a different uniform. "I really don't feel as much out of place here as at Oakland or some park like that where I never played." His comments were obviously still noncommittal toward full reconciliation with the Boston fans and press, who had labeled him as increasingly aloof as his time in the city wore on. Full forgiveness from both Williams and the city—or at least something close to it—would not happen until many years later.

The local fans were excited about the Cubs returning to Chicago on April 24 to open a series against the Cardinals, but baseball interest in the city appeared to be limited to the areas north of North Avenue. Two days earlier the White Sox had played before their smallest crowd ever at Comiskey Park, as 619 faithful squatted in the nave—"plus the usual ghost registration that pushed the announced turnout to 1,058," the *Tribune* mocked. Apparently, the excitement of the introduction of artificial turf into

Chicago sports had already worn off. After his first visit a couple of days later, Billy Martin, the rookie manager of the Minnesota Twins, had nothing good to add about it. "This isn't baseball," he complained about the rug. "It isn't the way the game was meant to be played." Martin made his comments after two "squibbers" and a usual double play ball turned into hits on the swift artificial surface, helping give Chicago a 6-5 win in the ninth inning.

Bitter temperatures in the low forties continued to hit Chicago as the Cubs held a light voluntary workout instead of the regularly scheduled game (which Banks chose to skip, excusing himself to go home and tend a nagging cold—an ailment he had acquired while playing in the rain-drenched games at Pittsburgh). Because of the poor conditions, it would be another one-day "series" for the Cubs before heading to New York to face the Mets. Durocher took advantage of a day's postponement to meet with Holland and other club officials about some possible trades. This reportedly was the first mention of Leo's desire to deal Phillips, as the skipper made it clear to Holland that he wanted Don Young to be his center fielder.

But, ironically, it was instead the pitching staff that experienced a change. Joe Niekro—still insisting on throwing his knuckleball, which would never allow him to become a Durocher favorite— was dealt along with Ross and Francisco Libran to the Padres for Selma, as the Cubs were beaten, 3-2, by Cardinal right-hander Dave Giusti. Selma, a brash talker and quite a different style of pitcher from Niekro, relied on his overpowering fastball to challenge hitters. He had waffled with the Mets for four seasons before coming to San Diego in 1969, not yet finding his niche as a starter or reliever (this despite striking out a then—Mets record of 13 in a 1–0 shutout in 1965 as a twenty-one-year-old in only his second Major League start; Selma again had recently struck out 13 batters on Opening Day for the Padres in 1969 against the Astros). Durocher planned to immediately put the promising Selma into the number-four spot in the rotation behind Jenkins, Hands, and Holtzman—a spot the search for which, according to Markus, "seemed almost as long as Galahad's search for the Holy Grail." Holland affirmed that "Selma *is* the fourth starter we have been seeking for so long. . . . Leo always had a very high regard for him, and we came close a couple of times this spring to making a trade for him, but never quite made it."

Holland continued: "I thought a lot of the three boys we gave up, and there is no doubt they will do very well—if not this year, next year. But we are looking at *right now.*" Durocher publicly agreed. "Sure, in the long run we probably gave up too much for Selma," he said in reference to the promising youngsters who left Chicago. "But we absolutely had to have a real, down-to-earth fourth starting pitcher, and we got him." But now, with the loss of Niekro and Ross, the number of pitchers on the roster was down to nine, so Holland also alluded that another move was imminent.

The Mets were coming off a 73-89 season in 1968, finishing only a game ahead of Houston for the basement dwelling in the National League standings. In the eight years that the Mets had been in the Major Leagues, there were only two months in which they had won more games than they lost, with the first one not occurring until their fifth season (July 1966), and the next not until June 1968. But they were now building possibilities around a formidable young pitching staff led by Seaver, a tireless workhorse and skilled craftsman. Seaver, who emitted quiet confidence from his very first professional appearance, had captured the 1967 Rookie of the Year award with 16 wins and 170 strikeouts; he followed up with an impressive encore in '68, posting another 16 wins, 205 strikeouts, and a 2.20 ERA, good for All-Star selections in both campaigns ("He won't make it," a Cubs scout had said about Seaver in 1966 when asked about his chances for the Major Leagues). Joining him were fellow third-year man and hard-throwing lefty Jerry Koosman (who in some ways outperformed Seaver in '68 with 19 wins and a 2.08 ERA) and Lynn Nolan Ryan, a twelfth-round pick of the Mets in the 1965 amateur draft whom most teams had dismissed as too wild despite possessing great velocity on his fastball. Several writers were calling it the most promising staff in history, as Seaver, Koosman, Ryan, and fellow youngsters Jim McAndrew and Gary Gentry were twenty-four, twenty-five, twenty-two, twenty-five, and twenty-two years old, respectively. The club weaknesses were found, conversely, on the offensive side. Their team batting average of .228 was last in the National League in '68, made less glaring with the dominance of the league's pitchers during the season. In 1969 youngsters Ken Boswell and Wayne Garrett were inserted into the lineup at second and third base by manager Gil Hodges, but nothing could seem to lift the team's lifeless bats. Hodges knew that he would have to win games by scores of 1-0 and 2-1, and he started off by taking aim at the first-place team, the Chicago Cubs.

Somewhat-unlikely power sources emerged in the opener against the formidable Seaver, as described by Langford: "Don Kessinger, who only had two home runs in 2,155 previous major league at-bats; Ferguson Jenkins, who hasn't taken batting practice in two years; and Ron Santo, struggling thru [sic] another early-season batting slump." Santo's power shortage was expected to be short-lived, of course, but the knocks by Kessinger and Jenkins were truly surprises. Fergie went the distance on the mound for a 3–1 win, upping his record to 3-1. This mark was equaled by Hands the next day as he bested Don Cardwell, 9–3, in a game in which Nate Oliver got two hits while making his first start in the big leagues since the previous July. He was in Beckert's place, who was now suffering with a 102-degree temperature. Although barely able to stand without having dizzy spells, Beckert still managed to get out of his hotel bed, make it to the stadium, put on his uniform, and sit on the dugout bench.

After the game it was announced that the Cubs had acquired pitcher Don Nottebart from Cincinnati for Minor League infielder Jim Armstrong and cash. Nottebart had actually been pitching for the Yankees but remained the legal property of the Reds while being in New York on a "conditional" basis. The thirty-three-year-old Nottebart was in his ninth Major League season, achieving a career high of 11 wins with Houston in 1963, which included a no-hitter against Philadelphia on May 17 of that year—the first in big league history for the city of Houston. Two years later Nottebart would surrender the 500th home run in the career of Willie Mays. On the day Nottebart had joined the Cubs in 1969, Mays had crushed home run number 590 off Wade Blasingame as part of a 2–1 win over the Astros; the next day Minnesota's Harmon Killebrew belted number 400 of his career off Gary Peters of the White Sox.

Since spring training Giants first-year manager Clyde King had been experimenting with Mays by placing him in the lead-off spot for the first time in his career, save for one regular season game in seventeen years and the several All-Star games in which he batted in the first slot. Billy Williams thought that the move would benefit the "Say-Hey Kid." "The pitchers are going to be in a hole to Willie before they throw the first pitch," Williams explained. "They don't want to start him off with a fastball. The first pitch to him will probably be a curve and right away the pitcher could be behind. Willie will then get better pitches to hit."

Selma was not sharp in his Cubs debut, giving up six earned runs in four innings as Chicago entered the ninth inning with a 6–4 deficit. The bats rallied, however, as Kessinger led off the frame with a walk. It was already his 13th on the season, a point of emphasis from Durocher after Kessinger had walked only 38 times in 160 games in 1968. "The walks are coming now because for the first time I've learned the strike zone from the left side," Kessinger pointed out. "That may sound strange, but I haven't been switch-hitting that long, and although you would think the strike zone looks the same from both sides, it doesn't."

His free pass was then followed by two Met miscues in the field. Banks deposited an RBI single, Hundley smacked a two-run homer for the lead, and Regan held on for an 8–6 win. Nye was firing well in the nightcap of the doubleheader, taking a shutout against Jim McAndrew and Tug McGraw into the ninth inning. But with one out, Mets outfielder Cleon Jones smacked a three-run homer for a split of the day. Nye had allowed only four hits and three walks, keeping the New York hitters off balance for the entire game. But for the time being, he was going to be left out of a regular job; Selma was still the pitcher of choice for the fourth starting spot. "I figured since Selma got rocked and I had pitched so well that I'd be in the starting rotation," Nye would later reflect. "Instead, Leo went with Selma, and I went to the bullpen."

Nye would have found it tough getting work elsewhere, for it seemed that the master moundsmen were strutting their stuff all over the majors—the domination of the bats from the 1968 season appeared to have carried over to the current campaign. While the Cubs were leaving New York and Shea Stadium for Philadelphia on April 30, Jim Maloney of the Reds crafted a no-hitter against Houston; it was nothing new to Maloney, however, for he had previously thrown two no-hit games in 1965 (both in extra innings, ironically—one a victory and one a loss). Considered one of the hardest throwers of the 1960s, Maloney also had set the Reds' single-game strikeout record in 1963 with 16, only to raise it to 18 with his first no-hitter in '65. In an ominous message to batters for the rest of the summer, however, Don Wilson of the Astros shockingly turned the table on the Reds and kept them hitless the very next day after Maloney's gem (Wilson had also authored a no-hitter before, first turning the trick as a rookie in 1967 against Atlanta). Even more bizarre was the fact that Wilson had been pounded for six runs as part of a 14-0 barrage by Cincinnati against Houston just the previous week, on April 22.

As April came to a close, the Cubs finished the month with wins of 2–1 and 10–0 over the Phillies, the latter coming thanks to two doubles by Kessinger (now batting .311) and the fifth homer and four RBI from the surging Santo, who while still just being over the .200 mark had been batting .172 a week earlier.

Thus the Cubs had ended the first month of the season in the same position in which they had started—first place:

National League East	W	L	Pct.	GB
Chicago	16	7	.696	—
Pittsburgh	13	8	.619	2
New York	9	11	.450	5.5
St. Louis	9	12	.429	6
Philadelphia	8	11	.421	6
Montreal	7	13	.350	7.5

Things were indeed looking up for the North Siders. The important bats in the lineup were starting to produce, and Hundley was finally able to take the support bandage off the ankle he had sprained three weeks prior. Before they left to come back home, a few of the players had pinned a note to the bulletin board in the visitors' locker room at Connie Mack Stadium in Philadelphia. It was left there for the Detroit Tigers, as the defending American League champions would be dropping in for an exhibition game on May 5.

> See you in the World Series if you can make it.
> Signed, The Vulture, The Cannibal, and
> The Spinner

Perhaps when John Holland had signed the "Three-Headed Monster" relief corps of Regan, Abernathy, and Aguirre, this had not been what he had in mind for their activities. Nonetheless, he was still confident that the trio would ultimately seal the pennant for the people of Chicago.

5

Shades of Scoreless '68
—Chicago Style

> Tom Seaver does everything well.
> He's the kind of man you'd want
> your kids to grow up to be like.
> Tom's a studious player, devoted
> to his profession, a loyal cat, trust-
> worthy—everything a Boy Scout's
> supposed to be. In fact, we call
> him 'Boy Scout.'
>
> —Cleon Jones

May was here, but with the growing interest in the team, Cubs
fans thought it was September. Or maybe even October.

"Wrigley Field's switchboard is handling more than 600 calls
an hour," Langford noted about the brisk rush for tickets to see
the first-place club, a few decades before fans could point and
click for tickets over the Internet. "Sacks of mail containing at
least 2,000 letters and cards are being dumped daily at the famous old address on Clark and Addison Streets. . . . The Cubbies
won more games last month (16) than in any other April in their

94-year history [and also had just finished their finest April in terms of winning percentage since 1934, when they had opened the year with a 10-2 mark], and returned home from a road trip early yesterday to a riotous greeting from more than 300 fans at O'Hare Airport."

While some of the big bats were still in hibernation, the Chicago pitchers had topped the National League with a 2.58 ERA (including an 0.71 mark out of the vaunted bullpen) for the first month of play. "Am I going to have to do it ALL?" joked Hands, who had just recorded his first RBI in two years in the last game at Philadelphia, a 3–1 loss.

The Cubs had not been back in town an hour before a big announcement came from the South Siders: Al Lopez was re-signing as manager of the White Sox, effective immediately, while the team was playing the Twins in Minnesota. A "reluctant news conference," as it was called, was summoned by White Sox vice president Ed Short, who notified the press that Lopez had "requested that he retire from the ball club due to his health." Lopez had complained of numerous stomach ailments, which physicians recently had attributed to the stress of his job. He had been the Chicago manager since the previous July, when he had taken over for Eddie Stanky, and he had led the team to a 21-26 record and an eighth-place finish in the American League. He left the current club with an 8-9 mark, passing the torch to his longtime coach and Major League veteran Don Gutteridge, who had been associated with the Chicago organization off and on for the previous fourteen years. "I've been on pills continually since last November when I had a terrific pain in my stomach," Lopez informed the papers. "My doctor in Tampa said it was a muscle spasm. Now, it's just nerves. But it doesn't seem to get any better, and I feel dopey a lot of the time. I've got to get off these pills, and I guess this is the only way I can do it."

"He just wasn't the same," noted Aparicio about his manager in recent weeks. "He used to run out to argue with the umpire. This year, he walked."

The Cubs' homestand got off to a roaring start on May 2 against the Mets, as home runs by Santo and Spangler led the team to a

6–4 win. It was Santo's 14th RBI in the past seven games, the product of a straightaway-center blast off Gentry that traveled nearly 440 feet. Despite his low average Santo was second in the league in home runs and RBI at this point, with 6 and 21, respectively (McCovey was pacing the circuit in both categories with 8 and 22 after the first month of the season). The Cubs limped into the winner's circle again the following day, 3–2. All four Cubs pinch hitters that day struck out, as it was left again to Santo to triple home the tying run in the eighth; Phillips later was walked with the bases loaded to prove the difference. Pitchers around the league were trying to throw Phillips inside because they believed his hand was still sore. New York pitcher Ron Taylor tried it four times, and missed.

Also in the eighth inning, Regan (who had entered the game in that frame to relieve Jenkins, who had yet to win at home on the year) was accused by Hodges of not keeping his foot on the rubber when he pitched. Time was called, and Regan was instructed by the umpires to take a few practice throws in his normal delivery as Hodges and umpire Davidson observed. The Cubs survived the outing despite leaving nine runners on base. "We've got to win games like this if we're going to be a winner," Durocher said in the locker room in reference to his team's erratic play.

"Now, when we're in a close game like that in the late innings, we have confidence we're going to pull it out," chimed in Santo, as excited as anyone about the Cubs' early luck in '69. "A few years ago, we didn't think like that, especially in games against the Cardinals. For some reason, we were always the ones that made the mistake." Regan already had picked up his fifth win on the young season, and Abernathy his second save—despite taking a line drive off his knee from the bat of J. C. Martin in the ninth before he closed the game.

Durocher issued an announcement on May 4 that he would be wed for the fourth time, on this occasion to Lynne Walker Goldblatt. Lynne had previously been married to Joel Goldblatt of the Chicago department store chain of the same name and had three children. Two of Durocher's previous marriages had included bonds with socialites Grace Dozier and Lorraine Day, the former a prominent St. Louis businesswoman (they were married in 1934 and divorced in 1943) and the latter an actress (whom Durocher wed in 1947 and divorced in 1960). A ceremony was being planned for later in the summer, one that Leo promised would only minimally disrupt his baseball duties.

The Mets series ended that day with a Sunday doubleheader in store for what was expected to be a full house at Wrigley. The Mets came and battled cool weather, and when the home team sprinted out to their positions, 40,484 spectators stood in the aisles and ramps to watch the first "big day" in the 1969 season so far. Koosman, McAndrew, and Ryan—three of the mainstays in the Mets' fine young rotation—had been fighting a rash of injuries, so Hodges had to fiddle with his plans and start usual-reliever Tug McGraw in the second game. Seaver was healthy, so he was given the ball for his regular turn in the opener. What was to follow symbolized the hatred that would grow between the two clubs over the coming months.

As the Mets batted in the top of the third, Seaver was dusted by a hard, high, inside fastball from Hands ("I'm telling you, it missed his chin by half an inch, if not less," Hundley admitted later, surprised that the ball actually found its way to his mitt). Two pitches later the Mets right-hander was struck in the left arm. In the bottom half Hands led off for the Cubs and was smote in the leg with a Seaver pitch; later, with Santo batting with an 0-2 count, Seaver sent the Cubs third baseman sprawling with a high, inside fastball. Santo barely got to the ground in time, as Seaver admittedly threw another "message pitch" in retaliation for Hands's hitting him. Both benches and pitchers were warned by plate umpire Frank Secory. Hodges and Seaver, meanwhile, used the course of events to fire up their lethargic team.

"I think when Hands hit me, it helped our whole ballclub," Seaver said afterward. "The whole dugout suddenly came alive. It gave us a lift."

Seaver and McGraw went the distance in the two games, each effectively scattering nine Cub hits and each walking away with an important 3–2 win (with McGraw beating Selma) as a tide of momentum ignited the men of New York. Kessinger was able to extend his current hitting streak to 12 games—and his team lead in hits with 35—while striking out just six times in batting in the lead-off spot the first six weeks. "People who have underestimated him also have become accustomed to annually raising his value," Langford affirmed about the Cubs shortstop. "Right now, Kessinger's stock is blue-chip."

But the Mets had seized two critical contests that Durocher feared would be mourned later in the season. He decried his team's inability to deliver in the clutch, as a total of sixteen Chicago runners were left stranded on the day. After the heads cooled off from the rhubarbs on the field, it was noticed that it would be more than two months before the clubs met again, as both teams angrily anticipated their mid-July meeting at Shea Stadium in New York.

§

It was Kessinger and the surprising Spangler—who had helped Kessinger for twenty minutes every day in spring training with his bunting—who righted the ship by supplying Holtzman with six hits in a 7–1 win over the Dodgers on May 6, a game in which Don Sutton had a string of twenty-seven straight scoreless innings snapped (as Hundley added his fourth homer as well). Spangler, a part-time role player for most of his career, now had his batting average up to .362 (25 for 69), which was good for fourth in the National League. "I've never been a fast starter," admitted Al, as Jenkins hollered out Spangler's new batting average for all to hear in the locker room. "And if I'm doing something differently, I hope I never find out what it is!" Despite his newfound success, Spangler still fully expected to maintain his platooning role and sit on the bench in favor of Hickman when left-handers took the hill.

With Spangler's surprising emergence, Durocher had more leverage in his desire to rid himself of Phillips, who had an error and went 0 for 3 with two strikeouts in the win over the Dodgers, and who continued to underachieve, in his manager's opinion. Holland and Durocher had met for over an hour in Leo's office before the game, a sign to the players that some kind of deal was in the works. Durocher had recently berated Phillips outside the dugout and in full public view, making it known to one and all that this was his last chance to hold on to a roster spot. "All he has to do is show me he wants to play," the frustrated manager said to the press. "That's all. I don't expect him to make spectacular catches, or bat .300, or knock in 95 runs, or hit home runs. Just give me 100 percent. I know his timing will be off since he broke the bone in his hand, but the doctors tell me there's nothing wrong with him now. . . . I don't know what else to do. Does Don Young have Phillips' talent? Of course not. But Young wants to play. He's shown me that."

Leo continued: "It's a bigger sin on my part if I give up on a man with this much talent. I don't sleep at night thinking about it. My coaches, everybody, have tried every avenue with this man. I told Pete Reiser to tell Phillips he was in the starting lineup. And you know what Phillips said? 'I want to talk to Leo.' Hell, don't talk to me—go out on the field and *show* me."

Further making Durocher's case was the fact that Gamble was hitting .340 in the minors at San Antonio.

As the NBA's Bulls were making guard Norm Van Lier of St. Francis College of Pennsylvania their first pick in the NBA draft on May 7, Jenkins was concurrently dropping a second game to the Dodgers, 4–2. During the afternoon Los Angeles center fielder Willie Davis made good on his bet to strike back at the Bleacher Bums for their abuse of him, as he hit two homers. "Those fans in left field are crazy," Davis was quoted as speaking with a furious voice. "They've been yelling at me for three years about some girl named 'Ruthie,' and I don't know any girl by that name. They throw stuff and get personal about my family. They made me mad—I wanted to hit one in the middle of them so bad"—which he did to tie the score in the sixth inning. His second blast won the game for the Dodgers in the twelfth.

The Giants were next in town, coming from St. Louis, where the great Mays had just turned thirty-eight years old during their series with the Cardinals. The San Francisco team had cooled considerably in the past week, losing five of their last six after ripping off a nine-game winning streak. On the night of his birthday, Mays was struck out twice by Bob Gibson; the initial time in the first inning sent Mays spinning into the dirt, and in the process he pulled a back muscle that continued to bother him as the team headed north to Chicago. As Mays and other stars around the league were beginning to age, more thought was given to the "designated pinch hitter" rule that had been experimented with in spring training. However, according to Cronin, managers and general managers in the American League unanimously voted against installing the rule. And with an equal show of nonsupport in the National League, the idea of a permanent hitter for the pitcher in the lineup seemed dead.

After an 11–1, rain-soaked Giants win on May 9, the clubs were given the next day off as the torrents continued. Only Abernathy was in the locker room, as he was getting treatment for the line drive that had struck his leg in the previous week. Up in the front office a roster move was made as catcher Bill Heath was promoted from Tacoma and as Alec Distaso, the team's only rookie pitcher, was sent to the other high farm team at San Antonio. Distaso had appeared in only two games, as Durocher was looking to include another bat off the bench (even though Heath had only one Major League at-bat on the season—a ground out off of pitcher Gaylord Perry—and that had been in spring training). With the pitching staff now down to nine members, it was decided that this number would suffice with the team encountering seven off days in the next four weeks, and with the batsmen currently suffering. The offense was down; Williams and Banks were continuing to struggle at the plate, with each hitting .272 and .264, respectively, and only three home runs between them. Combined with Santo the three stars had a total of only eight RBI in the past eight games, with the next one for Banks to be the 1,500th of his career. But Spangler and Kessinger remained sixth and tenth in the league, respectively, with .354 and 334 averages. This productivity notwithstanding, the club knew that its big guns would have to start producing.

Williams answered the bell when he drove a pitch from Ray Sadecki into the bleachers in the first inning the next day. It was his first homer since April 15, and it staked the Cubs to an early 2–0 lead. Conversely, the hot-hitting Kessinger had his hitting streak halted at 15 games. In addition to Williams, also coming along was Hundley, batting at a .350 clip over the previous ten days. Holtzman continued to be the best pitcher of the young season to date, as he wound up disposing the Giants, 8-0, in less than two hours for his second shutout of the year.

A glaring weakness for the team continued to be center field, where Phillips was still not getting the job done. "Dolf is a confused young man," Langford reported, "cautiously unaggressive at the plate and the Cubs' patience is finally wearing out." The man waiting in the wings was nineteen-year-old Gamble, who was ahead of schedule in hitting a blistering .370 at San Antonio. Langford continued: "The feeling now is that if Durocher can convince the Cub brass that it is not premature to give Gamble a try, the 155-pound Alabama native will be on his way to the Cubs by week's end or next week at the latest."

Durocher, however, had no plans to make Gamble an everyday player right away. "It is likely if and when we do call him up that we will start platooning him," Leo noted, addressing the probability of the young left-handed hitter avoiding lefty pitchers for the time being. Phillips's demise was accelerating because of the continued fast start for the Cubs, as Holland and Durocher did not want any weak link to spoil to the momentum; as a result Phillips saw his chances to hold onto a job becoming fewer and fewer. Phillips had only one hit in his previous nineteen at-bats— the lone safety being an infield hit—while striking out in nearly half of those plate appearances.

Jenkins followed up Holtzman's gem with a shutout of his own, a 2-0 blanking of the new Padres, who had arrived in town. It was Fergie's first win at Wrigley Field on the year, as he bested former Cubs Niekro and Ross to gain the triumph. The Cubs pitching staff had already posted seven shutouts on the year. But it was another tough day for Beckert, as the hard-luck second baseman was struck in the jaw on a pitch by Ross. Despite later X-rays being negative, the blow opened a gash on Beckert's face, which required fifteen stitches to close. He insisted he was fine but was ordered by doctors to stay out of action until the team went to Houston three days later.

It was the following day—Tuesday, May 13—that suggested that 1969 was going to be the "Year of the Cubs." It was a watershed moment, a point in time at which the Chicagoans announced to the rest of the National League that they had better stand up and take notice. Not only did Dick Selma deliver the Cubs pitching staff their third straight shutout—the first time the team had performed such a feat in sixty years—but the bats boomed like an artillery barrage, with the San Diego players looking less like fielders and more like refugees looking for cover. "Ernie Banks, that cheerful humanitarian, instigated a massacre yesterday that would have elicited the admiration of all the Indians at Little Big Horn," Langford wrote of the scene. Banks indeed led the charge, knocking two three-run homers, with a total of seven RBI on the day (vaulting him beyond the 1,500 mark, leaving him just three behind Mantle on the career list, with 1,506), as the Cubs cruised to a 19-0 shellacking of the Padres. Ernie's daughter Jan, along with her classmates from Faulkner School, were part of a small crowd of just over five thousand assembled at Wrigley Field to witness the bombardment in the particularly chilly May weather. Even little Nate Oliver chipped in with four RBI. "When you're a backup man like I am, you have to have games like this," he told the press, "and you have to realize with Glenn Beckert, Kessinger, and Santo in the infield, I'm not going to play too often." The score tied the National League record for the most one-sided shutout in history, equaling the score that Chicago levied on the Giants in the year of the Cubs' last World Series triumph in 1906. It was the first time since Selma had won on Opening Day for the Padres that he had gone a full nine innings, and he matched Jenkins's and Holtzman's strikeout totals of ten from the shutouts of the previous two days.

Teams around the league—particularly the Cardinals—marveled at the well-balanced team the Cubs had suddenly become, a club now with equally destructive hitting and pitching. "What makes the Cubs good?" Cincinnati manager Dave Bristol was asked in an interview with the national media. "They know how to play, and they give all-out effort," he replied simply. It was Oliver and Banks riding to the fore the next day too—in comeback fashion—as Ernie homered to lead off the ninth and Nate was driven home by a Willie Smith hit after doubling, giving Don Nottebart (in relief of Hands) his first Major League win in three years, 3–2. The Padres had missed a chance to increase their lead in the seventh, when a missed squeeze bunt attempt by Jerry DeVannon led to two San Diego runners being tagged out on the play.

It was the middle of May, and the owners of the twenty-four Major League clubs had finally met at the Sheraton-O'Hare Hotel outside of Chicago to ratify the deal that had been struck with the players' union back on February 25. And as the Cubs set off on a two-week road trip to the West, they had won more than two-thirds of their games so far and had their largest lead in the division to date:

National League East	W	L	Pct.	GB
Chicago	23	11	.676	—
Pittsburgh	17	15	.531	5
New York	15	17	.469	7
St. Louis	14	18	.438	8
Philadelphia	12	17	.414	8.5
Montreal	11	19	.367	10

The Cubs were a sickly 19-44 all-time in Houston, with most of the games occurring in the Astrodome, the home of the Houston club since 1965. Called "The Eighth Wonder of the World," the dome had been the site for the All-Star Game in 1968, during which—in keeping with the lethargic offense seen all that summer—the lone run had been scored on a double play ground ball. It was no mystery to the press that Durocher didn't like the place. "It's a $35 million park with a nickel infield, a nickel outfield, and a nickel scoreboard," he said. The Cubs players, too, did not have great enthusiasm for the strange building—even though Banks's family had driven over from Dallas to take in a couple of the games. "They are a just a wee bit suspicious of the air conditioning system," a Chicago writer noticed about the Cubs, "which they sometimes imagine sends a steady stream of air towards home plate in the top half of an inning then reverses direction when the home favorites are batting." In an attempt to shake off some of the demons, Cubs traveling secretary Blake Cullen booked the team in a different hotel; even junior club executives such as himself wanted to do nothing to halt the current hot streak. The players were reminded that, when the Cubs had ascended into first place for that brief moment in 1967, it had been a four-game sweep in July at the hands of the Astros in the dome that had restored St. Louis to the top spot permanently.

The Houston management took particular pride in the scoreboard at the Astrodome, which played cartoons (much to the further disgust of the traditionalist Durocher) and was advertised in the Astros' media guide as "an attraction in itself, featuring all pertinent sports information." Durocher himself had a laugh at the scoreboard's expense after the first game of the series. The scoreboard—the costliest one in sports, at $2 million—didn't have a "tens" column in which to display the ten runs the Cubs scored in the seventh inning, the meat of an 11-0 thrashing of the Houston club, prompting Astros manager Harry Walker to call Chicago "the best team my club has faced this year." It was yet another dominating performance by the left-hander Holtzman, who was now 6-1 on the season and had not allowed a run in his last twenty-four innings pitched. It was also the fourth shutout in the last five games for Chicago, with the Cubs sending fifteen batters to the plate in the decisive seventh frame. Don Young was part of the fun, replacing Phillips in the starting lineup and recording two hits, one of them a double. "The kid gave the whole team a big lift," Durocher said of Young's performance. "They were tickled to death to see him out there. He's not afraid of anything." And three safeties by Hundley extended his own personal hitting streak to ten straight games.

On Saturday, May 17, some big news came from back home. It was announced in Chicago that the teachers' union for the city's public schools was posing to strike, leaving the system short of the

176 days required for a full school year and threatening graduation for high school seniors. It also threatened student attendance at part of the summer schedule of Cub games, games that the high schoolers looked forward to. The vote to strike, taken by the union of its members, was strongly passed with a more than two to one margin—10,944 in favor of striking and 5,438 opposed. The main sticking point with the school board was actually the money spent on pupils; the union wished to see the amount raised from $400 to $600 per student, an increase that the board viewed as "practically impossible." Also locally, demolition had begun that day on the old Chicago Union Station, which had served trains entering and leaving the city since 1925. "The big Elgin clock that overlooks the marble staircase was stopped at 6:30 a.m. yesterday," the *Tribune* reported, "precisely the same time the station was opened 44 years ago on May 16." It was that recognizable large clock, manufactured in the suburban community of Elgin, that first greeted travelers when disembarking from the inbound trains.

The Cubs reverted to their typical misery in the Dome, concluding their trip to Houston with heartbreaking losses of 5–4 and 6–5. Jenkins could not continue his personal four-game winning streak on the road in the middle contest, which also ended a five-game Cubs winning streak in which they had outscored their opponents 43–2. In the final tilt, two throwing errors by Santo helped disintegrate Cub leads of 3–0 and 5–3 en route to the loss. Four hits by Kessinger (which raised his average to an even .333, ninth best in the league) could not offset what was called "the worst display of baseball on the year" in the visitors' portion of the press box. Two Cub runners were thrown out at the plate, and Regan walked in the winning run for the Astros in the eighth inning. Both games were saved by Fred Gladding, who like Regan had been recently accused of possessing a spitball in his repertoire. A pitcher who had thrown in only seven games in 1968 (with an ERA of 14.75), Gladding had found unexplainable success in '69, as his two saves had left his opponents scoreless in his last twelve innings of work. The good Houston news was passed along to one special Astros fan, Eugene Cernan, who was orbiting the earth as part of the crew on the *Apollo 10* mission.

A West Coast swing starting in Los Angeles was next as the team left Houston, with Santo (30) and Banks (29) topping the RBI charts in the National League. There was an open date before the first game of the series with the Dodgers, so Coach Reiser hosted a large barbecue for Durocher, the other Cub coaches, and the media at his home in L.A. His daughter Sally stole the evening by proudly showing off her room full of baseball memorabilia. It had been ten years since the Dodgers and Giants had made their controversial move west, and now the long airplane jumps to the Pacific had become second nature to clubs around the league. The new "Taj Mahal of Baseball," as it was called, was Dodger Stadium. The site at Chavez Ravine—a hilly, three-hundred-acre plot of land handpicked by Dodgers owner Walter O'Malley before the move from Brooklyn—was originally designed by the contracted architectural firm to hold close to ninety thousand fans.

The people who had ventured inside Dodger Stadium for the previous ten years had been fortunate to witness the rise of the great left-hander Koufax. Sandy had been a statistically so-so reliever and spot starter during his three years in Brooklyn, having arrived in 1955 at age nineteen. Through the rest of the 1960s, southern California was privy to the best pitching in baseball, as Koufax, Drysdale, Sutton, and Bill Singer threatened to completely shut down any opponent on any given night. Things had changed drastically in recent years, however—and also in recent days. Koufax hung up his cleats abruptly and without much explanation in 1966 at age thirty, during a season in which he continued to dominate (a 27-9 record, a 1.73 ERA, and a league record 317 strikeouts—the season before, he had set the modern-era Major League strikeout record with 382). Now Drysdale, who had been complaining since spring training of stiffness in his right shoulder, thought that the end might be near for him as well. "There's no use kidding myself," said Drysdale after a 6–0 loss to San Francisco back on April 22. "But when the good Lord says 'That's it,' well, that's it." Drysdale had broken in with the Dodgers in 1956, a year after Koufax arrived (and like Koufax, he had made his Major League debut when he was nineteen years old). It was hard to imagine the Dodgers' pitching staff without either one of them, let alone both.

So local fans were naturally curious about the arrival of the Cubs and their "Koufax clone" in Holtzman. The Dodgers were a definite threat to end Holtzman's hot streak, as they were 12-3 at home so far on the year and had pounded left-handed pitching to the tune of a .314 team batting average. Undaunted, however, he strutted out to the mound in the first game of the series to face Sutton.

Holtzman was not intimidated by the surroundings, the Dodger bats, or the aura of Koufax in the arena. He sent Walter Alston's men back and forth from the plate to the bench with great regularity, and the hometown fans were duly impressed as he posted yet another blanking, a 7–0 dash of the L.A. men. Overwhelmed by the talent of the Chicago players, Alston told the press, "If they left it up to me, I'd pick the entire Cub infield and their catcher for the All-Star team."

It was Holtzman's third straight shutout (a feat he had already performed in midsummer of 1968), his fourth overall on the year, and his fifth victory in as many tries. His string of consecutive scoreless innings had begun exactly two weeks earlier on May 6 against the Dodgers and Sutton, as he had shut them out from the fourth inning on for the 7–1 win. Holtzman now led the league in wins (7), as well as ERA for starting pitchers (1.44), and was making a strong case for early consideration as the All-Star Game starter. His battery mate Hundley had quietly been putting together quite a streak himself, having hit safely in the last thirteen games and batting .440 (22 for 50) over that stretch, including three hits (and his sixth homer) in Holtzman's latest dazzler. Kessinger, who tried to ignite some semblance of the Cubs' "running" game, stole his third base of the year—which was only the fifth for the entire team. Arkansas Don had two hits, as did Beckert, Williams, Santo, and Banks, as more balance was starting to return to the lineup.

The fifth member of the Dodgers' rotation, left-hander Claude Osteen, was looking to rebound from a tough 1968 season, in which he had posted a 12-18 mark. The veteran was off to a good start in '69, reportedly having developed a "slow curve and screwball" to add to his repertoire, and he beat Hands and the Cubs, 3-1, on the second night, May 21. Showing great resiliency, Osteen now owned half of the complete games performed by the otherwise-famous Los Angeles staff on the year. The Dodgers won despite the second homer in as many nights by Banks, now with seven on the year, as he also passed Mantle on the career RBI list.

It was also a historic day for the New York Mets. For the first time in the club's history, the team reached the .500 mark; the team sat in third place in the National League East with a record of 18-18. Seaver, however, wasn't impressed. "To me, it's nothing," the pitcher said, seeking greater heights for himself and his club. "What's .500? It's right in the middle. It's neither here nor there."

Meanwhile, that same day in Indianapolis, Indy 500 favorite Mario Andretti narrowly escaped death when he was dragged from the fire-engulfed wreckage of his crashed vehicle following an accident during a practice session. According to observers he had hit the wall at a speed of close to 175 miles per hour. Andretti returned to practice the very next day and promptly resumed rehearsing at high speeds. But after Andretti got himself into a new car, he threatened to quit the race because Indy 500 officials outlawed a special radiator that he installed.

When Jenkins shut out Singer and the Dodgers, 3–0, in the series finale on May 22, it was the sixth blanking of an opponent by the Cubs' pitching staff in the team's last seven victories. It tied Fergie for the league lead with Holtzman, each holding the opposition to zero runs four times on the year. Jenkins also continued to lead the National League in strikeouts, with 72.

Overshadowing the sport was an ominous feeling for the rest of the National League; a repeat of the batting death of '68 seemed in order, yet with a different team providing most of the poison. The previous year it had been Gibson and his mighty entourage leading the Cardinals to numerous 1–0 and 2–1 wins, games that seemed to be over before people in the ballpark knew what had happened. It was no secret that the team to beat in 1969 was the Chicago Cubs, a team that was having its pitching staff develop and come together at just the right time. Even "replacement parts" were working flawlessly, as Selma proved in his next outing when the club went down the coast to meet his former team, the San Diego Padres, for the first time ever. As in Montreal, Kansas City, and Seattle, the residents of the San Diego area in 1969 were being treated to, for many of them, their first visits from big league superstars—although a disappointing early showing in attendance was noted. Nearly one year prior, on May 27, 1968, the city had been awarded a National League franchise. Long a member of the Pacific Coast League through the 1930s, 1940s, and 1950s, San Diego was now getting a chance to witness the very best in the game. San Diego Stadium had opened in 1967, envisioned by local sportswriter Jack Murphy as a venue for both the NFL's San Diego Chargers (who had arrived from Los Angeles in 1961) and—hopefully, at the time—a new expansion team for Major League Baseball (when Murphy died in 1980, the stadium was renamed in his honor).

Selma was as brilliant in the opening game as any Cub pitcher—including Holtzman—had been in a single game on the year. Less than a month since he had been traded, he downed his former friar friends on two meager hits in yet another shutout for the Cubs, 6-0, powered by Williams's fourth home run and three more RBI by Banks. With their 27-14 record, the Cubs' lead in the National League East stood at a full six games ahead of Pittsburgh, and seven in front of the defending champion Cardinals. "The nicest sort of epidemic has infected the Chicago Cubs' pitching staff," Langford cheered. "And they are in the total type of isolation that is the envy of pitchers everywhere. The people who can't touch them are hitters." After the latest win the team sent greetings and get-well-soon wishes to Halas, as the seventy-four-year-old owner of the Bears was recovering from his second hip surgery, performed in England. Halas had his son-in-law, Ed McCaskey, at his side throughout the entire recovery process, and the doctors were very pleased with his progress. "Mr. Halas is as fit today as he was five days after the first operation," one of the attending physicians noted.

One of the superstars that San Diego natives were eager to see was Banks, and the fans were grateful that Ernie had not yet retired from the game by the time the Padres joined the league. He received a rousing ovation when his name was first mentioned over the public address system at San Diego Stadium, and in the second contest it was "Mr. Cub" who came to Holtzman's rescue. The hottest pitcher in the game, no less, still needed the bat of Banks. "Old Ern' initiated another major league city today," Langford proudly announced. "He did it with a snap of those still-powerful old wrists, which remain as quick as his smile and as inspiring as his sunny disposition." Holtzman was on the hook for a rare loss, ending a streak of thirty-three consecutive scoreless innings, as he left the game with a 4–2 deficit in the fourth. In the next trip to the plate for the Cubs, however, Banks lofted a "floater" that sailed high into the California sky and dropped softly into the yellow bleacher seats for four Cub runs and an instant Chicago lead. It was Ernie's eighth homer of the year, leaving him only 19 shy of the prestigious 500 mark. Ernie himself acted as if he had been taken to the amusement park. "Isn't this great?" he asked reporters in an abrupt conversational change to topics he felt were more important. "Is there anything better than playing baseball in the major leagues?" It was Abernathy who picked up the win in four solid innings of relief, raising his own record to 3-0. In addition to Holtzman's performance, another Cubs streak ended this day—it was the first time in forty-one games that Kessinger did not reach base.

The two teams split a doubleheader the following day, with Nye (0-3) losing the opener, 10–2, but Hands and Abernathy (4-0) combining for yet another shutout, 1–0, in the nightcap. With all the success of the pitching staff, scoring was hard to come by for Hands, who had received only seven runs of support in his last six outings. Abernathy had gotten yet another win when Santo crushed a long home run, his ninth on the year, leading off the ninth inning. The game was kept close by Padres outfielder Ollie Brown, who made a remarkable throw to gun down Hundley at the plate on a potential sacrifice fly, called by Durocher "one of the greatest defensive plays I ever saw."

And, unlike in Houston, Durocher was also impressed with the new ballpark in San Diego. He commented while leaving town that it appeared to him to be "very fair for both hitters and pitchers."

Some executives around the game, however, were starting to have second thoughts about San Diego's place as a Major League city, concerned that its general tourist attractions would never allow for full attention to big league baseball; in fact, one local bar owner mentioned that he "had not had a customer from out of town who came to see the Padres play." The Padres' crowds had averaged between eleven and twelve thousand, not a pace that would prove profitable for the owners, Arnholt Smith and Buzzy Bavasi. Bavasi, however, remained positive. "We are pleased with the city's acceptance up until now," he proclaimed to the newspapers, "mainly because we feel the acceptance and interest is growing all the time."

"I hoped they would stay over 15,000," added San Diego mayor Frank Curran when asked what he thought of the early returns on attendance figures. "Perhaps a little warmer weather will make the attendance jump. But people who weren't interested in baseball are talking about the Padres. That wasn't true as [when the Padres were] a PCL [Pacific Coast League] club. Another factor, I think, is Bavasi's personality. He has the ability to sell himself and the club to the community."

The series in San Diego raised some interesting macro points of discussion in the newspapers back in Chicago concerning the greater state of the game. Specifically, the baseball world was reflecting on the impact of involving the West Coast, in consideration of passing the ten-year mark of Major League Baseball's appearance there and now with expansion in 1969 broadening the sport even further. Some owners were calling for a complete overhaul of the Major Leagues—including the idea, growing in popularity among the CEOs, that the twenty-four teams should divide into *three* major leagues of eight teams each. Phil Wrigley was among those who thought this was a good idea, and his fellow members of the "old guard" had a sharp new ally in the rambunctious owner of the Oakland A's, Charles O. Finley. Finley, who had finally gotten what he wanted in 1960 when he wrestled the Kansas City A's under his own control, originally had attempted to move the A's to Dallas in 1962 but had been denied by league officials. Claiming over the next five years that he was losing too much money in Kansas City, Finley ultimately succeeded, in 1967, in bringing the team to Oakland. As the team left Kansas City, local loyalist Symington berated Finley on the floor of the U.S. Senate, calling him "one of the most disreputable characters to ever enter the sports scene."

Finley certainly was not afraid of change—be it using orange baseballs for night games, giving his players bonuses for growing long mustaches, or other oddities—and he welcomed the idea of comprehensively realigning the leagues, which would be, he predicted, "the greatest to come along in baseball since the invention of the concession stand." The airplane—viewed in the 1930s as a future panacea for long sports travel and as the saving mechanism that would ultimately bring Major League Baseball to the West—was now being denounced by Finley as an inhibitor. "Major league baseball today extends from the eastern seaboard—from Boston and Baltimore—to the golden West, where it ranges from Seattle to San Diego," he explained. "Major league baseball extends from Montreal to Houston. At first, the jet airplane seemed the answer to our travel problems. Then we found out that constant travel by jet can fatigue you more than travel in a covered wagon. . . . We are treating players like cattle. But instead of putting them in a truck, we put them in a bus to get to the point of departure. At the point of departure, we put them in a jet plane instead of a boxcar. Except for these differences, we're handling players like livestock."

Nothing more in the immediate future would be made of the realignment idea, but owners like Finley, Wrigley, and others were sure it would occur soon, with all Major League teams being more geographically compacted. Attendance at Major League parks had been suffering, and the owners were scrambling for plans to enhance fan interest. Kuhn was given a vote of confidence that same week by the owners, as all twenty-four chief executives approved permanently installing him as the fifth commissioner of Major League Baseball.

Stark challenges lay imposingly ahead of Kuhn, as a relatively new competitor was on the block, competing for a nationwide audience. Not coincidentally, the NFL announced that same week that thirteen "weeknight" games would be televised nationally on Monday evenings starting with the 1970 football season. A three-year agreement worth $18 million had been reached with the American Broadcasting Company (ABC); hence, what would become the longest-running television series was born, soon to commonly be known as "Monday Night Football." The National Broadcasting Company (NBC) and Columbia Broadcasting System (CBS) had been offered the deal but had turned it down, with one of the networks reportedly scoffing that the idea "would never get off the ground." Nonetheless, forward-thinking NFL commissioner Pete Rozelle wanted the two other networks involved, so he began creating an offer to include one or both in a national Sunday night television package. Roone Arledge, president of ABC Sports, was more than happy to accept the deal, calling NFL games "one of the prime, if not the prime, sports attractions on TV." Soon after the announcement, work crews at various NFL parks around the country hustled to make their stadiums conducive to live color television at nighttime. The move was lauded by other people in the business world as new, exciting, and progressive thinking.

Was baseball beginning to lose its fan base to professional football? Some writers, including Edward Prell, thought that it might have already occurred. "There are those who say it long since has yielded to football," Prell mused about the state of baseball in the late 1960s. "Plus, one must add the many do-it-yourself activities [that are here] in an expanding sports-minded and time-free populace." Even C. C. Johnson Spink, editor of *The Sporting News*—a publication that had always been referred to as the "Baseball Bible" by those who followed the game—admitted: "Most fans either regard baseball as their favorite sport or believe it is the country's number-one sport, yet they would rather watch football in person or on television."

When the Cubs arrived in San Francisco to finish the western swing, good news arrived all the way from Martinsville, Virginia, the home of Randy Hundley. Mrs. Hundley had given birth to an eight-pound, four-ounce baby boy named Todd Randolph. The new father made good in celebration, belting a grand slam as part of a seven-run third inning of the second game, a 9–8 win, after the Cubs dropped the opener, 5–4, in an error-filled contest. The Giants had been victimized by many injuries on the year, to the point where their Opening Day starting lineup had been on the field together only four times in their forty-three games. But they still had the imposing McCovey looming large at first base, and his 450-foot homer to right field, his league-leading 13th of the year, made the difference in the opener.

The Cubs left the two-game stop in San Francisco to return home and open a nine-game homestand on May 30 with the Braves, Astros, and Reds coming to town. Hundley raced back to get a look at his new child. "I've been waiting for a son for seven years," Hundley told one local writer. "I felt like when I saw Todd for the first time, all of my dreams had come true. When I went into that waiting room at the hospital when our first daughter was born, I was sure that God didn't make anything but boys. Well, He fooled me twice, but this time I came out a winner. I love my daughters, but wait until you see Todd."

The Braves, despite losing the All-Star Joe Torre, had become a more well-rounded team, already looking vastly improved from their 81-81 club of 1968. Like the Cubs in the Eastern Division, Atlanta stood atop its circuit in the West, winning two out of every three to date (28-14) behind the consistent Aaron, the enthusiastic Cepeda, and an improving pitching staff led by Joe Niekro's brother, Phil, who had three shutouts on the year and was a boyhood friend of Boston Celtics basketball star John Havlicek in Ohio. "Cepeda has accounted for the biggest change in the Braves," an Atlanta representative told the *Tribune* as the club arrived in Chicago. "Not only has he delivered the clutch hits [nine game winners so far on the season], but he has been a much better first baseman than we ever dreamed." Aaron, who was continuing to threaten the all-time home run chart, was feeling well as the 1969 season was starting to roll. "I can play just as well as I ever could," the thirty-five-year-old outfielder said, "but

I can't play as much. I need a rest more often now. If I play three or four days in a row, I get tired. I think I could play three or four more years and play good baseball."

Lead-off hitter Felipe Alou was doing his part as well, knocking the ball at a .352 clip. Leading the moundsmen was Niekro, in his fifth full season with the Braves (he had taken part in the club's move from Milwaukee to Atlanta before the 1966 season). Niekro had spent the winter working as a consultant for the National Science Institute, where he claimed that he received increased powers in positive thinking. "As much as three days before I pitch," he revealed about his new attitude, "I start saying to myself, 'I can beat this team.' Every night before I go to bed, I say this to myself." While Niekro possessed his brother's knuckleball, other members of the pitching staff were trying to gain an edge through another strategy. The Braves coaches, frustrated by the National League umpires' failure to enforce the ban on the spitball, had recently directed their hurlers to use the illegal pitch.

Niekro had quality company on the starting staff with Pat Jarvis, a young fireballer and former rodeo rider from Carlyle, Illinois. Jarvis agreed with the assessment that Cepeda had been the difference in the club's fine start. "He's added something extra that really helps the team," he said. "He keeps us in good spirits and on our toes." Another formidable starting pitcher for the Braves was Ron Reed, a former basketball player for the University of Notre Dame from LaPorte, Indiana, who competed for three seasons in the NBA. As with the Cubs, the only major weakness for Atlanta coming into the season was the lack of a quality left-handed reliever; Chicago believed they addressed the issue by acquiring Aguirre, while Atlanta chose to focus its off-season transactions elsewhere.

As May was winding to a close, only the Cubs had scored more runs (224) than the Braves (193). Large crowds were expected at Wrigley for the Memorial Day weekend, previewing what many thought could be a National League playoff matchup. "[Atlanta manager] Luman Harris said it back in March when hardly anyone was listing the Braves as pennant contenders," wrote Jesse

Outlar of the *Atlanta Constitution*. "He said that 'We've got just as good a chance of winning the league as anyone.'"

It was the second-to-last day of May, and as Hands walked to the pitcher's mound, he had not been a winner since April 26. The squad had complete confidence in his "stuff," but Hands's run support had been meager and the defense behind him marginal. Most in the packed house of 36,075 at Wrigley sensed things were about to turn for the right-hander. The bleachers, as always, were the prime general admission seats to be purchased; fans had lined up outside the bleacher gates beginning at four o'clock in the morning to be the first inside the bricks. It was not a complete sellout of the stadium, as a few sprinkled unfilled seats dotted the corners of the upper deck. Hands had battled Reed pitch for pitch through six innings in front of the holiday crowd, with each team remaining scoreless, when Braves second baseman Felix Millan reached second with nobody out in the seventh. Before the game, as Reed was doing his warm-up jog in the outfield, Banks had yelled to him, "You should still be playing basketball. . . . You can't beat the Cubs!!!". Hands went behind the mound, gathered himself, and promptly nailed Hundley's mitt on the outside corner to strike out Aaron, forced Clete Boyer to tap weakly to third, and fanned Cepeda to end the threat as the fans thundered an ovation.

The Cubs parlayed a collection of hits in the bottom half (initiated by Hundley's bunt single to lead off the inning), and Hands cruised through the final two frames for another shutout for the staff, 2–0, the fourteenth scoreless game the Cubs had thrown at an opponent on the year. Hands truly dominated, proving himself still on equal par with Jenkins and Holtzman, as he walked nobody and allowed a mere five hits to the Atlanta men. It was also the third loss in three decisions to the Cubs in Reed's career. Batting stars for the club included Williams and Beckert, with two hits apiece, as Williams was riding a twelve-game hitting streak and had pushed his average over the .300 mark during the day. "I'd have to say this is the best hitting lineup we've seen all year," Hundley stated in the locker room about the Braves, very happy in the sparkling performance of his pitcher. "In the seventh inning, we just decided to match strength against strength. He didn't shake off a single sign. His slider was breaking real good, and we just stuck with it." Durocher was laughing heartily in his office, celebrating the triumph with friends and his fiancé, Lynne Walker Goldblatt. Meanwhile, Hands was over at his locker, impervious to Hundley's comments and already figuring to himself what he needed to do in June to make up for May—and here was a start, indeed.

More of the same destruction fell on the Braves the next two days. In a 2–2 tie in the ninth inning on May 31, Santo tripled to lead off the ninth inning and subsequently jumped and stomped on home plate with both feet after Don Young singled over a drawn-in infield, providing a victory for Jenkins (7-2), with Young claiming that Braves starter Niekro had "only the second knuckleballer I've ever faced. When I went to bat in the ninth, I looked back at Mr. Durocher. I thought they would pinch hit for me. Why was I playing instead of Dolf Phillips? I guess Mr. Durocher just plays hunches."

The game was also highlighted by spectacular defensive plays by Kessinger, in which he robbed both Cepeda and Aaron by making quick dashes to his right to snag balls that were sure hits (Aaron had also homered on the day, his tenth, giving him 520 for his career and only one behind Ted Williams for the number-five all-time spot). Banks was asked whether he could have made those plays at short in his heyday, as Kessinger did. "Not in my palmiest days," he responded, grinning. "It's plays like those that give a ballclub a lift." Jenkins was a bit more humorous in his assessment. "It's a good thing Don's six-foot-three," the pitcher joked. "If he was an inch shorter, he never would have gotten either of those." The contest had been delayed for nearly two hours at the beginning by torrential thunderstorms, which "kept the 29,778 customers and the ground crew moving around like mice in catnip." A window of calm had pacified the Wrigleyville area for the next couple of hours; then, with Santo batting, a sudden Wrigley gust of the famous southern variety picked up Santo's ball and startled Alou in center field. The Braves outfield was visibly surprised when the ball carried way over his head and landed at the base of the wall, where the ivy was just beginning to bloom.

So with weather conditions also now on their side, who was going to stop the Cubs? They had just manhandled the best from the West in three straight and now had widened their own division lead to seven-and-a-half games when the newspapers hit the stands on the morning of June 2:

National League East	W	L	Pct.	GB
Chicago	33	16	.673	—
Pittsburgh	25	23	.521	7.5
New York	22	23	.489	9
St. Louis	22	25	.468	10
Philadelphia	18	25	.419	12
Montreal	11	33	.250	19.5

The team's confidence was growing every day, as winning was starting to become a habit for the Cubs under Durocher. "The way I see it," the manager told the press about his talented ball club, "the only way we can lose is if we beat ourselves."

The 1969 Chicago Cubs. Top row (L–R): Popovich, Decker, Holtzman, Hands, Hickman, Abernathy, Johnson, Nye, Kessinger, Regan, Nottebart. Second row from top (L–R): Scheuneman (trainer), Qualls, Hall, Jenkins, Smith, Young, Hairston, Aguirre, Rudolph, N. Oliver, Spangler, Cullen (traveling secretary). Third row from top (L–R): Kawano (equipment manager), Williams, Hundley, Santo, Banks, Becker (coach), Durocher (manager), Walker (coach), Amalfitano (coach), G. Oliver, Selma, Beckert. Front row (sitting) (L–R): Murphy (batting practice pitcher), Gamble, McGuire (bat boy), Rigacz (bat boy), Pinkus (bullpen catcher). (Courtesy National Baseball Hall of Fame Library, Cooperstown, New York.)

Don Kessinger, the steady
Cubs shortstop and former
All-American in two sports at
the University of Mississippi.
(Courtesy National Baseball Hall
of Fame Library, Cooperstown,
New York.)

Glenn Beckert, a quiet leader
who became one of the best
second basemen in the game
in the late 1960s. (Courtesy
National Baseball Hall of Fame
Library, Cooperstown, New
York.)

Nothing could dampen the spirit of Ernie Banks, perhaps the most beloved Cub of all time. (Courtesy National Baseball Hall of Fame Library, Cooperstown, New York.)

Ken Holtzman delivers a pitch. (Courtesy National Baseball Hall of Fame Library, Cooperstown, New York.)

Billy Williams, whose sweet swing excited crowds at Wrigley Field for many years. (Courtesy National Baseball Hall of Fame Library, Cooperstown, New York.)

Ferguson Jenkins, pitching in the fourth inning in the infamous game at Shea Stadium against the Mets on July 8, 1969. (Courtesy National Baseball Hall of Fame Library, Cooperstown, New York.)

Ron Santo makes a play at third base in front of the charging Rusty Staub of the Montreal Expos. (Courtesy National Baseball Hall of Fame Library, Cooperstown, New York.)

Bill Hands, who became the team's best pitcher during the turbulent latter months of the 1969 season. (Courtesy National Baseball Hall of Fame Library, Cooperstown, New York.)

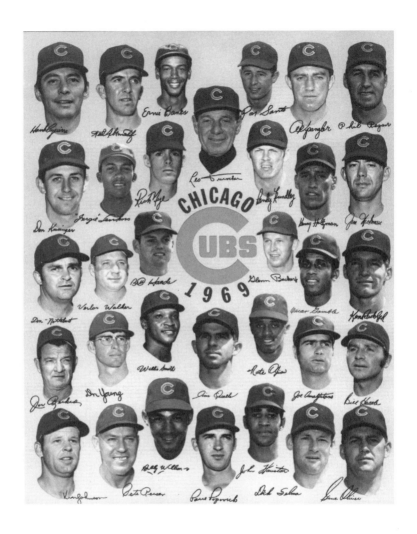

A popular yearly souvenir at Wrigley Field
was the "Head Shot Card" of the Cubs
players, with this version showing the 1969
team. (Courtesy National Baseball Hall of
Fame Library, Cooperstown, New York.)

6

Cub Power

> I like my players to be married and
> in debt. That's the way you moti-
> vate them.
>
> —Ernie Banks

Those lovable Cubbies.

It was a negative label placed on the North Side team forever, meant more as a pejorative than a boost, a label that implied
an unconditional tolerance of their typical losing manner. But
they were losers no more—and that being the case, they fierce-
ly guarded their newfound, first-place hive of honey like a pack
of full-grown, starving grizzlies. As the series with Atlanta rolled
the calendar into June, the Cubs wanted nothing more than to
destroy their fellow pennant contender from the West, and tem-
pers flared when it was thought that the Braves were seeking to
maim their icon in the series finale.

In the process of the Cubs building a 9–3 lead in the sixth inning, Banks stepped to the plate to face Claude Raymond, a former All-Star reliever who was now in the waning days of his ca-

reer. Raymond came in tight with a fastball, and as he was taught for so many years, Banks turned inward—and the stinging ball nailed him right in the middle of his back. In the next inning Selma, who had just entered the game in relief of Holtzman, fired two pitches close to the knees of Aaron, who stepped out of the batter's box and started barking at the Cubs pitcher. Hundley then took off his mask and got in Aaron's face. Aaron thought he had been singled out, as there had been two hitters to come to the plate before him; Hundley reminded him that he, like Banks, was the big bat in the Braves' lineup and thus he shouldn't be such a whiner about it. This was Hundley's birthday, and he was going to let nothing spoil his mood; he was shocked by the number of true fans he never knew he had, having received a total of twelve birthday cakes from fans in the stands before the game. Although he gave most of them away to local children's hospitals and orphanages after the game, he did save a couple for himself and his newborn baby son, Todd.

The next inning, when Selma came up to bat, he was sent to the ground on a toss from rookie pitcher Paul Doyle. This emptied the benches. Durocher was first out of the dugout; he was going not for a Braves player but, rather, for home plate umpire Ed Vargo. Almost cartoonlike, Leo skidded to a stop in front of Vargo after sprinting full speed, greeting him with a bobbing head full of obscenities. After the field was cleared of sparring players five minutes later, the Cubs resumed their more traditional assault on the Atlanta pitching staff with homers by Williams, Hundley, and Hickman (his first), demolishing the way to another win, 3–4, and a three-game sweep of the Braves. Banks knocked in two more runs to push his league-leading total to 43. The Cubs were now seventeen games over the .500 mark, as the Braves had lost four games in a row for the first time on the year.

"For the good of baseball," smirked Condon, "let's break up those Wreckers from Wrigley Field, the Chicago Cubs, before they make a farce of the national pastime. If the Cubs maintain their current pace, they figure to win the division crown going away." It was not just the local media extending the plaudits, however; unanimous concessions were finally being made around the league on who was the team to beat, and some were wondering if there would be room for players from any other teams on the All-Star roster come July. The most indomitable group in the collection of stars was the infielders, who appeared indestructible, and the most impressed members of the National League faculty were the hosts of the Cubs' recent West Coast trip. Alston again suggested that "it would save a lot of time and trouble if everyone would just vote the entire Cub infield," including Hundley, as the National League starters for the Mid-Summer Classic on July 22. Preston Gomez, the head man of the Padres, echoed the sentiment by calling "the Chicago inner defense the best in baseball." If it happened, it would be the first time all four infielders and the catcher from the same team started an All-Star game since 1948. It was the consensus that Banks would have the most difficulty being selected, with rivals McCovey, Torre, and Cepeda all posting their usual outstanding seasons at first base. And the slot at catcher wasn't a lock, either. "Hundley's competition is supplied by only one man but it is formidable," Langford pointed out. "His name is John Bench of Cincinnati, and most baseball people think that the youngster may soon be the sport's most outstanding all-around catcher. . . . Baserunners do not steal on either man. Bench is the only catcher to throw out St. Louis' Lou Brock this year, while the Cardinal speedster has yet to even test Hundley's arm."

Five years later Brock would smash the single-season stolen base record with 118, removing the mark set by Maury Wills of the Dodgers in 1962. On June 4 Wills—mired in a sea of losing with the expansion club in Montreal—announced his retirement, saying he wanted to allow the Expos to develop some of their younger players. His exit, however, took place under some unsightly circumstances. Batting under .200 and having been booed relentlessly by the Montreal fans, Wills purposefully arrived late outside the Expos locker room before the game on June 2, waited until all of his teammates had dressed and headed for the field for batting practice, and only then entered the locker room to put on his uniform for the last time and subsequently announced his decision to the club when he entered the stadium. Five days later the pitiful Expos lost their twentieth straight game, which tied the Major League record. In a strange twist of events, however—and one that would impact the Cubs directly—Wills, after announcing his retirement from the Expos, would resurface with another Major League team just one week later.

Since the Astros had beaten the Cubs in the two late-inning heartbreakers in Houston on May 17 and 18, they had gone on to win ten in a row inside the Astrodome. They did not play as confidently on the road as in their strange home, however, and the Cubs took advantage when they came to Wrigley on June 3. Hands and Jenkins made quick work of them in two games, winning 4–2 and 5–4, before smallish crowds of just over eleven and thirteen thousand, respectively. In between the games Durocher took time out for his bachelor party at Jack Mooney's restaurant. He playfully opened gag gifts from well-wishers, including a toy bear from Halas, a wig from actor Yul Brenner, a nose guard from an anonymous donor (the nameless note directed Leo to use it during future arguments with umpires for protection), and a concocted pair of 1969 World Series tickets from August A. Busch Jr.—the owner of the St. Louis Cardinals—with the name of Busch's Cardinals printed on the ticket as presumably having a rematch with the Detroit Tigers. Nearly all of the Cubs players attended the party and were mostly doubled over in laughter the entire evening as Bill Sullivan, a former basketball player from Notre Dame, roasted the groom-to-be. Leo would marry Miss Goldblatt in two weeks.

Hundley, to whose bat nobody ever seemed to pay much mind, provided a two-hit effort in the first game to raise his average to .311 with 27 RBI; he then homered the next day (his ninth on the year, and third in the last six games) to provide the margin in Jenkins's victory. Jim Hickman, who had entered the day batting only .143 (10 for 70), contributed a clutch two-run single as well. Hickman had been receiving extra playing time with Spangler nursing a bruised heel. And it was two more complete games from the starting staff, as the Three-Headed Monster of Regan, Abernathy, and Aguirre had not been called upon for a week. (This was an unusual move for Durocher, who preceded George "Sparky" Anderson as one of the first managers who used his bullpen liberally. "You don't save any pitcher for tomorrow," Leo said often. "Tomorrow it may rain.") Jenkins's opponent in the second contest was impressive rookie Tom Griffin, a twenty-one-year-old from Los Angeles who was coming off an outstanding performance in which he struck out thirteen Mets in a 7–0 shutout of New York in the Astrodome on May 23.

Despite being dominated by the rookie Griffin, the Mets had recently crept past Pittsburgh in the standings; after losing to Griffin and leaving Houston, the Mets went on an eleven-game winning streak, leapfrogging the Pirates for second place behind the Cubs.

It was at this time that Selma, already recognized in the clubhouse as an irrepressible character, became known as the "official cheerleader" on the field. When he felt that the team needed a lift, he would grab a towel and rise from his seat in the Cubs bullpen, which was located down the left-field line. The excitement would build from the Bleacher Bums in the left-field seats as, at any given moment, Selma would begin frantically waving the towel over his head, which Langford likened to "an airport ground crewman giving the signal for a pilot to rev up his engines." The hollering of the crowd would rise to a great crescendo, at which point Selma—at a split second of his own discretion—would throw down his arm like a track official starting a race and, on cue, the fans would start into a song—the usual favorite was "Don't Keep Kicking My Dog Around."

With threats of a teachers' strike gone and the Chicago Public Schools almost out for the summer, these stands would soon be even more filled—including the members of the Schurz High School baseball team from the North Side, who under the direction of second-year head coach Cliff Pierce had just won the state championship with a triple play to end the final game. "I'm not surprised by anything these kids do anymore," Pierce told the *Tribune* of his juggernaut. They would soon join the other Cub fans at Wrigley, whose bleacher antics were even bringing stiff grins to the face of the traditional Durocher, who could enjoy more unconventional activities with his club holding a ten-and-a-half game lead in the standings. After his club limped out of town to St. Louis, Astros manager Harry Walker added to the litany of impressed observers: "I just can't see how the Cubs are going to fold. They have not one but three pitchers who are stoppers [Holtzman, Hands, and Jenkins], who will keep them from going into any prolonged losing streak." He reminded the press, however, that when he was a player on the Cardinals in 1942, his team had trailed a Durocher-managed Dodger club by ten-and-a-half games in *August* and had ultimately caught them to win the pennant.

§

Meanwhile, even during its off-season, professional football was grabbing the sports headlines. It was announced on June 7 that Joe Namath, the flashy American Football League quarterback who led the New York Jets to the world championship the past year, was quitting the game. Namath, from Beaver Falls, Pennsylvania, had ventured from there to the University of Alabama and then on to an unheard-of sum of $400,000 to sign with the New York team in 1965. The Jets had just stunned the Baltimore Colts in Super Bowl III in January 1969, and their next order of business was to play the current college all-stars at the annual event at Soldier Field in Chicago in August, against the likes of O. J Simpson of Southern California and the Bears' own Douglass out of Kansas. Namath was suddenly larger than life in the city that never slept, as the Jets had—albeit temporarily—supplanted the Giants as the football kings of Gotham. But Rozelle had wanted Namath to relinquish control of his newly established New York nightclub, Bachelors III, because of the disreputable characters that regularly patronized it and the ongoing rumors that it was a haven for gambling. Former U.S. ambassador to the United Nations Arthur Goldberg offered to mediate the case between Namath and the NFL but was refused. Wagering within the major team sports—even in the socially-loosening days of the late 1960s—was still not viewed favorably in the athletic world and was described by Condon as "a dark cloud that has hovered over the sports scene since the first Christians were tossed to the lions." Namath stubbornly refused to give up the club—which had been open for less than a year—and claimed that Rozelle was threatening him with ultimatums that would force him to sell his interest in the club or face suspension from the league. According to a spokesperson for the New York City Police Department, the establishment on Manhattan's lower East Side "was crawling with the worst set of characters. There were a lot of things going on there that Namath didn't know anything about." Rozelle made it clear that Namath himself was not being named in any improprieties.

"It is obviously impossible for a player to be aware of the background and habits of all persons to whom he is introduced," Rozelle went on to explain. "However, *continuation* of such association after learning of a person's undesirable background and habits is cause for deep concern."

At the time, Bowie Kuhn was on a nationwide tour, visiting each Major League clubhouse and reminding the players of the dangers that could result from associating with gamblers. Kuhn, in no uncertain terms, denounced any presence of wagering in the game of baseball. He was also successfully convincing the owners of the Oakland A's (Finley) and the Atlanta Braves (William Bartholomay, Delbert Coleman, and John Louis) to relinquish their stock shares in certain Las Vegas casinos.

What would happen if Namath took his case to court? Kuhn was asked.

"I stopped practicing law four months ago," Kuhn responded. "I don't know the facts, but a commissioner's foremost responsibility is the retention of the integrity of his sport. He must protect the good image."

As news of the Namath situation was hitting the press, one of the most famous speakeasy dwellers in New York—Mickey Mantle—was having his number 7 retired in a ceremony at Yankee Stadium on June 8. "Namath is just talking off the top of his head," the Mick said, thinking that all would be fine in the coming days. With Mantle soon to open a restaurant of his own in Lubbock, Texas, long-simmering rumors resurfaced about he and Namath opening an establishment of their own together in New York City. "That's a bit premature," Mantle responded.

Namath would stand his ground for six weeks before succumbing to Rozelle's demands on July 18, when the quarterback would finally agree to sell his interest in the nightclub and return to play for the Jets, who would soon begin their summer drills at Hofstra University in Hempstead, New York, in preparation to face the college all-stars in Chicago on August 1. Both sides appeared relieved. "Joe and I and professional football have gone through six difficult weeks," Rozelle would announce with the grinning Broadway Joe by his side. "We are happy to say that the situation is resolved; I consider the matter closed."

§

The Cubs appeared concerned not about gamblers or unseemly nightclubs but, rather, only about keeping their strong club intact. Only an injury could break up the fun, and it occurred on June 6 at Wrigley Field against the Reds. "It was one of the things baseball experts have said all season the high-flying Cubs could not afford to have happen to them," the *Tribune* mourned. The casualty once again was Beckert, but this time his injury was far more serious than the wooziness he endured from the collision in St. Louis back in April or from the flu of weeks past. In the third inning of the Reds game, Beckert charged forward to field a tapper off the bat of Pete Rose. In trying to complete a double play, Beckert tagged Tony Cloninger as he was running from first to second. Beckert properly held the ball in his bare hand as he tagged, but the impact broke his thumb. As he was taken to Wesley Hospital for X-rays, Beckert also revealed that he had been playing with a sore back since the third game of season, when he had collided with Richie Allen of the Phillies. The discouraged Cubs still cruised behind Holtzman (9-1) for a 14–8 pyrrhic victory, although Holtzman was sloppy in allowing ten hits and five runs in five innings.

In the locker room after the game, Williams (who, with two hits on the day, was again above the .300 mark) and other veterans were walking over to Nate Oliver's locker, encouraging him for the task he was about to undertake—being the new starting second baseman of the Chicago Cubs for the foreseeable future. It was, however, the most subdued that the locker room had been all season.

That lackluster feeling continued the next day. While Wrigley Field maintained the adorable novelty of being the only Major League stadium without lights, nature constantly reminded observers that there was no electrical help to be had. Such was the case on Saturday, June 7, as the Cubs were battling the Reds before a national television audience. "Mid-afternoon looked more like midnight," as one witness put it. The teams had fought to a 5–5 tie in the ninth inning, when a light drizzle of rain became a hard downpour. The umpires then sent the teams off the field, with no decision about the outcome of the game—for they felt there was no chance of enough daylight being left to finish the contest fairly. "At 3:50 p.m., time was called, and most of the 29,908 fans knew that was all the baseball they would see this particular afternoon," Langford pecked on his damp, cold typewriter, "and they abandoned the dank park as if it were the *Titanic*." The game, as either a win or a loss, would never appear in the record books; rather, it would be replayed as part of a doubleheader on August 26 during the Reds' only other trip to Wrigley Field on the year. The players, on the other hand, were permitted to take their base hits and other personal statistical laurels from the game with them. This included Kessinger, who had extended his errorless streak to forty-seven consecutive games, just five shy of the National League record for shortstops held by the Giants' John Kerr.

As the Cincinnati club exited the field and made its way to the visitors' locker room along the right-field line, Reds pitcher Jose Pena had his nose struck and broken by a ball hurled from a Cubs fan, a perceived result of Pena's multiple inside pitches to Chicago batters in the game two days earlier. Things were more peaceful around the Cubs' clubhouse on the left-field side, where Phillips triumphed in a makeshift golf-putting contest that Willie Smith had organized in the hallway, as bettors flicked their nickels and quarters toward Adolfo in disgust. The putting tournament continued the next day, as the rain also continued and the ballplayers never removed their street clothes. The Reds finally ended things on June 9 with a 4–1 Cincinnati victory, with Jenkins (8-3) suffering the loss. After the game the Reds announced the signing of their number-one draft choice, left-handed pitcher Don Gullett out of Lynn, Kentucky. The Cubs soon also came to terms with their top selections in the June draft—Doug Ross, another left-handed hurler from Arizona Western Junior College, and their top overall pick, shortstop Roger Metzger. Joining the Major League roster the following week was the Cubs' (and the entire draft's) number-one draft choice from 1968, twenty-year-old pitcher Dave Lemonds from the University of North Carolina. "We wanted to bring him up two weeks ago, but they [the Cubs' Minor League coaches] told us he wasn't sharp enough," Holland said. "We think he is ready, and will do a better job than some we have now. Last night I got a call from a scout who said he is ready." Lemonds had struck out 12 batters in his last appearance for San Antonio in the Texas League. When he arrived with the Cubs, however, Lemonds would throw in only two games. After returning to the Minor Leagues and subsequently being traded, Lemonds would not reappear in the big leagues again until 1972 with the White Sox, his final showing in the majors.

The San Francisco Giants had made Irving (Texas) High School senior Michael Phillips their first-round selection in the draft. This was not especially noteworthy except for one point: Phillips was a left-handed shortstop. He signed quickly and was sent to the Giants' rookie league team in Great Falls, Montana.

When the Cubs arrived in Atlanta on June 10 to open a three-game series with the Braves, everyone knew that bragging rights for the entire National League were at stake. Under the warm Atlanta sky, Hundley approached Banks during batting practice.

"Ern, this is a big ball game for us," the catcher said.

"Sure is," Banks replied.

A moment later, Kessinger wandered over.

"Ernie, this is a big game for us," the shortstop said.

"Sure is," Banks responded again.

And even the minor actors had a role to play in the upcoming drama that was building.

Little had been heard from Willie Smith since his Opening Day dramatics, when he sent home the Wrigley faithful with a 7-6 win over the Phillies with his home run in the bottom of the eleventh. Since then Smith had been used only sparsely by Durocher, mostly as a left-handed stick off the bench. He had batted only forty-three times on the season, though hitting at a sharp .302 clip. In the series opener, once again his name was called late in the game. Holtzman had crafted yet another great game but had been surpassed by Reed, the Atlanta starter on the day, who held a 1-0 lead on the Cubs as Holtzman was scheduled to lead off the eighth inning. Smith grabbed a bat and promptly uncorked the longest home run in the short four-year history of Major League baseball in Atlanta–Fulton County Stadium—a rising shot that landed over 475 feet from home plate (the first batted ball to ever settle in the upper deck at the park)—to tie the score with a blast that Durocher described as "Ruthian," in reference to Leo's old roommate with the Yankees. (Only once before had such thing occurred in Atlanta. Back in 1965 Jim Beauchamp had hit a ball near that area of the stadium in a Minor League game.)

After an error by Cepeda, Santo came to the plate. Santo said later that Smith's homer "was the longest he had ever seen," but in the interim he tried to duplicate the feat. He walloped his own dinger, his tenth on the year, and Holtzman was granted a 3–1 lead that Regan nailed down in the final two frames for his sixth save, which included Williams's robbery of Aaron's sixteenth potential homer of the season with a leaping grab at the left-field wall. The umpires had been eyeing Regan very closely, having received instructions from Giles that day to be more mindful of ball-altering substances (such as petroleum jelly) that pitchers were suspected of smearing on their uniforms. Holtzman, who had recovered from a few shaky starts, gained the victory to become the first ten-game winner in the big leagues. The coaching staff had tired of Holtzman's apparently lackadaisical attitude when his team jumped out in front. "Once he gets a big lead, he eases up," claimed Becker after Holtzman's previous starts.

Phil Niekro matched the left-hander Holtzman's win total the next day as he knuckled his record to 10-4 on the year by beating the Cubs, 5–1, truly dominant in allowing only two hits and no walks with a Hundley homer being his only mistake. It was just two weeks earlier that Niekro had lost the heartbreaker at Wrigley Field when Santo had singled in the ninth for the 3–2 Cubs win that day. Hands (5-6) lasted only a third of an inning in Atlanta, as Nye pitched brilliantly the rest of the way to keep Chicago in the game. While suffering a lapse himself, Hands also continued to be hurting from a lack of run support as well, for the Cubs had scored only seven times in his last five starts. Niekro's ERA meanwhile, at 1.67, was the best in the league and nearly two runs better than the rest of the Atlanta staff.

Some of the players had noticed a change of attitude in Adolfo Phillips over the preceding few days, as he appeared to do more nervous talking than they had noticed in the past. Young was making great strides in center field, and the talented Phillips was very clearly hanging on his last threads under Durocher. The coaching staff knew that Young had all the "tools" defensively, but now his bat was coming along as well. This development had made the case even clearer in Durocher's mind. On June 11 Phillips and pitcher Jack Lamabe were traded to the Expos for Paul Popovich, who had just been acquired by Montreal from the Dodgers for Wills. When presented with the opportunity to return to the scene of his glory in Los Angeles, Wills suddenly reversed his retirement decision and allowed himself to be traded. Popovich, who had spent the last year and a half in Los Angeles, had actually begun his career with the Cubs in 1964. He epitomized the term *utility infielder*, as he could provide solid play at any position in a reserve role—just what Holland and Durocher had been lacking, and seeking, since spring training. But now with Beckert hurt and out indefinitely, Popovich would play a larger part than he had ever known before.

Meanwhile, in another sport, also coming to Chicago from Montreal that day was Tony Esposito, a promising young goaltender for the Canadiens who, like Popovich in the baseball business, was not in the plans of the Montreal hockey organization.

According to Chicago writer Jerome Holtzman, Phillips found out about his trade as he first entered the visitors' clubhouse in

Atlanta upon arriving in town. He was confused about the turn of events but still managed to shake hands with everyone in the room—except Durocher. "I've tried everything I can to wake him up," Leo said in final frustration about the young man's baseball ability. Phillips, who had not started a game since May 27, claimed that Durocher hadn't even talked to him in a month. After the news of the trade finally sunk in, Phillips was so distraught that he considered not reporting to Montreal. If he had decided not to go, it could have provided a scenario similar to the Donn Clendenon situation in spring training, whereby the Cubs would have to either send another player to Montreal or have the deal voided altogether. It was also revealed that Atlanta had recently turned down a deal that would have sent the Phillips to the Braves. But Phillips would ultimately find himself in Montreal, and Mauch appeared grateful to be able to work with him for a second time. "I'm going to give Dolf the chance I didn't give him four years ago with the Phillies," he told the press. "He's really going through spring training all over again, and he's just now beginning to show signs of coming around. He just has to get himself reestablished." Nonetheless, the turmoil of the circumstances had truly gripped the young outfielder. Later in the season, on September 12, he would have to remove himself from the Montreal club to undergo surgery for a benign growth in his stomach as well as be treated for an ulcer.

Qualls had also been recently recalled from Tacoma for extra support at the second base position, although he would have to leave once again in the coming days for two weeks of National Guard duty in California. Selma ensured a series victory in the next game against the Braves on June 12, as Spangler sliced two home runs through the hot, humid Atlanta night for a 12–6 decision, the Cubs' fifth win in six tries against the West-leading Braves. Spangler, who was not exceptional defensively, had been trying desperately to break in a new glove in hopes of better luck in the field. "I've been breaking it in for ten years," he joked. Unable to soften the stubborn leather any other way, he took the glove with him into the showers one day. Upon seeing this Gene Oliver told him, "Don't do that, Al—iron will rust."

The Cubs picked up two victories at Cincinnati on June 13 and 14, pushing their record to a season-high twenty-two games above the .500 mark, as rookie catcher Ken Rudolph's double (his first Major League hit) decided things in the opener. Regan gained both wins in the tenth inning, raising his record to 7-2, while Jenkins was called out of the bullpen to help as well—his first relief appearance in three years. Both Williams and Santo were injured during the sloppy, four-hour, 14–8 win on June 14, in which the Cubs scored six runs in the tenth to pull back ahead after letting an earlier four-run lead slip away. The first of the six runs resulted in a spectacular leap by Qualls over the reaching tag of Cincinnati catcher Pat Corrales; despite the heroics, however, Qualls would leave the team immediately after the game for his military obligations. He would be replaced on the roster by rookie outfielder Rick Bladt, who had been hitting .331 at Tacoma. "He doesn't excite anybody," Durocher said in complimentary fashion about the steady Bladt. "But he gets the job done, and everywhere he's been before, the manager at the end of the season always says: 'Bladt was my best player.' So, I gotta take a look at him." Durocher had it in mind that Bladt would give Young a reasonable challenge in center field.

Later in the tenth inning Santo jammed his elbow during another slide, and afterward he said, "I'm scared—it hurts like hell. I can't throw. It feels like something is wrong." Durocher held his breath, waiting for news on both Santo and Williams. Billy had fouled a ball off his instep in the sixth inning but had continued to play, homering in the ninth. He iced his swollen ankle and awaited the X-rays scheduled for the next day (on the positive side, Beckert returned to the club that day, showing up for batting practice with a cast on his broken thumb). Individually, things were particularly worrisome for Williams, who stood only 17 games behind Musial's National League record of 895 consecutive games played when he injured himself. He hoped desperately to be ready for the next day's game. In the 878 straight games in which Williams had played, he had been a starter in all of them; in the game on June 15, he hobbled to the plate as a pinch-hitter, keeping the streak going. The next day Williams would celebrate his thirty-first birthday. "Billy will probably play tomorrow if he improves as much overnight as he has since this morning," Cubs trainer Al Scheuneman announced later in the evening.

Meanwhile, Kessinger's errorless streak at shortstop reached fifty-four games—a National League record—the following day in a 7–6 loss to the Reds. "I've never played with a real good shortstop behind me until I came here," Aguirre told *The Sporting News*. "He's just one heckuva ballplayer. He makes the play in the hole better than anyone I've ever seen."

As Williams was recuperating that night, Juan Marichal beat the Expos 4–2 to improve his record to 7-2 on the season; the victory also pushed his career mark to 177-79, or a winning percentage of .691—one point better than the lifetime mark of Whitey Ford, the former Yankee great who had posted a career tally of 236-106, and second all-time only to another Yankee, Spud Chandler (.717 with a record of 109-43 from 1937 to 1947).

As the Cubs continued to play solid baseball, the surprising Mets had recently cooled off slightly since their eleven-game winning streak, but they still maintained the bridesmaid position in front of the Pirates. "Too far behind the Chicago Cubs to think seriously about first place," Leonard Koppett wrote skeptically about his Metropolitans in the *New York Times* on June 15, "but well-positioned to make a season-long fight for second."

The standings after the games on June 15:

National League East	W	L	Pct.	GB
Chicago	40	18	.690	—
New York	30	25	.545	8.5
Pittsburgh	30	29	.508	10.5
St. Louis	27	31	.466	13
Philadelphia	22	32	.407	16
Montreal	15	39	.278	23.5

An era had ended in professional basketball that week, as Bill Russell decided to resign as player-coach of the Boston Celtics.

He informed Celtics owner Arnold "Red" Auerbach that the decision involved his desire to pursue a Hollywood film career and was also made "in order to find new sources of income for the future." Auerbach was hoping that his big man would reconsider, but Russell was leaving his eleven NBA championships in thirteen seasons behind him.

As the Cubs played a four-game set in Pittsburgh against the Pirates beginning on the 16th, Mayor Daley (in town for a national mayors' conference) attended each contest, but Durocher did not. Selma was driven from the mound in a horrid first inning (during which he sustained a badly bruised ankle from a line drive off the bat of rookie Richie Hebner), as the Cubs lost the opener, 9–8. Pitchers Bob Veale and Steve Blass helped the Pirates sweep a doubleheader the next day, 1–0 and 4–3. With spirits plummeting among the Chicago players, Durocher could not be found on the morning of June 18. The manager had left the team hotel before anyone else had arisen and returned to Chicago to attend a party given in his honor by some of Chicago's "elite." Even though it was known that Durocher was going to be married the next day, the club panicked as game time approached and Leo wasn't there. They placed calls to Holland, who was also back in Chicago. "If he isn't with the club, I don't know where he is," Holland responded. Reiser was temporarily given charge of the team, although he was in no physical condition to handle everything; because of chest pains he had been suffering, Reiser had not even been in his typical third base coaching box since April 12. Added Phil Wrigley, "I don't like the way that Leo walked away from the team without saying anything in advance, but we'll just have to forgive him this time." Even the Cubs traveling secretary Cullen was not aware of the sudden departure until two hours before game time. Holtzman pitched solidly for nine innings, but Regan allowed Roberto Clemente to double in the tenth, which was followed by a Jose Martinez single and a 3–2 Pirates win. It was the ninth straight loss for the Cubs in Pittsburgh, and the Pirates ironically had the same-length losing streak at Wrigley Field. After the game the Cubs showered and dressed quickly as they attempted to catch up with their manager back west in Chicago.

In losing all four games in Pittsburgh, the Cubs had allowed the second-place Mets to climb within six games of the division lead. "The Cub bullpen, which became rusty in the Cub surge last month, suddenly became a foxhole as the Cub starters failed to stem enemy fire," the *New York Times* gleefully reported of Chicago's recent woes. To bolster their bench the Mets had recently acquired Clendenon, still somewhat reeling from his preseason odyssey of wondering where his final destination would be. "We'll just wait for the breaks," observed Mets manager Hodges about his team's assault on the Cubs. "The essential point is that we cannot lose ground."

Despite the contretemps with his whereabouts, the sixty-three-year-old Durocher was present on Thursday, June 19 (an off day for the Cubs) for his wedding in Chicago to Ms. Goldblatt, as the vows were exchanged in only three minutes in one of the fancier ballrooms of the Ambassador West Hotel. All of the Cubs players were present save Williams and Jenkins, who walked in late with their wives, despite the ceremony being twelve minutes tardy anyway (Banks chided his two teammates by bellowing out the tune, "Get Me to the Church on Time"). The nuptials were performed by Durocher's new stepbrother, circuit court magistrate John J. Kelly, with about two hundred relatives and friends in attendance—a list of dignitaries that was to include Sinatra, but the singer had sent his regrets while tied up with a previous commitment in Las Vegas. The entire crowd left the building in a happy mood, as the Cubs players thrilled a couple of children running a lemonade stand across the street by giving them some business. The Durochers announced that they would take a postponed honeymoon to the Far East after the baseball season. "No, I'm not nervous," the marriage-veteran Durocher announced. "I did not sleep all night. The only thing I'm worried about is tomorrow's ball game."

"I definitely will not second-guess his managing," Lynne added.

The team thought it could sharpen its claws at home against

a weaker team, as Hands posted a five-hit shutout in beating the Expos, 2–0, in the opener, already the fifteenth time in 1969 that the Cubs had blanked an opponent—with Hands being involved in four of them. But Chicago would lose two out of the next three to the lowly Expos, while the Mets continued their march by taking three out of four in Philadelphia—the Mets now stood only four games back. It was the smallest lead that the Cubs had held on the top spot since May 13. In the final contest of the series with Montreal (the second game of a doubleheader), the darkness of Wrigley Field came into play once again, with the game ending as a final score after the sixth inning with the Cubs trailing, 5–4, while the twenty-two thousand fans booed wildly at the umpires, who cited player safety as the reason for calling it off. "We would like to have seen the game completed," explained Tom Gorman, the chief arbiter of the crew assigned to work the series, "but somebody could have gotten hit in the head." Santo, and even the usually mild-mannered Williams, had to be restrained in their anger. "It's a lousy rule in the first place," said Gene Oliver, speaking of the league guideline that didn't allow a complete finish. "They ought to suspend these games. That's a sin to call these games when we had nine outs left." Changing the rule would require unanimous approval from all the clubs in the National League. Giles would receive this approval on June 26; from then on all nightcaps of doubleheaders were to be completed in a full nine innings, either on the original date scheduled or the next time that the two teams were planned to meet.

Causing Durocher equal concern was the team's fading ability to win close games; to date they had won as many such contests as they had lost (14-14). "We're making too many mistakes," he told the papers on June 24. Hauntingly, a headline in the *Tribune* offered a literal and figurative forecast:

DARKNESS CLOSING IN ON CUBS?

The news didn't appear to be getting any better, as the Pirates were next to visit Wrigley Field. The Bucs had just recently knocked off the Cubs in four straight at Pittsburgh and now trailed the Mets by only two and a half games for second place.

But the Cubs players refused to put any extra weight on the upcoming games. "Why is it a big series?" Kessinger asked. "What makes this any bigger a series than the one we just played against Montreal? As far as I'm concerned, the series you're in today is always the biggest series of the year."

"We have to play every game as hard as we can," added Hundley, who admitted feeling a bit tired in recent days.

Things started well for the Cubs at Wrigley. Chicago once again launched a come-from-behind win in the ninth inning in the first game. Pinch-hitter Bill Heath singled, and Kessinger followed with a bunt hit. After Williams—who had been hitless in his eight previous trips to the plate—knocked home Heath with a single, Santo did the same with a sacrifice fly for Kessinger, and Chicago was victorious, 5–4. It was the tenth time in a row that the Pirates had lost at Wrigley, as neither team could figure out the other's park. After a half-hour rain delay on the North Side of Chicago, Santo homered the next day while powering the Cubs to another win over Pittsburgh, 3–2, as Hands (7-6) lowered his ERA to a team-best (among the starters) 2.74. Nonetheless, the team still saw its lead on the Mets shrink to four and a half games after it had recently increased. The New Yorkers (who had played .800 ball over the past month) swept a doubleheader in Philadelphia by scores of 2–1 and 5–0 as Seaver and McAndrew dominated the Phillies from the mound.

Boxing had been on the minds of many the night before, on June 23, as Joe Frazier and Jerry Quarry met in Madison Square Garden. Frazier successfully defended his heavyweight championship, sending Quarry to the canvas for the final time in the seventh round. On the undercard was a young George Foreman, a gold medalist at the 1968 Olympics making his professional debut as he finished off Don Waldhelm with a third-round technical knockout. Foreman and Frazier would finally meet less than four years later on January 22, 1973, in Kingston, Jamaica, with Foreman winning by technical knockout in the second round to take the title. Ali, meanwhile, watched from afar.

The Cubs were digging their claws in for a fight, determined not to relinquish what had taken them so long to achieve and maintain—first place. Jenkins, who had not thrown a ball at all in five days because of soreness in his right elbow, stifled the Pirates on two hits and ten strikeouts for a 5–2 win on June 25. Regan equaled Jenkins's record (9-5) with a win in relief the following day, completing the sweep over the Pirates and handing Pittsburgh its thirteenth consecutive loss in Chicago. During Jenkins's work Durocher had to come to the mound with an expletive-filled tirade, because he (and Santo as well) felt the Canadian wasn't concentrating on his job when a wild pitch allowed a run to score. "You couldn't print what I told him," the boss said in the locker room afterward, "except that I told him he had gotten lazy."

In the final contest Hickman homered behind a twenty-eight-mile-per-hour tailwind in the tenth inning for the 7–5 triumph during "another deafening, hysterical afternoon in Wrigley Field," as Langford described the jubilant scene. Nearly thirty-eight thousand fans had come to the ballpark on the Thursday afternoon (including about thirty thousand paying customers), the largest crowd on the season after Opening Day. Hickman had gotten his chance when he had been sent up as a pinch hitter against Bruce Dal Canton. "I was just happy the team had won," the Tennessee native told everyone later on. Once expected to be a big power source on the team, Hickman had been batting only .216 with two homers when he took his big swing to end the game, although it was his fourth game-winning hit on the year. His playing time had diminished substantially, but Durocher still had plans for him as the summer wore on.

The fans in the left-field bleachers had been waving a large Confederate battle flag all game long, intended as good wishes for Hundley, as the catcher from Dixie had been unusually left off the starting lineup after spraining an ankle the previous day on a play at the plate. Rudolph sweltered in his place behind the plate as he took over the catching duties in the ninety-four-degree heat. Although he started to feel dizzy, he knew that he had to finish the job. "I took some salt pills in the fourth inning, and sort of got my second wind," he revealed. It was Rudolph's homer that tied the game 3–3 two innings later in the sixth. He then kept the decisive frame alive with his walk on a 3-and-2 pitch that allowed Hickman to come to the plate in the tenth.

Willie Smith celebrated the sweep in the dressing room by swilling some soda pop. "I really think the guys wanted these four games more than any others we've played all year, because there were some things said by the Pirates last week when they beat us four in a row . . . and none of us forgot what was said," he stated proudly with a towel draped around his neck and one foot up on the stool in front of his locker. Smith was referring to an anonymous statement by a Pirate player that announced, "The Cubs belong to us—for this series, and for the season."

§

Meanwhile, the Illinois legislature was sweating on the senate floor down in Springfield, dismissing the bill calling for the construction of a domed sports stadium in Chicago. The state senate had stopped the idea in its tracks with a vote of sixteen to two— from "suburban Republicans and Mayor Daley Democrats," as the *Tribune* described it—ending the discussion. The proposed $100 million arena was intended to hold eighty thousand spectators and be surrounded by twenty-five thousand parking spaces, but it was deemed by opponents to be a threat to the existing horse racing tracks in the Chicago area (thoroughbred meets had been planned for the site in addition to football, basketball, hockey, and potentially baseball events). In addition, Democrats voting against the bill had angrily cited the codicil that provided a tax-exempt status for the building for the first two years of its operation, a point they considered unacceptable. While a physical site had never been finalized, Chicago sports officials had been looking at plots of land in the northwest suburbs of Chicago, given the area's growing population of wealthy residents and expansive freeway access. It was becoming well-known that Mayor Daley wanted the dome to be built within Chicago city limits, and he and his cohorts sought such an amendment to the plan for future consideration.

Lou Brock had to deal with the confines of the *current* Chicago sports structures, and he became the next victim of the Bleacher

Bums as the archrivals from the South came calling next in Wrigley Field. The Cardinals always drew well in Chicago, but this was a beautiful weekend in June and overflow attendance was expected as five thousand standing-room-only tickets were sold for each of the four games, including a doubleheader on Sunday the 29th. Meanwhile, other baseball fans were visiting the National Baseball Hall of Fame and Museum in Cooperstown, New York, that weekend—including Arthur Greenwood of Chelmsford, Massachusetts, who became the three-millionth visitor to baseball's shrine since it had opened thirty years earlier in 1939.

In the third inning of the first game in Chicago, Kessinger drove a long ball to left, as Brock turned and sprinted for the ivy-covered brick wall. The outfielder made a tall leap as he robbed Kessinger of an extra-base hit, reaching just below the spot where the "basket" would hang after 1970. Lunging over the wall was a fan holding a plastic batting helmet, trying unsuccessfully to spoon the ball out from Brock's glove. When Kessinger went out to play defense in the top of the fourth, he was told by second base umpire Lee Weyer that, even if Brock had not caught the ball, Kessinger still would have been ruled out as a result of fan interference. After making the catch Brock incurred the full wrath of the Bleacher Bums as he returned to his original left-field position. As he watched an orange roll between his legs, he became a bit nervous. "Somebody's going to get hurt out there, and it's too bad," the shaken Brock said afterward. "The Cubs are going great, but the fans may spoil it." The taunts had increased in the eighth inning, when Brock misplayed a fly ball off the bat of Santo that fell for a double.

"The thing that really bothers me about it," Brock went on later, his anger deepening, "is that they are showing you people [the press] up. You have glorified them, and they show their gratitude by behaving like that."

Brock's neighbor Flood added that a quarter had whizzed by his ear in center field earlier in the game. "I have a family to feed," Flood pointed out, "and when you're out there it makes you kind of frightened when getting hit in the eye by a thrown object might end your career. . . . I think it's great to see people having fun like that at a ball game. But when they start throwing things at the performers who are trying to entertain them, it's not right." And while Mudcat Grant was signing autographs in the bleacher area before the game, he had been hit in the head with a rubber ball. Grant retaliated by throwing a few fastballs into the stands, and the Bums scattered as if grenades were going off. As a result of a formal complaint made by Brock to the Cubs organization, several inconspicuous security guards were placed in the left-field bleachers for the remainder of the series. Brock felt that the crowd monitoring had become too relaxed in the bleacher section and had now led to some dangerous circumstances. But Bob Wisniewski, chief of the security force at Wrigley Field, vigorously defended himself and his staff against Brock's charges. "I was out there for an inning and a half, and I didn't see anybody throw anything," he asserted after the first game of the series. "I put six extra men out there because we had reports of people throwing things. If we had seen anybody throw anything, they would have been immediately ejected from the park and arrested, but we didn't see anything like that."

Some thought that Brock needed to relax, as even Schoendienst didn't take the incidents so seriously. "He [Brock] was having a good time with them," Red reminded the writers about Lou's interaction with the left-field faithful. "He yelled back to them, 'We'll beat you bums,' after they'd called him by the same name." Schoendienst had always been good-natured about his rivals in Chicago; as an example of how he liked to motivate himself in a humorous tone, Schoendienst had affixed a sticker that read "CUB POWER"—a decoration that was becoming popular in Chicago during the year—to his shaving mirror in the restroom attached to his office at Busch Stadium.

Perhaps concerned about their "image," the Bums hurried to elect one of their own, Don Alger, as their public relations director. "Look, we know that you can't sit in the press box and see everything that's going on out there," Alger challenged Markus, the *Tribune* writer who had given Alger a mouthpiece for the group's cause. "From there, it looks like a mass of yellow helmets. We'd like you to come out and sit with us some day, so you can see what's really happening. . . . This isn't the only place where they throw things at the players. Billy Williams almost got hit with a lead pipe in Atlanta, but the papers didn't make a big deal out of that."

It would preface a day of tremendous frustration for the home team, as Holtzman (10-2) went from holding a perfect game in the seventh inning to being a 3-1 loser, the victim of hits in that stanza by Pinson, Torre, and Shannon that put the Cards ahead to stay. Holtzman was bettered by another left-hander, Steve Carlton, who struck out ten—including the last three Cubs—to end the game. "Their man pitched a great game," Santo admitted. "My two hits were just luck, and he only gave me one pitch to hit all day." Utterly dejected in the locker room, Holtzman bent over and stared silently for forty-five minutes at "two pairs of baseball shoes and a stack of unopened letters" between his feet, not speaking to any teammates or reporters. But the Cubs righted things the next day with a 3–1 win behind Hands as Kessinger and Santo logged two hits. Santo had now taken the National League lead in RBI away from Banks and stood one ahead of Ernie with 64 on the year. But the big blow came from Smith, now batting .291 in spot duty as he nailed his sixth homer to break a 1–1 tie in the sixth inning. Smith credited his success to having a stiff neck, which resulted from his new strategy of sleeping with his head propped on two pillows instead of one. "It makes me keep my head still when I'm swinging," he explained to the writers, while Williams laughed in disbelief as he listened.

Earlier in the day a twelve-year-old boy named Earl Grant had been standing behind the right-field bleachers during batting practice, after having strolled over from his Wrigleyville home only half a block away. As he always liked to do, Earl was trying to catch home run balls that left the park, using his new baseball glove that he had received on his birthday only two weeks prior. He hadn't been paying attention when Smith cracked a long one during warmup, however (and this time Willie did not have a chance to holler, "Look out, *Earl!*"). The ball plunked the boy square on the head, and Earl was rushed to Illinois Masonic Hospital, out cold but with no serious injuries. "He's always wanted to catch a ball," his mother said, with no one in the family holding a grudge against Smith. "But he never even came close until now." Because of his mishap Earl thus missed the excitement of Smith's home run that actually counted later in the day. When Willie later heard what had happened, he hurried over to personally deliver an autographed ball to the Grant's home; as always, a visit from a Major Leaguer was the perfect medicine for an injured child.

The victory set the stage for a brilliant, festive, cheerful day for a doubleheader at the ballpark on Sunday, June 29. Glenn Beckert was finally returning to the starting lineup, as his broken right thumb had healed. To make room for him on the active roster, Gene Oliver was sent to the farm team at San Antonio, although Oliver would return on July 11 when Rudolph would need to leave the team for military duty. But Beckert's return was only part of the cause for celebration, for on this day it was presumed that Billy Williams would tie and break the National League record of consecutive games played, setting a new standard with 896 straight contests—a streak that had continued since September 21, 1963. It was designated as "Billy Williams Day" in Chicago, and many fans and friends were waiting to shower the beloved outfielder with gifts. Instead of receiving gifts, however, Williams asked that well-wishers contribute to college scholarship funds that he was setting up for students at high schools near his home in Alabama. As fans headed to the concession stands, they were offered commemorative pins of the event for a cost of 25 cents, with the proceeds headed to these funds. Still, Williams graciously accepted a large trophy from Warren Giles and a new Chrysler Imperial from the Cubs; he also received gifts that included a fishing boat and outboard motor, a pool table, a washer and dryer, a Weimaraner puppy, a television, a sterling silver pitcher, and a gold wristwatch.

At the same time, heated emotions were being stoked on both sides—along with the recent trouble in the bleachers, it had not been forgotten by the St. Louis men that it was a Cardinals legend in Stan Musial whose record Williams would be breaking during the day.

With not an inch of elbow room to be had amid the 41,060 spectators, the biggest crowd of the year squeezed into the old stadium (some fans had stood in line for tickets at six o'clock the night before). The first game offered a match-up of two of the best fireballers in the National League in Jenkins and St. Louis ace Bob Gibson. Gibson, who had already long established himself as one of the premier "inning-eaters" in the game, had for the first time in his career been getting regular rest by Schoendienst. He had been pitching every fifth day to that point in the 1969 season, as opposed to every fourth. With what Schoendienst viewed as a pivotal game—not just for the series but for the rest of the season as well—he decided to place Gibby head to head with the Cubs' leading man.

It was simply one game at the end of June in 1969, but it would remain in the hearts and memories of many fans for seasons to come. June Cardinal-Cub meetings always seemed to be classics; fifteen years later, in June 1984, Ryne Sandberg would stun Bruce Sutter and the Cardinals with two home runs in a thrilling come-from-behind victory for Chicago. But 1969 was a time for other heroes, and Gibson and Jenkins—like Dizzy Dean and Lon Warneke before them, or John Tudor and Rick Sutcliffe afterward—went toe-to-toe in a sun-splashed heavyweight match that remained a draw into the eighth round. The intimidating Cardinal moundsman struck out seven of the first ten Cubs he faced, as Fergie more democratically—but as effectively—spread the ball around to his mates behind him. Williams was one of his most trusted fellows, as he threw out Brock, who had tried to stretch an important single into an ill-fated double in the sixth. Sensing the gravity of the moment, day, and season, the Cubs hurled themselves all around the field that day. The most fervent was Hundley, who charged into the stands to grab a pop foul off the bat of Flood. Taking matters into his own hands, Williams opened the Cub eighth with a ringing double to the wall. Banks sent him home with a single, and when Smith followed with yet another clutch home run, Jenkins entered the ninth with a 3–0 lead. A Vada Pinson solo homer with two out was all that could be mustered to spoil the shutout, however, and game one went to the Cubs in just over two hours. In head-to-head competition over their careers, Jenkins had now beaten Gibson in three out of four tries, with his lone defeat occurring by a 1–0 score.

Williams made a tearful gesture of appreciation to the crowd in between the historic contests, pivoting from the microphone with his number 26 jersey doing a quarter-turn toward the crowd as his emotions got the best of him. His teammates handed him a towel to wipe his eyes and then got ready to head back to business. "It was the first time I had ever seen Bill nervous," Santo remembered.

As the second game got under way, some in the bleachers began throwing lighted firecrackers onto the field. Taking command early, umpire Harry Wendelstedt had instructed public address announcer Pat Pieper—who had been on the job at Wrigley Field since 1916—to inform the crowd that the game would be forfeited to St. Louis if any such action continued. The pyrotechnics ceased, but they may have helped spark a Chicago offensive barrage early in the game as a four-run first inning was capped by a long ball from the swing of Banks (his 13th home run). Santo (15th, with five RBI to increase his league-leading total to 69) and Hundley (12th) added their own round-trippers later. But it was truly Williams's day, as he amassed four more hits that included a double and two triples. Selma (8-3) was the benefactor, cruising to a complete-game, 12–1 triumph with 10 strikeouts on just two days' rest. The St. Louis starter was the bleacher antagonist Grant, who left the game to a predictable cascade of jeers after he was able to retire only one batter. Once again the only Cardinals run came on a home run, this one off the bat of Shannon in the fifth inning. The North Siders had held the St. Louis men to a single run in each of the last three games.

"The Cubs just kicked the hell out of us," a dejected Schoendienst said, as his club was now a full fourteen games behind division-leading Chicago. "We had to win at least three games here. . . . We are simply not hitting the ball. It's just one of those years, I guess. I just can't understand it." Schoendienst had ordered his hitting coach, Dick Sisler, to temporarily give up his first base coaching duties and observe the Cardinals batters from the dugout bench in the hopes that he might see something to reverse the team's woes at the plate. Sisler, however, was just as befuddled as Red. "There are at least three guys in our lineup who have had over 200 hits in one year before," he commented, "so I know they can do it." The Cardinals had batted .233 in April and had improved to only .248 since. The glimmer of hope for the club rested in the fact that twenty-seven of their next thirty-four games would be in St. Louis, giving them a reasonable chance to close the gap in the standings and defend their National League championship.

At 7:00 p.m.—an hour after the sweep was completed—Banks emerged from the Cubs locker room to find "only a field littered with paper and seven people in the press box," as Langford, one of those still in the press's perch, recounted the scene. Ernie was singing, audibly and happily, as he strode to the pitcher's mound in solitude and let out a big laugh. He exited the field, walked up one of the aisles, and then down the ramps and out of the ballpark—still laughing and singing and whistling all the way. This was Ernie Banks playing on a first-place team.

Back inside the locker room Williams took the opportunity to make up for his relative national anonymity. "You say I haven't gotten the publicity I deserve over the years, and that I'm an underrated player," he told the newspapermen. "Well, that's up to you guys. I can't write about myself. For me, it's a matter of playing hard on the field every day, because in baseball, a player knows two things—today and yesterday. There's never a tomorrow in a player's career until it gets here. I guess maybe it's better that way."

Williams fancied himself a "guesser" in regard to the pitches that came to him, but that didn't matter to his teammate Randy Hundley. "He may be guessing at the plate," the catcher pointed out, "but he sure is guessing right a lot."

With the sweep it made seven wins in eight tries on the homestand for the Cubs, with the loss to Carlton being the only blemish. As the lights were turned out on "Billy Williams Day" and June came to a close, the standings looked like this:

National League East	W	L	Pct.	GB
Chicago	49	26	.653	—
New York	39	32	.549	8
Pittsburgh	38	37	.507	12
St. Louis	35	40	.467	14
Philadelphia	32	39	.451	15
Montreal	20	52	.288	27.5

The Cubs looked unstoppable, with no team seemingly able to check their advance. They had an All-Star infield, a deep pitching staff—and now, the iron man of National League players in the outfield. "The records are nice, but there's only one record I really want," the standard-setter Williams punctuated in a serious tone. "That's the one that shows us with four victories in the World Series."

7

Reaching New Heights

> Any culture which can put a man
> on the moon is capable of gather-
> ing all the nations of the earth in
> peace, justice, and concord.
>
> —U.S. president
> Richard M. Nixon, July 1969

When the Major League season rolls into July, the rising temperatures are accompanied by the heating up of the pennant
races. It is a time of year when the contenders begin to separate
themselves from the also-rans, and in 1969 the Cubs—with the
newfound "killer instinct" that Durocher had wanted and that
had not been seen for some time on Clark and Addison—sought
to make the Eastern Division of the National League a one-horse
race.

The team sputtered on the road, however, when opening
the month with a split of a four-game set at Montreal. The first
game did not begin until 10:00 p.m. local time due to a heavy
rainstorm. In the second inning Banks drove a ball to the wall

that appeared to be a home run, but second base umpire Tony Venzon ruled that the ball had actually rolled under the fence, and Banks was granted a double. Durocher sprinted out of the dugout like a startled hare, stopped for a moment to holler at Venzon, and then continued on a quick jog, with Venzon trailing behind, out to the point where Banks's ball had landed. When both men reached the disputed site, they made for a comical scene for the fans watching from a distance. Venzon kicked the bottom of the fence repeatedly, trying to show Leo where the ball had struck; Durocher was jumping up and down and flailing both arms in a downward motion over the fence. When Venzon refused to change his mind, Durocher announced that the Cubs were playing the game under protest, which led to Mauch's exchanging words with Santo and Hundley and, eventually, to both dugouts clearing into a minor shoving match on the field.

Durocher never wanted the game to be played in the first place, feeling that the conditions were "deplorable" after the ground crew did seemingly little work after the storm. He was further annoyed by a group of photographers who had nested themselves inside the Cubs dugout during the first two games of the series; in a phone conversation, Fanning assured Durocher that the cameramen would not be allowed to return. Leo soon after opened a telegram from Giles saying that his protest had already been denied. Giles was trying to prepare for his retirement in a few months, and the last thing he wanted was more headaches from Leo the Lip. Still in a bad mood, Durocher had words for the league president too, as he felt that his pleas were falling on deaf ears. "I'm going to write Mr. Giles a nice letter," he told his coaching staff in his office, "telling him I'm going to file his letters and bulletins in the same place he puts my protests."

Holtzman, having studied French at the University of Illinois, had struck up a conversation with a pretty female usher working at Jarry Park before the third game of the series. The left-hander had little work to do for the rest of the trip, having lost to Steve Renko the night before, 11–4 on Dominion Day (the 102nd anniversary of the confederation of Canada), and in what was only Renko's second Major League start. Naturally, the weather was much better than when the Cubs had made their first visit to Quebec in April, and Durocher—though recently married—was interested in innocently seeing the sights of the city with a companion. Holtzman mentioned to the skipper that the girl had a friend who would be happy to accompany Durocher, and the four wound up having a raucous, albeit platonic, night on the town. After Leo paid the tab in every bar they entered, the group wound up back at the Queen Elizabeth Hotel at four in the morning. When the team bus revved its engine at the front door a few hours later, ready to take the team to the ballpark for the final contest, Holtzman was right on time while Durocher was nowhere to be found. According to Holtzman, Leo remained in his room all day throwing up, ultimately missing the game and claiming to have "the flu" (Santo had been stricken with a bug as well, holed up in his bed during Holtzman's loss with a one-hundred-degree temperature). Three newsmen from the *Montreal Star* had called Durocher's phone for most of the day, and after encountering a "DO NOT DISTURB" sign, knocked on his room door for the remainder of the afternoon, never to get an answer.

Reiser once again took the reins in the manager's absence, and Hands once again busted up a losing streak in silencing the Expos, 4–2, as Williams made it nine hundred straight. Hands was beginning to eclipse Jenkins as the stopper on the staff, having allowed only five runs in his last four starts. The Cubs won again the next day behind Selma, 8–4, although rookie Mike Wegener had held them hitless for the first five innings. In managing to win the final two games of the series, the Chicago club was now only an unimpressive 7–7 against the expansion Expos.

While the name was not bestowed in honor of Leo's late-night revelry—or toward the manager in any regard—one of the streets that ran behind Jarry Park ironically was named "Rue Durocher."

§

In 1961 and 1964, respectively, as construction had begun on the new Gateway Arch and Busch Stadium in downtown St. Louis, the two edifices were intended to symbolize a revitalization of the area. Cardinals owner August A. Busch Jr. had pledged $5 million for the stadium project, to be augmented by $20 million from the city. Both the arch and the stadium would open for business in 1966, as the last piece of the arch was put into place on October 28, 1965, ready for visitors the following summer, which coincided with the first Cardinals game at the new ballpark on May 12, 1966. The arch was likened to its brother in Busch Stadium in that it was symmetrically perfect—630 feet tall at its apex and 630 feet wide at its base. It remains the tallest human-made monument in the Western Hemisphere, sitting on national park grounds as part of the Jefferson National Expansion Memorial. The arch had been designed by Finnish-born architect Eero Saarinen, who had only recently finished his plans on the ultramodern terminal for Dulles Airport in Virginia.

With these efforts, business slowly crept back into the riverfront area of downtown St. Louis over the rest of the decade, a place that had started to become crime-ridden and blighted. Not long after, summertime riverfront festivals became a regularity; the best of these usually occurred over the Fourth of July holiday, with bands, fireworks, and vendors celebrating Independence Day by the end of the 1960s and beyond.

This was where and when the Cubs crossed the midway point of the 1969 season, halfway home to a long-desired pennant for Chicago fans. Following are some of their individual statistics as they ventured into Busch Stadium with a 52-28 record, leading the Mets by seven and a half games and the defending-champion Cardinals by nearly twice that much:

Batting	Avg.	AB	R	H	2B	3B	HR	RBI
Smith	.336	107	16	36	6	1	7	17
Santo	.304	293	51	89	11	4	16	73
Beckert	.302	215	30	65	7	1	0	13
Williams	.302	318	55	96	18	6	9	46
Kessinger	.299	341	63	102	22	4	3	39
Hundley	.293	287	45	84	18	1	13	42
Banks	.262	294	33	77	10	0	13	67
Spangler	.250	160	22	40	7	1	4	17
Rudolph	.238	21	6	5	1	0	1	4
Qualls	.237	38	5	9	3	1	0	2
Young	.232	185	27	43	6	2	4	22
Hickman	.216	111	9	24	3	1	3	14
N. Oliver	.184	38	10	7	3	0	1	4

Pitching	W-L	ERA	IP
Jenkins	10-5	2.51	138
Holtzman	10-3	3.18	133
Selma	9-3	3.44	102
Regan	9-5	3.28	63
Hands	9-6	2.58	136
Abernathy	4-1	2.73	46
Aguirre	1-0	1.71	21
Nye	1-3	4.42	27

Santo's RBI total continued to lead the National League, four ahead of McCovey with Banks closing quickly in third. Santo was also chosen over McCovey as the National League Player of the Month for June, grabbing thirty-two of sixty votes from the nationwide panel of sportswriters (McCovey had garnered sixteen for second place). This occurred despite the fact that McCovey had more home runs before the first of July (26) than any player in National League history. In gaining his first Player of the Month award in five years, Santo had batted .395 in June with six home runs and 34 RBI.

It was ninety-seven degrees in St. Louis the afternoon of July 4, coupled with 85 percent humidity, but the infamous Busch Stadium field temperature pushed well over the one hundred mark (it was the legendary manager Casey Stengel who, at the 1966 All-Star Game at Busch, commented that the then-two-month-old ballpark "sure held the heat well"). The circular structure, while aesthetically pleasing, certainly did not cater well to the concept of air flow. The heat didn't stop two hundred Bleacher Bums from arriving at the park early for the 11:20 opening of the gates, however. Trying to pass the time before being allowed in the stadium, a Bum who had driven down from Rock Island, Illinois, put a woman on his shoulders as she sheepishly hung a "CUB POWER" sign from the bat of Musial's statue that stood outside the bleacher gates at the corner of Broadway and Walnut. A few minutes later they all planted themselves in the left-field stands, yellow construction helmets and all, chanting all sorts of tunes that echoed in the otherwise-empty ballpark. There was one player on the field—Cardinals veteran first baseman Bill White—who was taking some extra batting practice, and he was startled by the singing coming from someplace beyond the outfield that he initially could not discern.

The challenging weather conditions were just what the proud Gibson and Jenkins would have wanted, as the titans of the hill would clash once again. "Busch Memorial Cauldron" is what Langford called the site, fanning himself in the open-air press box that hung behind home plate. Banks was getting a day off, which had been planned in advance, as Durocher had felt that the first baseman had looked tired in recent games; Ernie agreed. The teams flailed mostly in vain with their bats at the trickery of the two pitchers, fighting most of the afternoon with a 1–1 tie. In the bottom of the eighth inning, Durocher went out to the mound for a conference with Jenkins and Hundley. After a moment Pelekoudas, the plate umpire on the day, strolled out and asked Leo in reference to Jenkins, "Are you going to take him out?"

"Hell, no," was Durocher's response.

After Fergie told his manager he was fine, Durocher walked off the mound and back toward the Chicago dugout. "That's great, pal," he said to Jenkins over his shoulder, "because you're going to win or lose this yourself." Jenkins worked through another inning without harm.

As the Cubs came off the steaming field after the bottom of the ninth, Jenkins walked calmly to the bench and placed a bag of ice behind his neck. Durocher then pulled Kessinger aside, who was to lead off the top of the tenth inning.

"Just get on base one more time for us," the manager told his player, "and we'll score."

"If I do get on base and we *don't* score, I've had it," the exhausted Kessinger joked in return.

The All-Star shortstop stepped to the plate and promptly singled on Gibson's first pitch. On Gibson's next offering—the first pitch to Beckert—Kessinger took off for second and beat catcher Tim McCarver's throw by an eyelash as he slid safely into the bag.

Beckert then laid a perfect bunt down the third base line, which he beat out for a hit, with Kessinger gliding into third. Next up was Williams, who laced a double off the dejected Gibson to score both runners. Schoendienst then came out to the mound and brought in reliever Joe Hoerner from the Cardinals bullpen. It was the first time in two years—through fifty-seven straight games—that Gibson had been removed in the middle of an inning. Horner then retired Santo, Banks, and Hickman to get out of the jam, but he was equaled by the indomitable Jenkins in his tenth inning of work to seal the 3–1 holiday win for the Cubs.

In the Cardinals clubhouse after the game, Schoendienst was still confounded about his team's play. "We just don't hit anymore," he muttered, continuing his lament from his Wrigley excursion the week before.

The team recognized Kessinger as the hero, as he had three hits and two amazing defensive plays in the game. He was the only Cub to have played in every inning of every game so far on the season. "He's the All-Star of All-Stars," Jenkins admired afterward. "He's my shortstop in any league."

Many of the Cubs were noticing that Jenkins's uniform—unlike those of some who didn't even play that day—was dry. "You were fantastic out there, and I don't mean your pitching," Willie Smith said. "I've never seen anything like you. It's a hundred degrees, you pitched ten innings, and didn't even break a sweat. Look at your uniform—it's not even wet. There were eight guys playing behind you, and their uniforms were so soaked with sweat they weighed ten pounds."

"I told myself it wasn't hot," Jenkins reasoned simply in return, which had the others laughing.

Smith had helped out on the grounds that day, but in sort of an unconventional manner. While scrambling after a batted ball that had dropped onto the ground, a fan had fallen over the outfield wall and into the field of play. Before an usher could seize the fan and cite him for trespassing on the field, Smith gave the man's bottom a boost and got him back up into his seat—apparently before charges were issued.

In another part of the Cubs locker room, Durocher leaned

back in his chair and took a deep breath with both hands clasped behind his neck. He then slowly shook his head and said to the reporters, "You won't see two better pitchers in your whole life than those two today."

Another masterful pitching effort by Nelson Briles landed the Cardinals a victory the following day, 5–1, over Holtzman. During the game a group of Bleacher Bums had brought in a load of blue and white balloons that spelled out the word "CUBS" in the left-field stands; unfortunately, the bouquet blocked the view of other spectators. The entire stadium watched as umpire Frank Dezelan confiscated the arrangement, cut the strings loose, and sent the balloons wafting into the downtown sky and over the Mississippi River into Illinois. Although the Cubs came up short in a ninth-inning rally, still no pitcher in the National League had fired a complete-game shutout against them in 1969. Holtzman (10–4), meanwhile, was now winless for nearly a month and had not even thrown a complete game in nearly eight weeks. Three of his four losses on the year had now come at the hands of St. Louis, as he was the only Cubs pitcher to lose to the Cardinals in '69. What was his recent problem, in his manager's eyes? "Control," Durocher said simply. "You can't be 2-0, 3-1 on every hitter and expect them to hit your pitch." Becker, who thought that Holtzman might be tipping off his pitches through inconsistencies in his delivery, even went to Durocher to discuss the possibility of temporarily removing him from the rotation. The starting pitching failed the team the next day as well, as neither Hands nor Nye could last four innings in the Sunday doubleheader on July 6. Losing both contests, 4–2 and 6–3, the Cubs limped out of sultry St. Louis with a trip to face the Mets on the road. The two losses meant that the Cubs headed to New York with only a five-game lead, and ahead of the Mets in the loss column by only three. And now, no one was counting out the defending champions either—even their formally despondent manager. "We started a new half of the season now," Schoendienst announced to the St. Louis writers. "The Cubs had a good first half, and now we're going to have a good second half. It's happened before, and there are a lot of games left to go."

The magnitude of the upcoming contests was apparent. The Mets would be visiting Wrigley in a week for a three-game series, so theoretically, the whole balance of the Eastern Division standings had the potential of shifting. "There's no question about it," Hodges told the *New York Times*. "The two series with the Cubs are bigger than any others, because they are the big team. We need to take two-out-of-three each time. . . . All of our people couldn't be more ready." He was referring to the fact that his club had just swept a doubleheader from the Pirates and now stood poised to attack the division leaders. On the way from the airport after the Cubs arrived in New York, Smith and Nate Oliver tried to keep the team loose. They stood up in the front of the bus and chanted made-up prayers while the group hummed along, finished with a strung out *"Ahhhhhhhhh-mmmmmmennnnnnnnnn,"* and started to pray in their own ethnic and religious verses—Jewish, Christian, Black, Hispanic, northerner, southerner, and others to which they didn't even belong, with Durocher just smiling and shaking his head in witness to the silliness. When that ended the team clamored for another song, so Banks took the front seat of the bus and led them in Johnny Cash's "Ring of Fire." Holtzman and Selma nearly found themselves on the floor of the bus, hysterical with laughter. They arrived relaxed at the Waldorf-Astoria Hotel, settled into their rooms, and from the windows watched a soft rain fall.

When Shea Stadium opened the next day, July 8, a good number of fans came early to check out the Cubs during batting practice. The crowd seemed quite large for so early in the day, but most of the players did not give it much thought. By the time they reemerged from the clubhouse for the start of the game, however, the throng had swelled to over fifty-five thousand crazed Mets fans, with every section packed. This included more than sixteen thousand children who were free guests of the New York team. When their heroes took the field, the stadium shook like thunder. "Their demonstration of lung power even drowned out the blasts of low-flying jets from landing and taking off from nearby LaGuardia Airport," Langford noticed. Jenkins was given the ball by Durocher and started sharply, allowing only one hit—a solo home run by New York's Ed Kranepool, which left him one shy of Hickman's career record for a Met—through the first eight innings and retiring the first eleven men he faced. Banks and Hickman had homered for the Cubs, and the game stood at a 3–1 Chicago lead entering the bottom of the ninth. But it was at this moment, Langford wrote, that the Mets "were on the threshold of their greatest day and Don Young, the rookie centerfielder of the Cubs, was on the verge of his worst."

Ken Boswell opened the Mets' last chance, pinch-hitting for the starting pitcher Koosman. Boswell took a chop at a Jenkins offering and floated a short fly to center. Having broken back two steps at the contact of the ball, Young realized immediately that he had misjudged the play. He dashed in to recover but could not get to the ball in time as the hustling Boswell stood at second base with a freak double. Jenkins was able to come back and get Tommie Agee to pop up, and the much-traveled Clendenon was next. On a 1-1 count he lifted a long fly ball toward Young in deep center. He looked as if he were camped under the ball at the wall, but it bounced into and out of his leather, falling free to the ground. Surprised by the turn of events, Boswell was only able to make it into third, as he originally thought the ball was going to be caught. Clendenon was at second, and the official scorer ruled another double, and no error on Young. Next up was Cleon Jones, leading the league with a .356 average, who subsequently "slammed the first legitimate hit of the inning down the left field line for a double, tying the score," as Langford watched in agony. It was Jones's 100th hit of the season. After a walk to Art Shamsky and a ground out to Beckert by Wayne Garrett, Kranepool strode to the plate once again. With Jenkins unleashing a blazing fastball on the outside corner, the left-handed Kranepool poked the ball over Kessinger's head at short. Jones came around to score, and the Mets had indeed won one of their biggest games ever, 4–3, as they closed the gap on the Cubs to a four-game margin.

"Yes, you can call it one of the most important victories in Mets' history," Hodges confirmed with a grin, as he stretched in his office chair after the game. "Of course, you've got to remember that I wasn't around for the whole eight years. . . . That's what we're all here for, to make believers out of all you unbelievers." Durocher and Jenkins were asked afterward why they had not walked Kranepool with first base open. The pitcher responded for himself. "I thought I could make him hit the pitch I wanted him to hit," Jenkins said simply. His pitching coach, Becker, was visibly sick. "It was the best he's pitched all season," he said. "It's a shame, a real shame he lost it."

"Somebody said the Cubs aren't taking us seriously!" Cleon Jones hollered in the midst of his mates in the New York locker room. "Maybe they'll take us seriously now!"

As expected, things were not pleasant over in the Cubs dressing room. Durocher entered to a roomful of drooping heads, and he started to quiver with anger as he got his speech going. "Let me tell you something," he began. "It's tough to win when your centerfielder can't catch a f_____flyball," he hollered. "Jenkins pitched his heart out. But when one man can't catch a fly ball, it's a disgrace. He stands there watching one, and then gives up on the other. It's a disgrace!" He then moved closer toward where Young was sitting. "My son could have caught those balls!!! My f_____ three-year-old could have caught those balls!!!" Things were quiet for another fifteen minutes after that, until Regan stood up and gave a quick wink to the rest of the club, telling them to stay positive.

Santo, however, could not hide his disgust any longer. When Durocher was finished, Santo found Young walking out of the clubhouse, as the dazed outfielder was not able to face his teammates any longer. Santo grabbed him and said a few words. Ron met the reporters moments later.

"I know the Dodgers won pennants with just pitching, but this Mets lineup is ridiculous," he began, conferring his belief that New York was an inferior team—which was actually the gist of his fury. "Maybe I'd better not say anything else because my mouth will get me into trouble."

But he continued. "He was thinking of himself, not the team," Santo blurted out, and the newsmen knew he was referring to Young. "He had a bad day at the plate, and he's got his head down. Don's a major leaguer because of his glove. When he hits, he's a dividend, but when he fails on defense, he's lost—and today he took us down with him. He put his head between his legs." While most of the writers heard the remarks, nearly all of them did not want them printed. "One career has already been ruined tonight," one told a colleague as they met for drinks in the hotel lobby later in the night. "I'm not going to ruin another." Inevitably, however, the story leaked. Santo was awoken by a phone call to his room on the tenth floor at the Waldorf-Astoria at three in the morning—a friend from Chicago was alerting him to the headline in the early edition of the *Sun-Times*, which announced that Santo had criticized a teammate for a loss.

The third baseman knew that he had made a mistake, and he churned sleeplessly in his room through the rest of the morning. At 2:30 p.m. he called selected members of the media inside his room and gave an informal press conference from the edge of his bed. "Don [Young] and I sat down for an hour today and talked," he revealed. "I apologized to him then, and I want to make a public apology now for what I said. I'm also going to call a team meeting tonight and give him a personal apology before the team."

PORTENT OF DOOM?

This was what the title above the Cubs box score would show for this game in the *Tribune* the next day.

Despite the reconciliation, the Cubs played that evening like a distracted team as Seaver overwhelmed them with a one-hitter, firing 71 strikes on ninety-nine pitches and never reaching a three-ball count on any Chicago hitter. Pelekoudas, who was working the plate that night, claimed that the pitcher "threw almost nothing but fastballs." Seaver had a perfect game until one out in the ninth, when it was disturbed by a line-drive single from Qualls, taking only his forty-eighth big league at-bat (and who, ironically but not surprisingly, had replaced Young on the lineup card in center field). The Mets won again, 4–0, as Holtzman's slide (10-5) continued. "I was aware from the fourth inning on that I had a shot at a perfect game, and I was going for it," Seaver said. Twice during the contest Santo had driven the center fielder Agee to the wall, 407 feet away, only to record an out each time. The deafening crowd had grown to over fifty-nine thousand for this contest, as the locals were sensing an upcoming opportunity to overtake the Chicago team in the standings. When Seaver came to bat in the eighth, the crowd was so loud that he had to wait two minutes before he could take his position in the batter's box. Seaver, now with a record of 14-3, had won eight in a row and was rightfully taking his place among the league's elite hurlers, on a level with Gibson, Marichal, and Jenkins. "Nobody was going to beat him tonight," Durocher said in stark conclusion.

Hands, once again summoned as the stopper, avoided a sweep for his club by beating the Mets, 6–2, in the finale, powered by Santo's seventeenth homer. "Are you over your hysteria now, Cub fans?" Markus wrote, as he tried to soothe fears. "That's good. Just sit back and enjoy the rest of the baseball season. The Cubs are not going to blow the pennant, not even if the Mets come in here and sweep three games in Wrigley Field next week—which they certainly are not going to do. . . . The only team with enough talent to take the Eastern Division flag away from the Cubs is St. Louis. St. Louis is too far behind to do it."

Markus continued: "There is a writer in New York, one of the best in our craft, by the way, who has allowed himself to be swept away in the thrill of it all. He thinks the Mets can win. He should know better, because it was he himself who once said: 'Over the course of a 162-game season, class will tell.'"

Despite Markus's confidence, the Cubs came home and dropped the opener of a series with the struggling Phillies, 7–5, notwithstanding Banks's 1,550th RBI, which moved him up to fourteenth on the all-time list. In some good news that day, it was announced that Santo and Kessinger had been named as starters for the National League All-Star team, who would take on the best from the American League on July 22 in Washington DC. The choices were the result of voting by the players, coaches, and managers in each league. The managers of the two squads—Schoendienst and Detroit's Mayo Smith—selected the pitchers and reserve players, with the results of the starting position players being released earlier. "I'm more pleased with getting on the team this year than the first time, because there are so many good shortstops in the league this year," Kessinger said in getting his second nod, while it was the sixth selection for Santo. As most had expected Bench was the runaway choice for catcher, outdistancing the second-place Hundley by a whopping 261–76 tally. Beckert had been beaten out by only 27 votes for the second base position, granted to Felix Millan of the Braves; this "disgusted" Durocher, who thought that his own man should have been appointed. Even more disturbing to Leo and to Chicago fans was that none of the Cubs' pitchers had been selected by Schoendienst. An omission especially surprising to many observers was Jenkins, currently leading the National League in strikeouts. Throwing instead would be Schoendienst's own Gibson and Carlton, in addition to Seaver, Marichal, Koosman, Phil Niekro, Larry Dierker from the Astros, Grant Jackson from the Phillies, and Bill Singer from the Dodgers. Of the current Chicago pitchers, Aguirre had been an All-Star in 1962, Regan in 1966, and Jenkins in 1967.

The Cubs rebounded to take the next three, including victories by Jenkins (12-6) and Holtzman (11-5) and a 6–4 win by rookie Jim Colborn in the final game of the set. Colborn, a graduate of Whittier College and erstwhile sociology graduate student at the University of Washington, had been recalled from Tacoma to take the place of the rookie Lemonds, who had been battling a sore arm. Colborn had once struck out 21 batters while pitching in a collegiate all-star game in the Netherlands in 1966. He claimed that, before coming to the Cubs a few days before, he had "never been in a major league training camp, or ever known a major league player. . . . I hope the next time I can concentrate more, rather than just standing around staring at Ernie Banks and Ron Santo."

While at his locker before the game, Banks read the following letter from a devoted fan. He also had it published in the Chicago newspapers the next day.

Dear Ernie:

You are receiving this letter from a long-time Cub fan who is 10,000 miles away, but still follows you guys every day. I'm in Viet Nam, serving my second tour with the Army. I'm 22 and can remember the Cubs as far back as the early 1950s. I follow the Cubs here because we have Armed Forces Viet Nam radio and our newspaper, the *Stars and Stripes*. My father and little brother also send clippings from the *Tribune*.

You get the 500th homer this year. I'll settle with Fergie Jenkins winning 24 and leading the league in strikeouts. I'll let you and Ron Santo battle it out for the runs-batted-in lead.

I'll be back in the "beautiful confines of Wrigley Field" in September. But if I'm a little late, please save me and my family some World Series tickets.

Remember Ern, the Cubs have the "Bleacher Bums" in Chicago, but your big fan is a member of the "Rice Paddy Rooters."

SP/5 Phil Guzzo, You Know Where

When the Mets arrived in Chicago on July 14, a horde of twenty New York newsmen had accompanied them on the trip. Durso was one of them, still marveling at the success of New York's new media darlings. "A new chapter will open in Chicago, where the Mets will open another three-game series against the Cubs. . . . For the second time in a week, people will be wondering how a team that lost 737 games in seven years could now be challenging for the top." Durso had started referring to the Mets almost exclusively in his articles as the "Urchins," comparing the New York baseball men to the playful, seemingly harmless sea creatures. Seaver had skipped the last start he was supposed to make (part of a doubleheader, the day before in Montreal) so that he could face Hands in the opener at Wrigley. It was one of the largest weekday crowds in Cubs history to that time—40,252 fans had assembled, some arriving at the park as early as six in the morning. "I haven't seen anything like this since those weekends when the Yankees used to come in to play the White Sox ten years ago," said one veteran of the Chicago Police Department on duty at the scene, in reference to the city's last pennant—won on the South Side—in 1959. All kinds of zealots were showing up, and all kinds of prodigal sons as well. "One fellow came in pretty upset because he couldn't cart his beer into the park," the officer continued. "I asked him if he didn't know the ball-park regulations and he said 'no,' that this was the first time he'd been to Wrigley Field in 25 years." An hour before the first pitch, standing-room-only tickets went on sale.

After Hands set down the Mets in order in the first, Seaver stomped to the mound with an air of supreme confidence and struck out Kessinger and Williams, sandwiching in a meek Beck-ert ground out in between. Seaver looked as if he would be just as dominant as the last time he faced the Cubs. By the time the sixth inning had rolled around, the game was still scoreless and Durocher knew that he had to manufacture a run. Kessinger planted a ball down the third base chalk—"that was as good as I can bunt a ball," he later said—and wound up on first. Beckert moved him to second on a hit-and-run play, and then, on cue, Williams singled for a 1–0 Chicago lead. Hands, while not pos-sessing an overwhelming arsenal of "stuff" on the day, kept the New Yorkers in check throughout. He picked up his second win in a row over Hodges's club by maintaining the shutout, as Re-gan notched his ninth save in recording the final out. But Selma (9-4) dropped a heartbreaker, 5–4, the following day to Gary Gentry as back-to-back homers by Williams (his 10th) and Santo (19th) in the eighth inning were the final blows that left the Cubs one tally short. It was Selma's first loss in eight decisions; the Mets had been the last team to beat him—over two months ago on May 4.

At 8:32 the next morning—July 16—a few of the ballplayers and park personnel were sleepily making their way into Wrig-ley Field for the final game of the series. At that very moment in Florida, rocket engines were heard for hundreds of miles as they boomed from the Kennedy Space Center. Trailing fire nine hundred feet beneath its body, and with the eyes of the world upon it, the seven-million-pound *Saturn 5* projectile zoomed out of sight in the high Atlantic sky at nearly 18,000 miles per hour, carrying with it men by the names of Neil Armstrong, Michael Collins, and Edwin "Buzz" Aldrin on the *Apollo 11* mission. The astronauts were on a 250,000-mile trip, seeking to be the first men to orbit and land on the moon. Within seconds after liftoff, they would need to get the craft up to 24,200 miles per hour, known as "Earth Escape Velocity," in order to free itself from the planet's gravity. "We can see snow on the mountaintops of California," Aldrin reported back to mission control a few minutes after liftoff. "It looks like L.A. doesn't have much of a smog problem today." Attention from around the globe was focused on the event, but particular amazement centered on the now-famous human beings in flight. "The Soviet Union called them 'courageous people,' Iranian hippies drank goat's milk to their health, and good many Italians feared that they might contaminate the earth," the *Washington Post* reported. The crew would attempt to land its excursion craft, called the *Eagle*, on the moon's Sea of Tranquility on Sunday, July 20.

As earthlings returned to their summer duties of lawn mowing and pennant watching, both Jenkins and Mets starter Don Cardwell were chased early from the premises on Addison Street in Chicago. But five innings of shutout baseball thrown by New York reliever (and former Cub) Cal Koonce paved the way to another Met victory, 9–5. Their catcher, Jerry Grote, scoffed in the locker room at the Bleacher Bums. "Notice where they all were in the ninth inning—they left, that's what. They're real great fans, aren't they?" Soon after, his teammates joined in with impromptu songs. "*Let's hear it for Leo! Let's hear for Santo! Let's hear it for the Bums!*" The Mets were enjoying the moment while they could, for they would not get another shot at the Cubs for nearly two months, with a September 8 date at Shea Stadium being the next time the two teams were scheduled to meet. The Cardinals, also needing other teams to beat the Cubs to get back into the race, would have to wait even longer—their next contest with Chicago would not be until September 12. "The Cubs have been in first place for 102 days," Langford reminded his readers, "and that requires something special in itself."

On July 17 the Cubs had their first day off in six weeks (and had barely played .500 ball during that time, with a record of 22-20). The National League East standings looked this way:

National League East	W	L	Pct.	GB
Chicago	57	36	.613	—
New York	51	37	.580	3.5
St. Louis	49	46	.516	9
Pittsburgh	45	48	.484	11.5
Philadelphia	38	52	.422	17
Montreal	29	63	.315	27

In what was becoming a following that would have made the Grateful Dead jealous, a caravan of nomadic Bleacher Bums had trekked to Philadelphia for the Cubs series with the Phillies. Not unlike the Deadheads, many of the wayward Bums parted with much—their money, their jobs, and in some cases, even their families—to be with their team at the next scheduled stop.

A most perplexing story was unfolding within the annals of Philadelphia baseball, and it involved the team's first black star ever, Richie Allen. The twenty-seven-year-old third baseman, who had arrived on the scene during the Phillies' noted pennant collapse to the Cardinals in 1964, had been suspended for the previous month for poor conduct. "Someone once called it the 'City of Brotherly Love,' for reasons known only to himself," Markus smirked. "In its relations with its baseball team in particular, Philadelphia has demonstrated repeatedly that if there is any family feeling at all, it is of the Cain-Abel variety." It was granted that Allen had suffered greatly in the past, in particular with his stint as the first black player on the Phillies' Minor League roster as well. He led the National League in runs scored, triples, and total bases in being named Rookie of the Year in 1964, and was an All-Star in 1966 and 1967, but he could not withstand the "boos" that his poor defensive play at third base brought from the Philly faithful (in his productive offensive rookie year of 1964, he had committed 41 errors). When relations with the fans and local media failed to improve, Allen went into hiding.

Allen's problems had truly begun back on June 24, when he missed a doubleheader with the Mets, claiming that he had been stuck in traffic after watching some horse races in New Jersey. He was losing $500 daily with the suspension that he was serving until July 20, and no one seemed to know exactly where he was from one day to the next. Three weeks later, on August 7, Phillies manager Bob Skinner would resign, feeling that front-office people with the team were not supporting his efforts to discipline Allen's tantrums. "All he told us was that, under the present conditions, he did not feel like continuing on the job," Philadelphia general manager John Quinn told the press. A couple of days earlier the Phillies had dropped a 19–17 decision to the Reds in a game in which the teams combined for 46 hits. "When you score 17 runs and lose," a frustrated Skinner said afterward, "something's got to be wrong." When Allen had heard the news about his manager leaving, he was not sympathetic. "He's a quitter," Allen said plainly. "He didn't show me much. I've been taking the rap for five years now, and I haven't quit. Who likes a quitter? All I know is everybody is getting out of here but me, and I'm the one who wants to go."

So the series began without the Phil's top slugger, and the Cubs seized the advantage. Regan picked up his tenth win in relief, aiding Holtzman in a 9–5 victory as Banks's four RBI tied him with Tris Speaker for thirteenth on the career list. After the game it was announced that Hundley, Banks, and Beckert would join Kessinger and Santo on the National League All-Star team, marking the first time in over twenty years that an entire infield from the same club would appear together in the Mid-Summer Classic. (It was also made known that Schoendienst had left Jenkins off the team to make room for Banks, as was suggested to the Cardinal manager by Warren Giles. Giles thought that it might have been Banks's last chance to play in an All-Star Game.)

Beckert was out to prove that he had indeed recovered from his broken thumb; his play was so stellar that he sent Popovich back to the bench at a time when "Popo" had been hitting .410

since joining the Cubs. Like Beckert it was the first appearance in the game for Hundley, and for a time it looked as if Hundley would get to start the game, as it was thought that Bench would be away for compulsory military duty when the 22nd rolled around. But the Cincinnati catcher received an unusual twenty-four-hour pass from Camp A. P. Hill in Virginia, clearing the way for him to play. From the South Side of Chicago, twenty-one-year-old rookie outfielder Carlos May (the brother of Bench's teammate with the Reds, Lee May) had made the American League squad for the White Sox, with he and Bench being the second-youngest All-Stars in the history of the game. Representing the veterans, it was the thirteenth trip to the All-Star Game for Banks. "I'm really thrilled," Ernie said. "I understand we're going to get to meet President Nixon. He's a real baseball fan, and I've got a couple of 'CUB POWER' stickers for him."

"This is a real honor," Beckert added. "There's only one honor greater, and I plan to get that one this year, too—playing in a World Series."

In the midst of the excitement of the *Apollo 11* launching two days earlier, the nation was conversely stunned on July 18 with the news that a car being driven by Massachusetts senator Edward Kennedy had crashed off Cape Cod in Chappaquiddick late that night. Found in the back seat of the car was Mary Jo Kopechne, a staffer in Kennedy's office who died as a result of the wreck while Kennedy was able to leave the scene unscathed (it was the second time he had escaped death—five years earlier, in June 1964, he had suffered only back injuries while involved in a plane crash). The vehicle crashed through the barriers of the wooden, one-laned Dyke Bridge, and the car wound up in a swift-moving current of water. Authorities later ruled that Kopechne's death was caused by drowning; investigators were baffled, however, because Kennedy did not contact the police or rescue units until 9:30 the next morning. After claiming that he had taken a wrong turn onto an unfamiliar road, the senator noted that he had jumped in the pond several times in an effort to save Kopechne but was so distraught with what he described as "a jumble of emotions" that he did not think clearly throughout the rest of the early-morning hours, nor did he remember how he got back to where he was staying in Edgartown—although it would have required a lengthy swim. "I was exhausted and in a state of shock," Kennedy told reporters later that morning. "I recall walking back to where my friends were eating. There was a car parked in front of the cottage, and I climbed into the back seat. I then asked someone to bring me back to Edgartown. I remember walking around for a period of time, and then going to my hotel room. When I fully realized what had happened this morning, I immediately went to the police."

What raised curiosity further was the fact that an autopsy was not allowed on Kopechne's body—the petition for which was filed by her family. "Medical Examiner Donald Mills quoted District Attorney Edmund Dinis's office as saying an autopsy would not be needed," Cornelius Hurley wrote for the Associated Press. "Mills said the cause of death was 'completely obvious.'"

Kennedy pleaded guilty to a charge of leaving the scene of an accident, and though given only a two-month suspended sentence, the incident was thought to ruin Kennedy's chance at the Democratic presidential nomination in 1972, for which many pollsters had him favored. "There is no truth, no truth whatever, to the widely-circulated suspicions of immoral conduct," Kennedy asserted as he went on national television. Kopechne's body was flown immediately on a plane chartered by the Kennedy family to her hometown of Plymouth, Pennsylvania, where the funeral was performed. Kennedy attended the funeral "with a neck brace he was never seen wearing again," according to further reports by the Associated Press.

But thoughts quickly turned to better news of national pride. After losing the next day the Cubs swept a doubleheader from the Phillies on July 20, the final games before the All-Star break. In the third inning of the nightcap with the Cubs batting, play was halted abruptly. It was seconds after 4:17 p.m. Eastern Daylight Time, and the two teams silently went and stood along their respective baselines and looked skyward. Word had been sent from Armstrong to mission control in Houston:

"Houston . . . Tranquility base here. . . . The Eagle has landed."

A prayer was said for the men over the loudspeaker at Connie Mack Stadium, asking for continued safety for the first human-made craft that had landed on the moon. The game resumed after a recording of Kate Smith's rendition of "God Bless America" followed the prayer over the intercom.

About six and a half hours later, at 10:56 p.m.—with hundreds of millions of people fixated on their television sets back on earth—Armstrong opened the hatch of the fragile, four-legged landing device.

"Okay, Houston, I'm on the porch," his voice crackled over the airwaves as he emerged.

He hopped carefully down the nine-step ladder, along the way releasing a robotic device from the module that set up a television camera on the moon's surface to record the historic event. Armstrong got down to the last step, took a final leap, and firmly planted his left foot on the southwestern edge of the dry lunar Sea of Tranquility. He contacted mission control once again.

"That's one small step for man . . . one giant leap for mankind."

"You're looking good in every respect," mission control replied from Texas.

Twenty minutes later Aldrin joined him outside, while Collins maintained his orbit of the moon in the command ship. "They first timidly, then almost playfully, walked about the strange new world," wrote Jeff Nesmith of the *Atlanta Constitution*. Armstrong continued his report back to earth.

"The surface is fine and powdery. I can pick it up loosely with my toe. It does adhere in fine layers like powdered charcoal to the sole and sides of my boots."

When asked by mission control how he felt, Armstrong quickly added that he was "very comfortable."

Television watchers gaped in utter amazement at what they had witnessed. "People back on earth found the black-and-white television pictures of the bug-shaped lunar module and the men tramping about it so sharp and clear as to seem unreal," wrote

John Noble Wilford in a special to the *New York Times*, "more like a toy and toy-like figures than human beings on the most daring and far-reaching expedition thus far undertaken."

The astronauts later received a congratulatory phone call from President Nixon, in what the president said "has to be the most historic phone call ever made. . . . Because of what you have done, the heavens have become part of man's world. And as you talk to us from the Sea of Tranquility, it requires us to redouble our efforts to bring peace and tranquility to earth. For one priceless moment in the history of man, all the people on this earth are truly one—one in their pride in what you have done, and one in our prayers that you will return safely to earth."

"Thank you, Mr. President," Armstrong replied. "It's a great honor and privilege for us to be here, representing not only the United States but men of peace of all nations."

Just ten days later, the unmanned *Mariner 6* and *Mariner 7* spacecrafts would make their closest approaches to the planet Mars, giving viewers from earth a close-up image of the south pole of yet another astrological wonder. Meanwhile, the moon craft was expected to leave for home at 1:55 p.m. Eastern Standard Time on Monday, July 21, allowing its crew one more beautiful gaze at the stars.

And on July 22 earthlings were allowed to see some stars of their own. By the time the *Apollo 11* mission had landed on the moon, the exhausted Cubs had played thirty games in the previous twenty-seven days. A break was needed, and the All-Star break was here. With Durocher authoring the same lineup nearly every day, the break was thought to do the Cubs the most good out of all the teams in the league.

The festivities began on the evening of July 21 with a black-tie dinner in Washington the night before the game. The dinner was celebrating the supposed one-hundredth birthday of baseball, and thirty-four out of the thirty-seven living members of the National Baseball Hall of Fame were present at the celebratory meal. That evening Banks had a chance to meet up with Kuhn and President Nixon. "He gave me three years," Banks said about the chief executive's misjudgment of his age. "The President thought I was only 35. Then the commissioner [who was about to receive a seven-year extension of his contract from the owners, at a salary of over $100,000 per year] said, 'No, Mr. President, I think Ernie is 38.' And Mr. Nixon said, 'Well, he looks 35, and don't tell any of those other fellows, but this man deserves a pennant.'"

Nixon continued on. "I like the job I have," he admitted, "but if I had to start over again, I'd like to have been a sportswriter." The press had bestowed on him an honorary membership in the Baseball Writers Association of America.

Scribes from all over the land continued to admire Banks for the sheer, unbridled enthusiasm that he still had for the game. "Banks . . . smiling and happy as usual . . . presents that wonderful world of sports that intrigues so many of us," observed Bob Addie of the *Washington Post* as he watched the playful scene of interaction among Ernie, Kuhn, and President Nixon. "The cheerful Cub says he doesn't understand people who say that baseball games are too long. 'I wish I could play three games a day,' he says happily." As a small poke at the Chicago team, Al Harvin of the *New York Times* suggested from another part of the room, "Ernie Banks has been a Chicago Cub since 1953, so he's learned to smile in the face of adversity."

A sellout crowd of over forty-five thousand was expected at RFK Stadium in Washington for the game between the leagues' best on July 22. The National League had won the last six games (the last four of which had been decided by only one run) and held a 21-17-1 all-time lead. The starting pitcher for the American League was supposed to be the Tigers' McLain, who was registering slightly behind his pace of 31 wins the year before but nonetheless entering the break with a strong record of 14-5. Because of phlebitis in his nonpitching arm, however, it remained questionable until game time whether he would indeed pitch. Schoendienst had chosen his own Carlton to start for the Nationals, because he had missed his last scheduled start in Pittsburgh due to a rainout.

The rains must have followed the Cardinals eastward, for four hours of showers in the District of Columbia postponed the All-Star Game until the following afternoon. The rains had stopped right at 7:00 p.m. on the 22nd, just fifteen minutes before the scheduled first pitch, but the field was too soggy to attempt the affair. Kuhn decided that 12:45 p.m. on the 23rd would be the meeting time for the start of the game. Nixon was unable to stay the extra day, as he needed to head to the Pacific Ocean to help greet the returning *Apollo 11* crew, scheduled to splash somewhere in the sea in the next twenty-four hours. So, instead, he transferred first-pitch duties to vice president Spiro Agnew. Before he left town, however, Nixon was able to meet with several more of the All-Stars; he especially enjoyed talking with Kessinger. "Your team is really doing well," he told the Chicago shortstop. "Keep up the good work."

The starting lineups were as follows:

National League	American League
Alou (PIT)—CF	Carew (MIN)—2B
Kessinger (CHI)—SS	Jackson (OAK)—CF
Aaron (ATL)—RF	F. Robinson (BAL)—RF
McCovey (SF)—1B	Powell (BAL)—1B
Santo (CHI)—3B	Howard (WSH)—LF
Jones (NY)—LF	Bando (OAK)—3B
Bench (CIN)—C	Petrocelli (BOS)—SS
Millan (ATL)—2B	Freehan (DET)—C
Carlton (STL)—P	Stottlemyre (NY)—P

McLain had remained the expected choice on the mound for the American League, but he ran into some trouble in trying to get to the ballpark. Piloting his own small plane, he was circling the area near RFK Stadium, waiting for permission to land. He had previously flown himself back quickly to Detroit in order to visit his dentist and have nine teeth capped. By the time he finally grounded the plane, got to the stadium, and changed into his uniform, Mel Stottlemyre of the Yankees had been given the ball by Mayo Smith and John "Blue Moon" Odom had already entered in Stottlemyre's relief in the third inning. By that time the National League had built an 8-1 lead. McLain was greeted by McCovey in the fourth inning, as the Giant first baseman slugged a long home run—his second of the game—to make it 9–2 in favor of the Nationals. "Will Denny ever settle down and give us the opportunity to find out how great he can be?" Condon asked about the carefree McLain in the wake of the incident. "If only someone will take Denny back to the woodshed and acquaint him with a few facts of adult life. . . . If Kuhn fails to reproach McLain for Denny's cavalier attitude about the game, then the All-Star production is a joker rather than—as baseball likes to term it—an attraction 'second only to the World Series.' . . . What other person do you know who would be in such a rush to sit down in the dentist's chair?"

In the next inning (the fifth), Willie Mays, making his twentieth appearance in the All-Star Game, flied out to right field as a pinch-hitter after receiving a roaring ovation. Bench had also homered to the second deck in left field and had a shorter one stolen away by Carl Yastrzemski, the American League Triple Crown winner from two seasons ago ("I could never jump any higher than that," Yaz admitted, in pulling himself up on the top of the wall with his throwing arm to make the catch). The young catcher added another hit and was given the MVP award, as the National League pitching staff shut the door the rest of the way for a 9-3 win. "I was nervous coming into today's game," Bench told Edward Prell for the *Tribune* afterward. "I'd been on military duty for a week. I hadn't swung a bat except for a few times. And I worried, too, about doing a good job handling all our fine pitchers." After showering quickly he changed clothes and made the two-hour drive to Camp Hill for a 4:30 reveille and regular army drills the next morning.

Beckert, Banks, Kessinger, Hundley, and Santo went a combined o for 9 in the game, although Kessinger (diving and grabbing a line drive off the bat of Oakland's Sal Bando) and Santo (reaching into the stands to catch a pop-up) sparkled in the field with outstanding defensive plays.

§

The Cubs would enjoy a ten-game homestand against the West Coast teams in resuming league play after the break. First in town were the Los Angeles Dodgers. The Braves had continued to lead the Dodgers by two games in the Western Division, and in Atlanta's first game after the break, Aaron hit home run number 534 to move him into fourth place on the all-time list, passing Jimmie Foxx and now sitting just two behind Mantle for third.

With the Cubs and Dodgers splitting the first two games of the series, the teams appeared in front of a national television audience for the third contest on Saturday, July 26. Durocher had approached Reiser that morning—it being Durocher's sixty-third birthday—and mentioned that he was ill. "I may stay one inning," Leo reportedly told his assistant coach. "Maybe two, maybe three." With the Cubs leading 1–0 in the top of the third, he addressed Reiser again. "Run it the way you want to—I'm going in." He made his way to the clubhouse as the two teams fought to a 2–2 tie into the eleventh inning. (Reiser did not feel constrained by the circumstances; in fact, he found it an opportunity to experiment, as he placed Popovich in center field for the only time on the year.) Then Williams, hitting safely in his fifteenth consecutive game, lined a double to the outfield to represent the winning run. Hundley followed a couple of batters later with a single, and the Cubs went home winners, 3–2, behind the relief work of Regan, who had won his eleventh game.

On Sunday the 27th Dr. Suker announced to the media that Durocher was being confined to quarters because of "gastritis" and would resume his managerial duties the following day when the San Francisco Giants came to town. Richard Dozer affirmed in his *Tribune* column that "Durocher stayed home in his apartment, still suffering from a painful bellyache." A crowd of 30,291—which pushed the club over the one million mark for the season, the earliest achievement of that number at Wrigley in forty years—watched as Drysdale, who had decided to postpone his retirement and make his first start for the Dodgers in three weeks, beat the Cubs, 6–2. "The shoulder felt fine and my arm didn't bother me at any time aside from getting tired," Drysdale told *The Sporting News*. Most of the Dodger offense for the series was provided by home runs from rookie Bill Sudakis, a native of

Joliet, Illinois, who had driven to Wrigley Field from his family's residence in the southwest suburb for each of the games. It was the second loss for Jenkins (13-9) in the past three days, as he had been knocked out early from the series opener when a line drive struck his thumb, badly bruising the digit. After the game it was discovered that Durocher wasn't really ill at all. He had secretly ducked out of town to Camp Ojibwa in the northern Wisconsin town of Eagle River to be at "Parents' Weekend" for the twelve-year-old son of his new wife, Lynne. He had chartered a small plane to Rhinelander, Wisconsin, which had taken off from Meigs Field, the small downtown Chicago airport, at 3:45 p.m. Durocher had always been at personal odds with Jim Enright, a writer for a local magazine named *Chicago Today*, and as chance would have it, a friend of Enright's had a son at the camp. When Enright's friend saw Durocher at Camp Ojibwa—with a Cubs game simultaneously being shown on national television—he could not believe it. He immediately phoned the writer, and the story took off in the Chicago media. After the ceremonies at the camp, Durocher, Lynne, and the boy returned to Chicago on the same plane, arriving at Meigs at 11:30 on Sunday morning. It was noted in the papers that the pilot of the plane had remarked that he heard Durocher say he was ill.

"Mr. Wrigley almost fired Leo that weekend," Jack Brickhouse would later recall. "For about two hours, Leo *was* fired. Wrigley was really upset, but Helen [his wife] calmed him down and warned him to cool off before making a decision. He did cool down, thought it over, and gave Leo a chance to explain. That's when Leo came back, met with John Holland and P. K., and almost got down on his hands and knees to kiss their shoes." It may or may not have been as dramatic as all that, for the media had reported that Durocher stopped by Phil Wrigley's apartment before the first game of the Giants series, offered an apology that was accepted, and the matter was put to rest. "It took only five minutes," Leo said of his meeting with the owner. "We understand each other perfectly—as we always have. It's as simple as that. This is a private matter, and I don't discuss my private life with anyone. If I have anything to say, I'll say it to Mr. Wrigley."

Wrigley had told Durocher that no apology to the team was necessary, since none of the players appeared to be very offended by the circumstances. Leo added that, as for his physical condition, he "still felt punk all over" when he returned on Sunday, and thus while he could have taken over the leadership of the team once again, he did not want to unnecessarily ruin the "winning streak" that Reiser had established.

Markus publicly defended the manager as well. "Leo has been getting bad press because he committed the unpardonable offense of calling in sick and playing hooky from a ball game," he wrote. "Well, what the heck, Leo didn't do anything that a lot of people aren't doing these days. Bus drivers. Cops. Air traffic controllers. They're all doing it." Then, in his most flagrant display of confidence for a pennant, Markus continued. "Durocher could set the Cubs on automatic pilot and spend the rest of the season in Wisconsin if he chooses without affecting the course of destiny."

Certainly all had seemed well and forgiven, as Leo's unit beat Marichal for the first time in nearly three years, downing the Giants 4–3. Hands had taken a no-hitter into the fifth inning but had grown tired and was replaced by Nye, who held on for his second win of the year against four defeats. But the Cubs lost the next two, the first of which involved a collision between Mays and Hundley at home plate that left Mays out for the remainder of the series. Jenkins righted himself with a victory in the final game over the Giants, 12–2, fueled by homers off the bats of Williams (his 12th), Hundley (15th), and Banks (16th) to gain a split. It was deemed critical that Fergie reestablish himself as the ace of the staff for the pennant run, for Hands had gotten the only two victories the club secured from the Mets during the month of July. The month closed with the standings showing that the Cubs had inched further ahead in their lead over New York, despite the fact that Chicago had only a 15-13 record for the last four weeks:

National League East	W	L	Pct.	GB
Chicago	65	41	.613	—
New York	55	44	.555	.5
St. Louis	55	49	.528	9
Pittsburgh	53	50	.514	10.5
Philadelphia	42	60	.411	21
Montreal	33	70	.320	30.5

Pete Rose, observing from a distance in Cincinnati and the Western Division, wasn't sold on the quality of the Cubs outfit. "Leo Durocher is an excellent manager," the defending National League batting champion stated, "but the Cubs have got to put a little faith in their gloves and bats and not so much in Durocher. He can't swing their bats for them."

But Chicagoans still maintained *their* faith in Leo and his Cubs, including one of the manager's most public cheerleaders—Markus. "Leo Durocher whipped home long shots in each of his three pennant winning years—1941 in Brooklyn, 1951 and 1954 in New York," Markus reminded the readers who still may have been unsure of the skipper's capabilities. "And he currently has another pre-season outsider, the Cubs, winging out in front in quest of his fourth victory."

"They can't wait to see him fail," Santo said about Leo's critics. "But I'll tell you this: he won't fail. Because for him to fail, we have to fail. And we won't as long as he's our manager."

Despite the Cubs' widening the stream a bit between them, the Mets hadn't lost conviction. "Ticket sales are booming," Koppett reported about the club from his desk at the *New York Times*. "The players are happy, confident, and determined. Club officials can hardly do their work because they are keeping their fingers crossed so desperately."

What would happen next would simply be two of the most perplexing months ever to end a pennant race.

8

No Time to Rest

> When you're eight games behind,
> it's like eight miles; when you're
> eight games in front, it's like eight
> inches.
>
> —Ron Santo

With two months between the Cubs and their first pennant in twenty-four years, most of the team's concern was directed at the Cardinals, who had gone 20-8 in July. The streak had prompted St. Louis broadcaster Harry Caray to constantly sing over the airwaves of KMOX radio, "*The Cardinals are coming, tra-la, tra-la . . .*" And while impressive, the young Mets were not considered by most to be seasoned enough to stay in the hunt. Even with the exciting race, the sports attention in Chicago shifted gears for one evening to an annually anticipated event.

On August 1, the thirty-sixth annual College All-Star Football Game took place at Soldier Field in Chicago, with the nation's finest collegiate players taking on the New York Jets and their prodigal son, Joe Namath. Tickets had been available since June for $10, $7.50, $5, and $3, and a crowd of nearly seventy-five thousand (the largest for the event in twelve years) turned out at the large—but usually dormant—stadium by the Chicago lakefront (a year later, the Bears would begin plans to make Soldier Field their permanent home, moving out of Wrigley Field). Making his final appearance as a collegian was O. J. Simpson, the flashy running back from Southern California who would take handoffs from the future Bear Douglass and fellow quarterbacks Greg Cook of Cincinnati and Terry Hanratty of Notre Dame, part of fifty schoolboys who would face the Jets. Namath had arrived in style, having the driver of his Cadillac cruise right into the stadium to drop him off, to the delight of early-arriving onlookers. "An Indian maharajah couldn't have done better parading in elephant-back," claimed Condon as he witnessed the spectacle. An Associated Press writer noted that Namath was "booed when he was introduced, cheered when he overthrew a receiver, and mauled when he tried to get to the dressing room."

Coached by former NFL quarterback legend Otto Graham, the college boys gave Namath and the Jets all they could handle, allowing the Super Bowl champions to escape with a hard-fought 26–24 win, missing the Las Vegas spread by nearly three touchdowns. For the game Broadway Joe—who had been practicing with his team for less than two weeks, since his reinstatement by Rozelle—was 17 of 32, passing for 292 yards and two interceptions. As the Jets left the field, Namath further angered the crowd when he gave an ornery look to a youngster who had grabbed the chin strap of his helmet as he jogged to the locker room. The game was not taken casually by the collegians; Graham's team, at one point, was penalized fifteen yards for his being on the playing field to argue a call. He then went face-to-face with New York defensive back Johnny Sample, who opened a gash above Graham's nose when his face mask bumped the coach. While they were walking off the field, his boys were calling over to the Jets, requesting a rematch down the road. "It really doesn't matter what it looks like," Namath scoffed about the close score. "We won."

The following night the Bears opened their 1969 preseason schedule against the Washington Redskins in RFK Stadium at the nation's capital. The Bears would play six exhibitions this year instead of the usual five, which included their second meeting ever against an American Football League team (to take place in Miami against the Dolphins the following week, on August 9; in 1967 Chicago was humiliated in the preseason by the Kansas City Chiefs of the AFL, 66–24, these being the two contests involving the Bears in advance of the leagues' merger in 1970). The Bears must have felt they were haunted, for much to their disbelief, their old coaching nemesis Lombardi stood across from them on the opposing sideline. Lombardi had been preceded in the Redskins' coaching position by Graham, who had directed the Washington club for the previous three seasons. Lombardi, who had led the Packers to five world championships in the 1960s, had been lured out of retirement with the offer of being the general manager of the Redskins as well. It was the complete control of personnel that Lombardi had always wanted in Green Bay but had never officially attained.

As the rains started to fall ten minutes before the opening kickoff, observers became concerned with the test that the elements would place on Sayers's reconstructed knee. But the "Kansas Comet" fielded that kickoff in the drizzle and raced sixty-nine yards down the sideline before being cornered off by a Redskins tackler at the twenty-five-yard line. It was a glimpse of heroics from a couple of seasons back, before his injury, when Sayers had been a threat to run for a touchdown every moment he took hold of the ball since entering the league. Dooley played him sparingly for the rest of the evening, as Washington sloshed its way in a constant downpour to a 13–7 victory in Lombardi's return.

One week later George Preston Marshall—longtime owner and president emeritus of the Redskins—passed away after a long battle with a variety of complications that stemmed from a stroke he suffered in 1963. It was an ironic (yet only symbolic) transfer of power in the organization to Lombardi. It was also the same day that Simpson came to an agreement for his first contract with the Buffalo Bills, which reported to be paying the star collegiate running back $350,000 over four seasons, the initial couple years of which would make him the highest-paid rookie in league history. "We came to a compromise," the reigning Heisman Trophy winner said diplomatically about the negotiations.

§

A visit from the San Diego Padres opened the month of August for the Cubs. The expansion Padres, still trying to feel their way through the National League, stood with a record of 34-71, a full twenty-five games behind the division-leading Braves in the West. It was a series that Durocher and the Cubs knew that they had to dominate, and the pitching staff responded. Hands, Holtzman, and Selma held the San Diego bats to a total of six runs, and Regan picked up his 11th and 12th saves, as Chicago swept all three contests from the friars at Wrigley Field, finishing their home games with San Diego for 1969 with a perfect 6-0 record. Hands (12-8) complained once again of shoulder tightness in the opener and revealed that he had spent his three previous off days with his right arm held under a heat lamp for therapy.

In the middle contest Santo belted his 23rd and 24th homers, which pushed his RBI total to 92, still the best in the league. In that game Holtzman (13-5), just back with the club after another National Guard stint with his unit (the 108th Medical Battalion) at Camp McCoy, Wisconsin, finished with a complete game and only two hits allowed. And, with Beckert and Santo receiving their 1968 Gold Glove Awards in a pregame ceremony, Selma (11-4) bested his counterpart from the April trade, Joe Niekro, by a 4–3 score. The Cubs pitcher fanned ten Padres in the process, as Williams erased a 3–1 deficit in the eighth with a home run. The victory opened up a six-game lead for Chicago over New York in the division. As the team prepared to depart for Houston, Selma offered to Durocher to pitch the third game of the series with the Astros on two days' rest—for that would have been Holtzman's turn in the rotation, and he was scheduled to leave for military duty once again (while at Camp McCoy on this trip, Holtzman would scratch his eye when a tree branch struck him, but with no serious damage).

Despite the typically unfriendly setting of the Astrodome, the

Cubs reeled off another sweep to make it seven straight wins, the first time that the Astros had been swept in their odd home in fourteen months (the Cardinals finished off the feat in June 1968). In the opener, a 9–3 win, Santo was hit in the little finger on his left hand by a pitch, but X-rays revealed only a minor bruise—an examination to which Santo originally objected but later accepted as necessary. "The doctor told me that if I had stayed in the game, I might not have been able to play for a few days." He was not able to take part in the sixteen-hit parade that was mustered by the Cubs, which included five off the bat of Beckert—the first time on the year that a Chicago player had produced five hits in a game—which raised the second baseman's batting mark to .302. The team equaled the sixteen-hit mark the next night as well, part of Hands's 13th win as Santo rejoined the fun with three hits of his own (over in Los Angeles that evening, Willie Stargell of the Pirates became the first player to ever hit a ball out of Dodger Stadium).

Despite pleas from Selma, Durocher gave Nye a rare start in the final game, in which Selma instead came out of the bullpen to close out a 5–4 triumph, with Selma fanning four and shutting out the Astros over the final three innings. A key moment earlier in the game had been the steal of home by Hickman, who jarred the ball loose from Houston catcher John Edwards. After the final loss, the Houston fans displayed their disgust for their team by littering the indoor park with a storm of wadded paper. In two weeks the Bears would make their debut in the dome while playing an exhibition game against the Houston Oilers. (The Bears had actually played one indoor game before—the 1932 NFL Championship Game was moved inside to Chicago Stadium when a blizzard hit the Windy City on December 18. The Bears beat the Portsmouth Spartans, 9–0, on an eighty-yard field in the "Madhouse on Madison.")

The wins left the Cubs eight and a half games ahead of the Mets on August 8—their largest lead since June 6, which was the date that Chicago had also finished crafting a seven-game winning streak. It was also announced on August 8 that plans had been made to prepare Dyche Stadium—the football home of Northwestern University in Evanston, Illinois—to serve as the Bears' home field for their date with the Minnesota Vikings on October 12 if the Cubs should be in the World Series, in an agreement reached between Halas and NU athletic director Tippy Dye. The measure was then passed—albeit narrowly—by the Evanston City Council with a vote of 10–6. The council's vote had been preceded by over an hour of discussion, primarily coming from two Evanston groups of citizens who were opposed to commercial interests (such as the Bears) using the campus facilities.

With a few scattered Bleacher Bums in attendance at Dodger Stadium in Los Angeles, looking "badly out of place way up there in the fifth deck behind first base," the Chicagoans traveled to Tinseltown and lost in Chavez Ravine, 5–0, as Singer fired a two-hit shutout, with the first safety not coming until the sixth inning when Kessinger broke up Singer's no-hit bid with a single (Qualls would later log the only other hit, a single with two out in the eighth inning). A cast of Hollywood luminaries, including Dean Martin and Milton Berle, had descended into the human-made valley to see the phenomenon from the Midwest known as the Cubs. Durocher filed a protest after the loss, claiming that umpire Tony Venzon—his nemesis from earlier in the season, when Venzon had taken the home run away from Banks in Montreal—had inappropriately allowed a Dodger runner, Willie Crawford, to take an extra base after an overthrow that went out of play. Crawford was running to second when Willie Davis hit a ground ball to Beckert and the second baseman flung the ball into the first base dugout. Crawford, who was rounding second, was ruled by Venzon to have been approaching third base and thus was awarded home plate. Leo shot off the bench and uttered several disparaging words in the face of the adjudicator. Once again, Giles denied the protest filed by Durocher.

The next evening, on August 9, the tables were turned as Hands authored his own shutout, a 4–0 tally, with a resurgent Hickman nailing two home runs. He had claimed the starting right-field job for the past few weeks, a position at which Spangler had been most regularly inserted. "I'm just in a hot streak now," Hickman noted, "and that's why I'm playing. Leo always plays the guy with the hot hand."

After the game the disappointed Los Angeles fans walked out of the stadium, got in their cars, and headed home as Dodger Stadium took on its typical postgame emptiness and silence. The peaceful nighttime quiet blanketed the area. Just a couple of hours later, however, the calm would be shattered down the street by a horror that would grip the entire nation. Around midnight local time, actress Sharon Tate—the wife of movie director Roman Polanski and considered one of the most promising young female stars of the cinema—was murdered along with five other people (including Abigail Folger, heiress to the coffee company of that name) by followers of Charles Manson at Tate's house on Cielo Drive in Beverly Hills. Polanski was away on business in England. Tate, age twenty-six, was eight and a half months pregnant at the time. As the attack occurred, she begged for the life of her unborn child, but the tormentors ignored her plea. Police had broken the case in the early morning hours after interviewing William Garretson, a nineteen-year-old caretaker of the home's grounds who was found sleeping in a nearby cottage; Garretson soon revealed the identity of the attackers. Ten people would be convicted of the crime, but it would be well into 1970 before Manson and his followers were brought to justice. He and three others were sentenced to death but were spared when California abolished the death penalty in 1972.

Despite the immense local sadness, the Cubs and Dodgers played on, finishing their series as Sutton beat Holtzman (who had just returned from his National Guard duty), 4–2, in a game that nobody seemed to notice. Afterward Drysdale announced that he was retiring, effective immediately and for good, having been unable to convalesce from a chronic sore arm that had been diagnosed as a torn "rotary" cuff (to be renamed in later years the "rotator" cuff). "I deeply regret having to retire," Drysdale told the news reporters. "But like they say, some things are inevitable—like death, taxes, and retirement from professional sports." A Dodger since 1956, Drysdale had been the winner of the Cy Young Award in 1962 and an All-Star eight times. His six straight shutouts in 1968 had broken a record that had stood for over sixty years.

On an off day on August 11, during which the Cubs left the mourning city of Los Angeles and headed down the coast to San Diego, the Chicago club purchased veteran pitcher Ken Johnson from the Yankees for slightly over the waiver price of $20,000. To make room on the roster, Rudolph was optioned to triple-A Tacoma as Hundley and Heath remained as the only two catchers on the squad. Coming to the Cubs with a career record of 90-103, Johnson in 1964 (as a member of the Houston Astros) became the first pitcher ever to lose a nine-inning no-hitter. He had first arrived in the National League with the Reds in 1961 at age twenty-eight after spending several seasons with the Kansas City Athletics. That year he helped Cincinnati win its first pennant in twenty-one years. Although Johnson had been primarily a starter over the course of his twelve-year big league career, Holland made the move in a simple, inexpensive attempt to add some immediate depth to the bullpen. The Cubs had been fortunate to avoid any serious injuries of late, pitching or otherwise. An exception was Nate Oliver, who was sitting in a Los Angeles hospital bed with a kidney infection. "Personally, I've always had trouble hitting Johnson," Banks told readers in his weekly column for the *Tribune*, "largely because he keeps his pitches off-speed and works on all parts of the plate. He has one of the best knuckleballs in the game, too."

Johnson was not needed the first night in San Diego, as Jenkins dominated the Padres in a 4–0 shutout while Hickman saved the goose egg with a great leaping catch at the right-center-field wall in the seventh. Hickman also continued his recent terror with the bat, pounding out his 10th home run of the year. In striking out ten batters Jenkins raised his league-leading total to 209, and his 6th shutout was the best in the circuit as well. "I want to lead the league in strikeouts this year," he said plainly after the game, "and I want to get more than 300 of them." Wouldn't that be a tough chore to accomplish? he was asked. "No, it shouldn't be," he snapped back. "I've got it all figured out. I will have twelve more starts, at least—and that ought to be enough." It was Hands who had been the really hot pitcher, however, and he continued his winning ways the next night with a 4–2 win over the Padres, his sixth victory in a row and his tenth in his last eleven tries. As the Cubs enjoyed an "off day" on Friday, August 15 (despite the fact that they still had to travel to Tacoma and play their triple-A team in an exhibition, a game that the Chicago club won, 7–4), there was excitement brewing on the other side of the country. At 5:07 p.m. local time, thousands of people who had been flocking from all over the nation finally heard the first instrumental sounds at the much-anticipated Woodstock Music Festival near White Lake in Bethel, New York. The event, organized by twenty-four-year-old band agent Michael Lang, eventually included an estimated half-million people, with traffic jams as long as twenty miles heading into the area. For the next three days, people of all sorts listened to music, acquainted themselves with strange substances of all kinds, and all the while attempted to maintain reasonable sanity and sanitation. It was truly a revelation for some in attendance; the turbulent 1960s, with all of its sorrow, bloodshed, and also hope, was indeed nearing its end. While the big weekend party was getting under way in Bethel, folks down in New York City thought their chances of partying for the Mets may have been dashed, for the Cardinals had caught their team for second place. The National League standings displayed the morning of the 15th looked like this:

National League East	W	L	Pct.	GB
Chicago	74	43	.632	—
St. Louis	65	52	.556	9
New York	62	51	.549	10
Pittsburgh	59	55	.518	13.5
Philadelphia	46	69	.400	27
Montreal	38	80	.322	36.5

Meanwhile, an amazing race was unfolding in the Western Division of the National League, with Cincinnati (63-50), Atlanta (66-55), Los Angeles (63-53), San Francisco (63-53), and Houston (63-54) all no more than two games away from one another.

Only the expansion San Diego club (35-81) was out of the hunt, trailing a full thirty games behind the Reds. This made nearly every contest that the Cubs encountered with a Western team a hard-fought endeavor, as each outfit was staking a claim to the top of its own division. Over in the American League, Minnesota (70-47) held a scant two-game lead on Oakland (67-48) in a two-horse race, while the imposing Baltimore Orioles (82-35) were running away with the East, leading the defending-champion Detroit Tigers (66-50) by fifteen and a half games.

After the team's warm stops in Los Angeles and San Diego, the weather in the north turned chilly on the evening of the 15th. After playing in Tacoma the Cubs made a final visit for 1969 to San Francisco to play a Giants team currently being decimated by injuries to its great stars. Dubbed "the Tape-and-Liniment Brigade" by Dozer, the Giants' lineup consisted of a banged-up Mays (sore knee), McCovey (pulled groin), and outfielder Jim Ray Hart (tendonitis in his throwing arm). Mays's knee problems stemmed from the collision with Hundley he had suffered at home plate at Wrigley Field back on July 29. Furthermore, their ace off the mound—Marichal—appeared to have lost his magic touch, not having won in his last five starts, dating back nearly four weeks. But, as he always seemed to do against the Cubs, the high-kicking Dominican found his best stuff and drafted a 3–0 blanking of Chicago, giving him 42 shutouts for his career, which broke the active-pitcher record that he had shared with Gibson since Drysdale's retirement. Beckert managed two hits against the right-hander, and Banks and Heath (giving Hundley a rare rest) one apiece, for the only offense Durocher's club was able to summon.

Substitute-extraordinaire Paul Popovich came to the rescue the next night, delivering his seventh hit in 13 pinch-hitting attempts (for a .538 average) as the Cubs rallied in the ninth to beat the Giants, 3–0, with Jenkins (17-10) advancing his season lead in the shutout race with seven. A loss by Hands (15-9) and a win by Selma (12-4) caused a split in the doubleheader to end the series on the 17th.

As Woodstock was winding down into the late evening hours of

Sunday night the 17th, a ferocious storm far to the south was preparing to smash the Mississippi Gulf Coast. With winds in excess of two hundred miles per hour and tides over thirty feet, Hurricane Camille smashed into the cities of Biloxi and Gulfport that night and continued its devastating path until the early hours of Monday. It was originally thought that the hurricane would veer west into the empty bayous of Louisiana, but at a final moment offshore it took an abrupt turn northward. The hardest-hit communities on the coast were the small towns of Pass Christian and Long Beach, just to the west of Gulfport, as the two communities suffered nearly complete annihilation. The Biloxi Yacht Club was destroyed, as was the famous Baricev's Seafood Restaurant and hundreds of other businesses. The loss of Baricev's was ironic, as the popular establishment had been previously demolished by Hurricane Betsy, which hit landfall four years earlier. When the winds finally subsided, Camille had killed over 170 people on the coast (including 41 victims who were never found) and left another 2,000 injured. As the storm crept to the north and east over Tennessee, it took a right turn and headed for Virginia; its final death count would tragically rest at 347 by the time it sputtered into the Atlantic Ocean. It was the most damaging storm seen anywhere in the world in over fifty years, the likes of which the Western Hemisphere had never experienced in recorded times, before Hurricane Katrina hit the same region in 2005.

Not in Camille's path was the city of Chicago, and the Cubs and Sox were able to play a charity game against each other on August 18 in front of 33,333 fans at Comiskey Park. The Cubs reclaimed bragging rights with a 2–0 win on homers by Banks and Williams. The starting pitcher for the White Sox was their nineteen-year-old farmhand Bart Johnson, who had recently struck out 17 batters in a Midwest League game for Appleton. It was the twentieth such midsummer meeting between the crosstown rivals, a charity affair that raised funds for youth baseball in the Chicago area. Only the All-Star Game that was held in Comiskey Park in 1950 had interrupted the tradition.

The 19th of August was a typically steamy, hot day at Wrigley. What was unusual about the day, however, was the large Tuesday crowd that appeared—41,033 Cub crazies—which well surpassed the structure's capacity. It was Holtzman's turn to pitch, with the Atlanta Braves in town, and the players and spectators alike had been recently unsure of which Holtzman would show up at the ballpark. Some had thought that the military obligations that Kenny fulfilled had disrupted his rhythm for the season, but he looked forward to throwing again in front of the home fans. He started the first inning crisply, as fly outs by Millan and Aaron followed a sparkling play in the infield by Beckert, who went far to his left to snag a ground ball off the bat of Felipe Alou. Santo staked the left-hander to a 3–0 lead in the bottom of the first, launching his 25th home run of the season off of a fluttering knuckler from Phil Niekro. As the innings wore on, wherever the Braves tried to bat a ball there was a Cub defender there to fill the hole. In the seventh inning a supernatural hand seemed to reach up and grab a ball that Aaron hit that by all accounts was destined for the left-field stands; witnesses claimed that the baseball had actually traveled *over* the wall, suspended in midair. The ball then dropped like shot duck into the waiting glove of a surprised Billy Williams, who had his back to the wall. Santo's homer stood as the only scoring in the game until two were out in the Braves' ninth. Holtzman stood one batter away from becoming the first Cub to throw a no-hitter since Don Cardwell on May 15, 1960, two weeks before Santo joined the club.

As the imposing Aaron stepped to the plate one more time, Vince Lloyd called the action on WGN radio: "A nervous crowd . . . an excited crowd here at Wrigley Field. Holtzman looks in for the sign . . . the pitch . . . ground ball to Beckert . . . he bobbles it momentarily . . . HE'S OUT! A no-hit, no-run game for Kenny Holtzman! He's being mobbed by his teammates out on that mound! Pandemonium on the field, as several fans have broken through the squadron of Andy Frain ushers and joined them on the mound!"

Like receiving a leaping hug from an excited puppy, Holtzman was planted by Santo in the grass with a tackle that would have made Butkus proud, as the fans continued to pour from the outfield walls and sprint toward the celebration taking place on the infield. Holtzman's no-hitter was the first in the big leagues in nearly fifty years in which no strikeout was recorded. Just five days earlier, twenty-three-year-old Jim Palmer had performed the hitless feat for the Orioles. To be certain, Holtzman was truly aided by that sixteen-mile-per-hour gale that was blowing in over the left-field wall—while not quite the strength of Camille, it was a formidable zephyr nonetheless. "Without the wind," Holtzman said of Aaron's drive in the seventh that got caught up, "that ball would have landed in Evanston. I thought it was gone, even with the wind blowing in." Kessinger saved the no-hitter in the ninth as he fell over Young in center field while catching a pop fly off the bat of the leadoff batter, Alou. "The crowd was making so much noise, we couldn't hear anything out there," Kessinger said. "Don says he called for the ball, but I didn't hear him. And that wasn't a spot where I wanted to back off and let the ball drop. If it was going to drop, I'd rather Don had run right over me. Then one of us would get an error."

Holtzman added that he threw "about 96 to 100 percent fastballs," as his curve actually had trouble finding the plate all day. Strangely enough, it was Heath and the recently activated Gene Oliver—not the iron man Hundley, who was resting a bruised finger suffered on the West Coast trip—who had the pleasure of being the catchers for the piece of history. Oliver entered in the eighth inning and, according to Dozer, "admitted he was nervous" in finishing up the no-hitter "because he had caught only ten innings all year."

"Break out the champagne!" Willie Smith exhorted from his locker in praise of the lefty. Only beer was to be found in the ice chest, however.

Durocher was asked by reporters how good Holtzman currently was as a pitcher. "He's this far short of Sandy Koufax right now," he said, holding his hands six inches apart.

The Cubs were now thirty-two games over the .500 mark with a record of 77-45, their highest such point for the season.

Jenkins lost the next day to Ron Reed, 6–2, as the Mets had jumped back ahead of the Cardinals for second place and now stood six and a half games behind the Cubs. And even though

Hands lost the next day to the Braves, fans in Chicago started counting down the "magic number"—it stood at 35 (that is, the combination of Cubs wins and the second-place team's losses needed to clinch the division). It slipped to 34 the following afternoon, as the largest crowd at Wrigley for the year—42,364—watched the Cubs get shut down by a relatively undistinguished third-year pitcher named Jim Britton, who allowed a lone unearned run in a 3–1 triumph for the Braves, powered by Aaron's 33rd homer of the season. The attendance was augmented by thirteen thousand women who were admitted free of charge as part of a "Ladies' Day" promotion. "It may be said with considerable concern," Dozer noticed, "that the Chicago Cubs have quit hitting." With Williams being 0 for his last 12 as one example, Dozer pointed out that the club had scored an average of only two and a half runs a game in the preceding two weeks, a pace that did not bode well for pennant hopes. The Houston Astros were next in town. Having their own hitting woes in just being shut out at Pittsburgh, the Astros walked onto the Wrigley Field turf for some extra batting practice an hour after the Braves, Cubs, and spectators had departed the stadium.

The practice worked for the Houston men, as Dierker led them to an 8–2 win on August 22, the third loss in a row for the Cubs as the Mets moved up to five and a half games from the lead. There had been speculation in the Chicago media that the Cubs were fatigued, in part from Durocher's managerial style that placed the same players in the lineup nearly every day.

As Durocher was shaving and running an informal press conference in his office restroom after the game, he suggested that one of the newsmen ask the entire room full of players if any of them were tired. Everyone knew it was a loaded question, but one scribe took him up on it. After a moment of uncomfortable silence, Williams—who hadn't missed a game since 1963—was the only one to speak. "Sure, everyone's a little tired, but we've just got to keep battling," he said back, sternly. "This is as far as we've ever gone. Nobody's going to quit for a minute in this race. We'll just hang in there."

When the questions turned back to Durocher, he was asked

about the physical condition of Hundley, who was trying to recover from a variety of ailments. Hundley had not been in uniform for three days, as Gene Oliver had gone o for 4 in his place for the loss to the Astros. It would be Oliver's last appearance as a regular player; he was retiring into a coaching role for the Cubs.

"I'm no doctor," Leo said gruffly as he put on his street clothes.

"We play at 1:30," he added in one of his favorite usual quips to the media, not willing to look beyond that day's game to a "bigger" one down the road.

The manager then walked slowly out into the players' dressing area and gazed around the room. At one end sat Santo with his right foot packed in ice, the result of catching it under the tarpaulin in the ninth inning while pursuing a fly ball. Durocher looked each player in the eye and then asked for a volunteer who wanted a day off from work. There were no takers.

Everyone—including Durocher—knew that Hundley was hurting, but Hundley wasn't going to be one to complain, spend a lot of time in sick bay, or even try to catch up on his rest. In addition to his busted finger, he had also sustained an ear infection in the previous two weeks. The next morning he had nearly had enough. As Hundley told writer Rick Talley years later:

> I'm on Demerol for the pain, and they've got a wick in my ear for the infection. They had me hospitalized for four or five days. So now it's Saturday, about seven o'clock in the morning, and they give me another shot for the pain before I check out. My wife picks me up and I say, "Let's drive past the ballpark so I can at least see what's going on before we go home." Well, I walk into the clubhouse and Leo is having a meeting. As soon as I walk through the door he says, "Randy, can you play?" Well, I've got the whole ball club looking at me, so what was I supposed to say?
>
> I say, "Well, my hand feels pretty good, Skip," and before I can say anything about my ear he says, "You're in the lineup." Well, I think I felt fine. The pain medication

was keeping my finger from hurting, so I go on bloomin' national TV, for cryin' out loud, with my bloomin' hand so taped up I can hardly put the ball in it. I had no more business playing that day than anything, but I played.

Hundley was indeed in the lineup on Saturday the 24th, catching Holtzman, with eyes across the country upon the left-hander who was going after his 15th win. Hundley's courage would not allow him to escape peril, however—he caught the entire nine innings while sustaining bruises from foul tips on his neck and inner leg. In the interim, those watching on televisions across the land, as well as those 27,665 who were in the ballpark, were treated to a back-and-forth affair as the Cubs and Astros switched leads five times. Continuing to emerge as Chicago's hottest hitter in the past three weeks was Hickman, who drove two home runs out of the yard—including a grand slam—which gave him 13 for the season and gave the Cubs and Holtzman a thrilling 11–5 win. Unlike in his no-hit performance in his previous outing, Holtzman was able to log a strikeout—ten of them, as a matter of fact. "I had a horrible curve against the Braves," he admitted, "but today I had as good a curve as I've had all year." Santo (26) and Banks (17) also homered, the former pushing Santo over the century mark in RBI with a league-leading 102. Santo was also able to laugh about a defensive lapse he committed in the third inning, in which he threw to the second base bag on a double play attempt—but no one was covering. "That was our secret play," he joked. "You can call it our '5–0–3' double play" It was the first time the Cubs had scored at least five runs since August 6.

The runs continued the following day in a 10–9 decision in the first game of a doubleheader with Houston, with Regan (12–5) taking the win in relief of Jenkins and with Aguirre picking up his first save. This time it was Banks's turn to knock out two home runs, giving him 493 for his illustrious career and tying him with Yankee great Lou Gehrig for ninth on the all-time list. Hickman added yet another, his seventh since permanently taking over the starting job in right field on August 3. Durocher provided some extra entertainment for the crowd in the ninth inning as he argued with umpire Tom Gorman. Gorman had charged Leo with a visit to the mound when Kessinger went to the dugout for a drink of water during a time-out in play. The momentum was short-lived, however, as a heartbreaker was dropped in the nightcap. Houston ace Don Wilson silenced the Chicago bats again to the tune of a 3–2 Astro win in Ken Johnson's first appearance as a Cub. With a Mets victory against the Dodgers in New York, the lead stood at an even five games.

Criticism about his usage of the bench and bullpen had been leveled at Durocher since his tenure with the Cubs began. In an effort to shake things up, he and Holland had reserve catcher John Hairston called up from Tacoma on August 25 (the first day of a home series with the Reds), taking the place of Qualls on the roster, who had a badly bruised thumb and shoulder after colliding with the outfield wall in the Houston series. Two days later it would be Oscar Gamble making his Major League debut, with the Cubs—on the verge of desperation and holding on to a waning lead in the division—turning to the youngster to provide a spark. In the approaching seventy-two hours, the Cubs could feel a free fall about to begin.

It started with Hands dropping a 9–8 decision to Cincinnati's Gary Nolan on the 25th, in which a four-run rally in the ninth inning fell one run short. The following day the Reds sprinted out to a 7–1 lead and held on to win, 8–7, despite Beckert's first homer of the year and Banks's 494th of his career as he passed Gehrig. Durocher left the premises early, after being ejected by umpire Shag Crawford in the second inning. Crawford's partner Pelekoudas jumped in between the two men when he saw that fists were starting to be clenched. Crawford claimed that "Durocher kicked me on purpose," later pointing to a mark on the outside of his foot. "If he says he didn't kick me, he's a damned liar," Crawford added.

"All I did was kick dirt *on* him, and I told him right away that it was unintentional," Durocher retorted to the writers. "If he says I kicked *him*, then *he's* the damn liar. Then he draws back his fist like he's gonna hit me. I wish he had. Nobody is gonna challenge me in the middle of the diamond. I just said, 'Be my guest. I dare you. Go ahead. I'll spot you the first punch.' So now he's gonna send in his report that I kicked him, but he's a liar. I just called him a dummy. I only kicked two umpires in my life—once on purpose and once on accident, and that time I apologized. Once, I did it intentionally. That was when I kicked Jocko Conlan in Los Angeles—only he had his shin guards on, and he kicked me back. It hurt me, not him. So now Shag says I'm a liar. It's a Mexican standoff. No way I can win. You think I'm gonna win over umpires?"

Interestingly, when the incident with Conlan occurred eight years earlier, in 1961, Pelekoudas had been on Conlan's crew as well, and again, he had been the one trying to make peace between Durocher and one of his colleagues.

In losing again on the 27th, the Cubs once again spotted the Reds a large early lead. This time Holtzman was the victim, giving Cincinnati a 5–0 advantage by the fourth inning. This day marked the debut of Gamble, as the young outfielder who had shown so much promise in spring training went 1 for 3 in his first big league appearance as the starter in center field. With the team starting to sour, however, there were those in the media who were beginning to wonder whether some of the Cub players were becoming too distracted with profiteering from their recent fame. A local fan named Jack Childers had started collecting a pool of money for the players from their product endorsements and community appearances, a fund that was to be redistributed to the players at the end of the season. The fund got larger and larger as the mystique of the pennant-chasing Cubs—both locally and nationally—continued to grow. As one example (and years before the Bears would shock the music video world with the "Super Bowl Shuffle" in 1985), the Cubs that week had released a record album, which Regan claimed had produced over $12,000 for the pool in the first few days alone.

Jenkins (18-11) turned things around with his twentieth complete game as the Cubs finally snapped the losing streak in beating the Reds in the final series contest, 3–1, on August 28. It was a game in which Wrigley Field attendance for the year reached 1,502,222—an all-time record for the park with a full month left in the season.

Meanwhile, the Mets had swept a pair of three-game series from the Padres and Dodgers, leaving the first-place margin at two games.

As the Cubs traveled to Atlanta to open a series against the Braves, the team management paid for nearly a hundred Bleacher Bums to make the trip, a brief tradition that had begun two years earlier. Some of the "officers" among the Bums had believed that they would have seats on the club's chartered plane, but this rumor proved false. In Atlanta they found a new object of their enemy scorn—the mascot—in addition to Braves outfielder Rico Carty (to whom they gave a yellow construction hat for his good-natured acceptance of the usual ribbing). The Braves mascot, Chief Knock-a-Homa, had grown comfortably accustomed to normally having his teepee free from projectiles. With the Chicago visitors in attendance, however, the Chief found himself ducking inside for cover as the missiles fell down upon him in his bullpen-area home. Also in attendance at the series were observers from American League teams, as the Cubs had scouts from the junior circuit contenders following them to every city, believing that Chicago would be representing the National League in the World Series.

Events opened ominously for the Cubs, as Williams lined into his second triple play in two weeks in the first inning (the first had occurred off Joe Niekro in playing the Padres on August 13; with this more recent occurrence, Reiser was prompted to ask Durocher, "What time is my base-running drill tomorrow?"). With the score tied 1–1 in the seventh, Hickman sent yet another ball over the fence—his 17th of the year, and his tenth in the month of August—which landed just in front of the yelping Bums, part of the largest crowd to see a ball game in Atlanta on the year (36,413 paid spectators). It was a special treat for the large throng of Hickman's personal fans from his home area in Tennessee, who had made their way to Georgia for the games. "There can't be anyone left in my little hometown," Hickman said after seeing the group assemble in the stands. It was not the most enjoyable of homecomings to the South for Willie Smith, however, as Smith received permission from the club to visit his ill son in Alabama. Hands (16-11) then shut down the Brave bats for the final three innings for a 2–1 win. The Cubs had gotten their other run earlier when Kessinger had tripled off a misplay by Atlanta outfielder Tony Gonzalez and had subsequently been sent home by a Beckert sacrifice fly.

Cub wins followed on the next two days for a three-game sweep of the Braves in their home park. In the middle contest Banks hit homer number 495 for his career, which helped Ken Johnson to his first Cub victory, 5–4. "We only wanted Johnson to go six innings or so," Becker said afterward, grateful to have the veteran's seven frames of strong work. In the seventh Johnson surrendered the 547th homer of Aaron's tenure, which the hurler claimed was "the worst pitch I've ever thrown in my life." Banks maintained great respect for Aaron, predicting that the Braves slugger would ultimately pass Willie Mays for second place on the all-time homer list behind Babe Ruth's 714. Ernie also started giving his preliminary thoughts about the postseason. "The team I would least like to play is Houston," he said before the game, in reference to a possible match-up in the "National League Championship Series," a new concept for the 1969 season. "They are awfully hard for us to beat in the Astrodome." The blast off Banks's bat traveled well into the left-field stands, only one section over from where the Bleacher Bums were situated.

By the time the ninth inning rolled around, the Bums were having such a frolicking good time that one of them fell over a railing and down twenty feet to a walkway. As usual in such a circumstance, the worst injury was to his pride. Then, to make matters worse (or better), Grousl—the king of the Bums, and their president—donned a bear suit and climbed down into the Cubs bullpen, where he was "unleashed" onto Chief Knock-a-Homa by Gene Oliver as Oliver opened the gate that normally cordoned off the chief's area. Grousl, trying to run on all fours in the costume, chased the Indian all the way to third base and tackled him. After he was escorted off the field by stadium personnel, speculative stories about Grousl's final destination that night—be it jail or hospital or otherwise—were as numerous as the Bums who remained in the stands.

Twelve days after he had no-hit the Atlanta team at Wrigley Field, Holtzman (16-8) struck another blow with an 8–4 win to close the trip to the South. He hit his first Major League home run in the sixth inning off Phil Niekro, which Kenny claimed to be his biggest thrill in baseball—even bigger than the no-hitter. "As I was rounding first base and realized that I had hit a home run," Holtzman reflected, "I said to myself, 'What do I do now?' I'm used to rounding first base and going to the dugout. I didn't know what to do. . . . I was going to make sure I shook hands with [third base coach] Walker three or four times because I knew I'd never be there again."

The Bleacher Bums arrived back at O'Hare Airport in Chicago later that night (with Grousl in tow, being released by whichever Atlanta authorities had been holding him), feeling as much the conquering heroes as the players on the field. "The voices were not as strong as they were on their departure," Stephanie Fuller noticed in writing her column for the *Tribune*, "but the songs were the same. In spite of the hoarseness, there was no mistaking 'World Series, Here We Come' sung to the 'Battle Hymn of the Republic'"

They were fortunate to have arrived back home safely. That very same night, former heavyweight boxing champion Rocky Marciano and two other men were killed in a plane crash in central Iowa, near the town of Newton. The flight—having taken off from Chicago and bound for Des Moines—had asked permission from Iowa air traffic controllers to touch down at Newton. It was the last communication received from the aircraft. Marciano had been away from his Fort Lauderdale, Florida, home for a total of ten days on business and had been looking forward to returning to his family after learning that his seventeen-month-old son, Kevin, had learned to walk on his own. Later investigations could not fully conclude whether mechanical failure or pilot error caused the crash, as plenty of fuel had been found leaking from the tanks at the wreckage site. The boxer had retired thirteen years earlier as the only undefeated heavyweight champion, winning all of his forty-nine professional fights, forty-three of them by knockout. Marciano had decided on a boxing career after a post–World War II tryout as a catcher with the Cubs had failed. September was here, with football and autumn and cooler temperatures arriving. President Nixon announced that thirty-five thousand more troops would be home from Vietnam by December 15 (in addition to the thousands that had already been recalled). "The time has come to end this war," he proclaimed. September also marked the final lap of the Major League Baseball season, and the Cubs were ready to throw everything they had into their slimming defense of the National League Eastern Division lead:

National League East	W	L	Pct.	GB
Chicago	83	52	.615	—
New York	76	54	.585	4.5
Pittsburgh	70	60	.538	10.5
St. Louis	71	62	.534	11
Philadelphia	52	78	.400	28.5

Was it permissible for Chicagoans to start getting World Series fever? If any man knew for sure, it was the ancient Pat Pieper, the public address announcer at Wrigley for over fifty years who had seen virtually every Cubs home game since 1906. His answer? Not yet. "I've seen too many things happen in this game," he cautioned. "You wouldn't believe it, but in the 1918 World Series between the Cubs and Red Sox—the home games that year were played in Comiskey Park because of the small seating capacity out here—I saw Babe Ruth lifted for a pinch hitter. You never know what can happen in baseball."

9

Collapse

It breaks your heart. It is designed
to break your heart. The game begins in the spring when everything
else begins again, and it blossoms
in the summer, filling the afternoons and evenings, and then as
soon as the chill rains come, it
stops and leaves you to face the
fall alone.

—A. Bartlett Giamatti

Two first-place teams strengthened and weakened their positions simultaneously on September 1—even while the game they
were to play against each other was rained out. The Cubs were
in Cincinnati to take on the Reds, and the Western Division was
taken over by a half-game by the Giants because San Francisco
had beaten Montreal. Chicago, meanwhile, stretched its lead to
five games with a Mets loss at home to the Dodgers. Entering
September the Cub regulars had maintained strong offensive

statistics, including those of Beckert (.310 average, 1 home run, 34 RBI), Santo (.294, 27 home runs, 110 RBI), Williams (.293, 15 home runs, 81 RBI), Kessinger (.287, 3 home runs, 54 RBI), and Hundley (.276, 16 home runs, 60 RBI). Banks (.262, 21 home runs, 92 RBI) had seen his average dip in the past two months, but he continued to be among the league leaders in homers and RBI. And Hickman, with his brilliant month of August, had solidified himself in the right-field slot.

On September 2 Gene Oliver was officially taken off the active player list and named an assistant coach. The Cubs took two games from Cincinnati that day—the first of which was the completion of the rain-shortened game from earlier in the year, 5–2, and the regularly scheduled contest that wound up a complete-game victory for Jenkins, 8–2. In the nightcap Kessinger pounded out his fourth homer of the year—twice as many as Don's total in his first four years in the Major Leagues combined—and he nearly missed another, doubling high off the center-field wall. After missing the next game of the series due to a military obligation in Chicago, Kessinger returned to the Cubs in Cincinnati for the rained-out makeup from September 1. Santo was sent back to Chicago as well, but Ronnie's trip was for examination of his sore knee by Dr. Clinton Compere; Popovich manned third base in his absence. The troops were held to two hits by Jim Maloney, as the Reds took the rescheduled game 2–0 with Hands (16-12) being the victim. Hands had stood with Maloney for half the game when speedy Reds outfielder Bobby Tolan—just acquired before the season from the Cardinals—beat out his 20th bunt hit of the season in the fourth inning to start the game's only scoring sequence. Already with 174 hits on the season, he was projected by some to be the next superstar outfielder in the National League. "When I told Bobby he was going to be a regular," Bristol mentioned to Earl Lawson of *The Sporting News*, "one of the first things he did was practice his bunting in the batting cage." Tolan was relishing the opportunity to play every day, as a crowded Cardinal outfield of Brock, Flood, and Roger Maris had limited his time over the past two seasons.

Despite losing the finale the Cubs had been a strong 13-5 in their last eighteen road games, a promising thought for coming home for a series against Pittsburgh that would begin on Friday, September 5, the beginning of the Labor Day weekend. This interlude at Wrigley would precede another trip out of town, as afterward the club would head east to Shea Stadium to face the Mets. With an off day on Thursday scheduled before the Pirates came to town, Jenkins and Williams took advantage of the free time to enjoy a restful fishing trip in Indiana.

The pitcher and the outfielder happily flung their lines into the lake, not appearing to have a care in the world. Their team stood with a record of 84-53—at thirty-one games above .500, their high-water mark on the year, save for when they stood 77-45 after Holtzman's no-hitter on August 19. The incoming Pirates were hardly a threat at ten and a half games back, while defending league champion St. Louis had dropped to fourth and was fading quickly. "The Cardinals are dead," proclaimed Markus, presumably trying to anchor the Eastern chase as a two-dog fight. "Make no mistake about that, they are as dead as a doornail—than which, once said Mr. Charles Dickens, there is nothing deader."

But Markus surprisingly continued to boldly comment on the other team left over. "And the Mets, though still kicking, are measured for the grave."

The Cubs' magic number was down to twenty-three, and the Mets peered at them from behind at a five-game distance.

Things started badly for Holtzman against Pittsburgh and quickly got worse. He was touched for a home run by opposing pitcher Steve Blass, who went the distance in allowing four hits—all of them to Billy Williams, which included two doubles and two solo home runs—for an easy 9–2 Pirate win, while Seaver won his 20th in the Mets' 5–1 victory over the Phillies (McAndrew lost the nightcap of a doubleheader that day for New York). Blass equaled Williams by knocking four hits himself off of Holtzman and his followers, as the left-hander (now 16-9) had given way to Abernathy in the sixth. The Pirate pitcher went for his fifth hit as he came to the plate in the ninth but was foiled as Don Nottebart struck him out. Just before Blass had fanned—when the Cubs had finished their eighth turn at bat—most of the 10,411 spectators at Wrigley Field had surrendered and left for home. "Nothing like that had been seen in weeks in the noise factory at Clark and Addison Streets," Prell noticed. Before the game Santo had been instructed by doctors to rest his knee for an additional day, leaving the Cubs with less offensive pop than normal.

When Jenkins went for his 20th win the next day, the 24,556 paying customers were joined by 3,000 Boy Scouts admitted at no cost. With the weak performance of the home club, Dozer found it ironic that those youngsters' promise was "On my honor, I will do my best . . ." The Cubs played like a beaten team, enduring a Pirate onslaught set in motion by a fly ball that Young and Hickman allowed to drop untouched in right-center. Jenkins was run out of the yard in the third inning, permitting six runs on eight hits. Nottebart, Nye, Abernathy, Aguirre, and Regan would mop up the mess in a 13–4 rout seen on national television, as the Mets moved to within three and a half games on the shoulders of Cardwell's six-hit shutout of Philadelphia, aided by the Met bullpen. To make matters worse for Jenkins, he learned that he was being sued for $30,000 in damages from an auto accident he had sustained in Lima, Ohio, as a Minor Leaguer five years earlier. At the time he had failed to appear in court to address the charges against him, and the judgment had been made in favor of the plaintiff.

Jenkins was visibly upset in the dugout, frustrated by the poor defensive play in the outfield. He then left the stadium early, an act for which Durocher would berate him. "It was actually meant for all of us," said one member of the team the next day, in reference to the lecture. When word of the tongue-lashing reached the press, it was implied that Durocher had thought of Jenkins as a "quitter." Jenkins was polite but adamant in his response. "I admit that I lost a little concentration," he said, "but I never quit on this club. . . . He's [Durocher's] got a right to handle the situation his own way. I know what my job is, and I'm not going to say anything. I want my five more starts."

With their empire seeming to suddenly crumble around them, the Cubs lost to the Pirates again, 7–5, in eleven innings, the first time all year that Chicago had been swept in a series at home. The "Friendly Confines" were suspect as the Cubs were 3-10 in their last thirteen home games. A home run by Stargell with two out in the ninth had tied the game at five, and the Pirates went on to score a couple of unearned runs two innings later, as several more mistakes—from missed signs to missed bunts to missed batted balls in the field—plagued the Cubs once again. "You could hear a pin drop as we walked into the clubhouse," Santo remembered about that day. "Everyone's head was down. Nobody said a word. Our usual routine of staying around and talking about the game was abandoned; we got out of there as quickly as possible."

It was now obvious that the race in the National League East would be a fierce struggle through the last month of the schedule and that a letup in intensity could not be permitted. "The last twenty games of the season are the toughest and longest in the world when the big prize is in sight," claimed Pirates coach Alex Grammas about the Cubs' situation. With another Met victory against the Phillies, the lead was down to two and a half games on September 8 as the Cubs prepared for a crucial two-game trip to New York. The red-hot Pittsburgh club had actually played its way back into the pennant race—albeit mathematically—as they themselves now stood only seven and a half from the top.

But even though the team's lead had shrunk in recent days, most of the Cub fans' enthusiasm had not. Across the street from Wrigley's home plate, at the CubbyBear Lounge, bartender Richard Hiller counted 175 times that "Hey Hey, Holy Mackerel" was played on the jukebox. "That's no exaggeration," he stressed. "People are coming in from Indiana, Iowa, Wisconsin—all over, and we can't keep enough Cub bumper stickers and decals on hand to supply them."

Tensions were rising. The Cub players, thriving on camaraderie and kinship the entire season, were nearly at one another's throats as they entered New York. One writer told of a story in which Aguirre stood up on the back of the team bus as it arrived at the hotel from the airport, threw his wallet on the floor, and screamed, "*You guys don't have the guts to pick up the money! This team isn't going to win! I've played with winners! You guys aren't winners!*" No one wanted to talk to the media; Durocher was close to banishing reporters in the clubhouse altogether, and he had only recently refused to allow photographers and tape recorders in the locker room. When a New York writer approached Oliver and asked when press privileges would be reinstated, the former catcher said, "Never."

Cleon Jones, while maintaining his second-place position in National League hitting with a .348 average, had recently missed several games due to a bruised hand. He would sit out the opener against Chicago but hoped to return in game two.

"The pressure is still all on the Cubs," Clendenon said. "This club has learned winning ways, and will stay close to Chicago. They know if they fall, we will be right there." Clendenon, taking over much of the first base duty for New York in the absence of the injured Ed Kranepool, had been one of the hottest batters in the game while producing nearly a .500 clip in the previous two weeks.

"We're too young to know what pressure is," added Mets shortstop Bud Harrelson, speaking to *The Sporting News*.

"I figure somebody has to have one good slump," proposed New York relief pitcher Frank "Tug" McGraw, "and the Cubs haven't had theirs yet." In addition to making a few key starts earlier in the season (including a complete-game win against the Cubs back on May 4 at Wrigley Field), the left-handed McGraw had won seven and saved ten more for his team, becoming New York's main force out of the bullpen.

The *Tribune* reported that twenty-seven different writers from seven states were in the press box for the big game, which started fifteen minutes late due to wet grounds. There were five thousand free attendees among the forty-three thousand fans at the park, the result of a local milk company offering folks free tickets back at the beginning of the year, before pennant implications could have been imagined for this fateful night. Pitching for New York was the team's deft left-hander Koosman, a twenty-six-year-old with two All-Star appearances in his first two seasons in the big leagues. He fought with Hands to a 2–2 tie into the bottom of the sixth inning; it was at this point that the Cubs' quest for the pennant looked ready to unravel.

Agee, who earlier in the third had barely homered over the left-field wall to give the Mets a 2–0 lead, had led off the inning with a double. He had lined a ball into the gap in left-center, and the tall grass had caused Williams to change his route to the ball and given Agee an opportunity for the extra base. He was followed to the plate by third baseman Garrett, who lined a single to Hickman in right field. The former Met fielded the ball cleanly on two hops and fired a perfect strike to Hundley at the plate after Agee had rounded third. Hundley grabbed the ball in plenty of time, whirled his mitt toward Agee, and then checked to see if Garrett would try to advance to second on the throw. Instantly, the catcher knew that something was wrong.

"I tagged him so hard, I almost dropped the ball. . . . The ball was rolling up from the pocket of my mitt to the webbing," Hundley later said. "That's when I felt so relieved that I turned toward the runner at first. Then, I turned around to toss the ball to Hands, and all of a sudden I heard this tremendous roar go up from the crowd. I guess that's when my quick, analytical mind told me something was wrong." Rookie umpire Dave Davidson had called Agee safe, which caused Hundley to jump up and down in protest, his head whipping from side to side in an attempt to control his anger. Durocher, of course, blitzed out of the dugout as he and his catcher struggled with each other to get closest to Davidson's face. The run stood—and it was the deciding run—as Koosman dominated the rest of way, logging 13 strikeouts in bringing his Mets within one and a half games from the top. In addition, Santo was banged up again—this time, after being hit by a pitch from Koosman on the forearm in the second inning.

Back in Wrigleyville, resident Wayne Pries walked out of Ray's Tavern and muttered to himself, "There's no joy in Bumville tonight."

Years later, Agee—the former American League Rookie of the Year with the White Sox in 1966—admitted to Beckert, "You guys had me."

Durocher figured that something drastic had to be done to thwart the New York assault, so he summoned Jenkins on only two days' rest to go toe-to-toe with Seaver the following night. It could be argued that the reason for the move was twofold: obviously, the team needed to place its best pitcher on the mound in this game, but Leo also saw a chance to reestablish trust and confidence in Jenkins after their spat just forty-eight hours earlier. To make things right in Jenkins's world, all the big right-hander wanted was the ball—and he got it. Dozer pointed out that Jenkins might have some extra motivation in this game, as Seaver had beaten him as the first Major Leaguer to reach the 20-win mark a week earlier. Nonetheless, the bad omens were all around, and one in particular of a four-legged variety was looking to place a hex on the visitors.

As the Cubs were getting ready to hit the first inning, a black cat sneaked onto the field and trotted menacingly toward the Chicago bench. Santo peered nervously over his shoulder at the intruder from the on-deck circle, as the feline appeared to have business with the rest of the Chicago men. The cat stopped at the edge of the dugout, a few feet in front of Durocher, and stared right into the eyes of the manager. It is hard to say who was more spooked; Leo twitched nervously as he got up and moved, and the cat darted across the home plate area toward safety on the Mets' side of the field and disappeared through the wall as quickly as it had arrived.

The Mets got to Jenkins right away as Agee led off their first inning with a walk, and a free pass soon followed to Jones, who was back in the lineup after his injury. Boswell then laced a double to right that scored both of them, and Hodges's troops were off and running. Clendenon homered in the third to double the margin to 4–0, and the Mets never looked back. After Seaver had retired the first ten batters, Santo singled home Beckert in the fourth to get the Cubs on the board, but the apple of New York's eye once again prevented Jenkins from getting to the 20-win mark. "Tom Terrific" went the distance just as his teammate Koosman had done the night before, beating the Cubs, 7–1, for his sixth straight win and the 53rd in his career with the Mets, which had not yet reached three full years. He performed the feat in front of over fifty-eight thousand cramped fans in Shea Stadium, most of whom had been waving celebratory handkerchiefs at each piece of Met success during the evening and who sent the Cubs packing with strains of a "Good-bye, Leo" song. Even when the Cubs fell further behind in the middle of the game, Jenkins wanted to take matters into his own hands, and he was not afraid to let his manager know it. "Before I went to the plate to hit in the fifth," he would recall, "Leo asked how I felt. I said 'fine' and he said, 'Go ahead.' If there had been anybody on base he probably would have hit for me, though."

It was the sixth loss in a row for the Cubs, their longest losing streak of the season. Some thought that the cat had indeed caused some mischief for the Cubs, for in an unlucky trifecta, the game was Jenkins's 13th loss to the season, caused in part by the 13th homers of the season by Clendenon and Met outfielder Art Shamsky.

The New York players were greeted in the locker room by the team's owner and founder, Joan Payson, who was as excited as any fan could be. She reached out to embrace her field general, Hodges, the son of a coal miner from Princeton, Indiana, who was keeping a lucky stuffed rabbit on his office desk. "I'm so happy—so thrilled—that I can hardly stand it," she blurted out. "This is just so wonderful. I never dreamed we'd be so good so soon. Can I kiss you???" She made her way around the room, shaking hands with all the happy players.

The Cubs' lead was now held by a fraying thread, the slimmest of all differences, at a half-game. They were now actually *behind* the Mets in the loss column, 58 to 57. A consolation for Fergie was that his nine strikeouts upped his season total to 250, a figure that continued to outdistance the rest of the league.

Even though it was time to head out of town, Holtzman still was furious with the Mets—especially their starting pitchers, whom he felt were throwing too far inside with no reprimands from the umpires and then boasting about it to the papers. "Koosman and Seaver are good pitchers," the Cubs left-hander told Murray Chass of the *New York Times*, "but they act like they run the league. They think they can intimidate our guys. But they're not the only guys in the league who can throw hard at somebody." He then issued a clear warning to the Mets: "I'll say one thing. If it's this close when they come into Chicago, I better not hear anyone popping off. I can speak for Fergie and Hands, too. If they start coming close to our big hitters in Chicago, their whole team had better watch out."

With the team facing a must-win situation in Philadelphia, however, it was the Cubs who were intimidated. Holtzman (16-10) and his teammates were humiliated in a three-single shutout by Rick Wise, a young right-hander enjoying a breakout year after first appearing in the Major Leagues as an eighteen-year-old in 1964. Dick Allen had since returned to the Phillies lineup after his "disappearance," with George Myatt now running the team in place of Skinner. Just over four thousand fans were present in Philadelphia—the second-smallest crowd to watch a Cubs game in any park on the season—and one observer noticed that the foul balls were "banging off the seats" in empty, old Connie Mack Stadium. "Philadelphia fans no longer come to ball games except as curiosity seeker," Dozer wrote, "or perhaps to boo the hated Richie Allen."

The Mets were in the process of sweeping a doubleheader from the Expos in New York. As news of the Cubs loss hit the stadium in Flushing Meadows, fists were clenched high in the air and shouts were heard on the Long Island Expressway—the Mets were in first place. The large scoreboard showed the new standings of the first two clubs in the National League East, above which a caption read "Look Who's No. 1" for all to see. "Paper fluttered from everywhere," reported Condon, covering the scene that Chicago fans had long feared they would witness. "Shea Stadium looked as if it had been hit by a snowstorm. . . . Old-timers said they had not seen anything like it since Lindy [Charles Lindbergh] was paraded through Manhattan. . . . This had to be the Mets' finest hour." People around New York were getting accustomed once again to having a team other than the Yankees in a pennant race. It was the Metropolitans, a group restoring hope to National League fans in the Big Apple. It was an ascension for the young team that took eight years in the making and was confirmed by the standings in the newspapers the morning of September 11:

National League East	W	L	Pct.	GB
New York	84	57	.596	—
Chicago	84	59	.587	1
St. Louis	77	65	.542	7.5
Pittsburgh	75	64	.540	8
Philadelphia	56	84	.400	27.5
Montreal	44	99	.308	41

That same night in the American League, in which ho-hum divisional races had Minnesota leading the West by nine games and Baltimore the East by fifteen, the Kansas City Royals used a Major League–record twenty-seven players in a nine-inning game. The Royals were sparing no expense in their search for talent; their owner, Ewing Kauffman, soon after announced that he was spending $3 million to open a "baseball academy" in Florida, a facility designed to identify and train players specifically for the Kansas City organization. It was part of Kaufman's timeline to bring a pennant to the city within five years.

Still looming ahead for the Mets were nine presumably tough games with the resurgent Pirates, who were intent on remaining a factor in the race.

The Cubs were out of the top spot for the first time all year, and there was no denying the fact that the club was exhausted—physically, mentally, and spiritually. The defensive lapses that had transpired over the previous few weeks (stemming more from mental than physical breakdowns) continued the next evening, as the hapless Phillies beat them once again, 4–3, with Selma this time causing the implosion. He allowed the score to be tied at one in the third inning when he threw to an empty third base on a pickoff play. "The best part was Leo," Beckert said years later in recollection of the scene the followed. "Those old dugouts in Philly were very small, and had tin roofs. Well, when that ball went over third base, Leo jumped up and hit his head on the roof." After the Cubs leaped back ahead on Banks's 22nd home run (Ernie had just snapped an o-for-22 streak the night before), Selma permitted doubles to Tony Taylor and Johnny Briggs, which preceded a long homer by Allen that sank the Cubs into an irreversible deficit. Immediately, many questioned why Durocher had chosen to pitch to Allen with first base open. The victorious Phillies pitcher was another unheralded hurler named Jeff James, a second-year man making his first start of the year.

Unable to face his manager afterward, Selma hid from Leo outside the locker room, peeking out from under a pile of clothes. "Durocher went nuts," Santo recalled. "Selma was so afraid of what Leo might do, he wouldn't go into the clubhouse after the game." Later Selma was found weeping in a broom closet in an obscure section underneath the old Philly ballpark. "Now in full retreat and losing confidence daily," moaned Dozer, "the Chicago Cubs were chased out of Connie Mack Stadium tonight with a 4 to 3 defeat, and first place suddenly looking for all the world like a small dot way out there on the baseball horizon." It was the longest losing streak for the North Siders in two years, and it was coming at precisely the wrong moment.

The Cubs' retreat continued as the Mets marched on, winning their seventh in a row on the right arm of Gentry, who spun a six-hit shutout of the Expos. Refusing to defer superiority, Condon still wasn't impressed. "Hodges isn't about to win a pennant unless baseball is sicker than we believe," he wrote. "The New York Mets are a gutsy ball club, and they have responded to great leadership, but they lack the real great players. Tom Seaver, the young pitcher who hurls aspirins, is the only Met who appears to have a reservation on the train to the Hall of Fame. The rest are a bunch of journeymen." This statement, it could be argued, summed up a lot of the recent frustration of Chicago media, fans, and even Cub players: that the Cubs obviously had more talent than the team they were now chasing.

Earlier in the week a fan had sent an anonymous letter to Beckert, with the writer claiming that he was going to have the FBI sent to Wrigley Field to investigate the Cubs' sudden free fall. Some players on the team were starting to have autographs mailed back to them, mementos that had earlier been sent out to previously grateful fans.

The Cubs limped into St. Louis with the ex-champion Cardinals swarming around the enemy like angry hornets, looking for revenge on one of the clubs that was going to preclude them from repeating as National League pennant winners. Hands rose to the occasion and tried desperately to reverse the direction of his club with a 5-1 victory. He scored the deciding run in the eighth inning, compliments of a Beckert single that snapped a one-all tie. Beckert's ball had been bobbled by Brock in left field, which allowed Hands—not normally accustomed to running to the bases—to head for home. Crediting "the cooler weather," Banks drove in the other four tallies for the Cubs, bringing him a total of 98 for the season and 1,578 for his career. The Chicago players recognized the efforts of their pitcher, presenting him with the game ball after the final out.

"It has been Hands," Dozer credited, "more often than anyone else, who has stepped in when the Cubs needed it most this year." He pointed out that Hands was the one who stopped the pair of five-game losing streaks during the season, as well as the most recent disaster.

The Cubs could feel the power of the demoralizing Mets even from far away. Although Chicago finally broke the drought, the Mets had gained ground once again in sweeping a doubleheader from the Pirates by the minimum score possible, 1–0 and 1–0. In learning of the games, the most frustrating news for Cub followers was that Cardwell and Koosman—the two starting pitchers for New York—drove in the lone runs, running the team's current streaks to three straight shutouts and nine straight wins. It was symbolic of a team on the rise, a team of destiny, for—as had happened for the Cubs so many times earlier in the summer—the Mets were now riding a wave of immense fortune.

Before the Cubs took the field in St. Louis, Durocher attempted another lecture to focus his club on the task at hand. This one was less fire-and-brimstone and more matter-of-fact in tone. In addition to laying down some new guidelines (which included the removal of all nonclub personnel from the Wrigley Field locker room an hour before game time after the team returned to Chicago), he also wanted to make clear his intentions of dealing with the press, for his policies appeared to be confusing the players. "They [the press] have had to ask you questions in the last 30 days that I should have been answering," he confessed to them. As part of the new clubhouse rules that Durocher was setting, card playing would be forbidden as the team bus arrived at the ballpark on the road and an hour before the start of any remaining home contests. Even Leo himself would abide by this mandate. Since his days of riding the trains with Dizzy Dean, Frankie Frisch, Pepper Martin, and the rest of the Gas House Gang Cardinals, Durocher loved to pull out the deck for a game of hearts. As manager of the Cubs, he often played with various people in the locker room while batting practice was occurring on the field. Beginning with the first game in St. Louis on this trip, however, Durocher was on the field for the entire pregame regimen, observing the players and suggesting what could be done to improve performance. The players tried to remain positive about their dealings with the Mets in the standings. "All we have to do is stay within two games of them," Hundley reminded everybody, "because we play them twice at the end of the season."

But while all the self-discipline may have improved the Cubs' perspective, the players could do nothing to check the advance of the Mets. Seaver (22-7) made it ten in a row for the Mets the next day, as the New York pitchers were approaching invincibility. Conversely, something smelled afoul in St. Louis. While the odor was later discovered to be wafting over from a chemical plant across the river in East St. Louis, Illinois, many thought it was the fading play of the Illinoisans that stank. Despite the first Busch Stadium homers for the Cubs on the year by Hickman and Hundley, the team blew an eighth-inning lead as the Cardinals came back to score four runs and beat Jenkins, 7–4, who failed once again to reach 20 wins. Before Regan permitted the go-ahead runs on a Cardinal hit that the tired Beckert would have reached earlier in the season, Jenkins was showing more signs of frustration as he jawed at the home plate umpire while leaving the barrage in the eighth.

Holtzman pitched valiantly the next night, on September 14, but fell to Gibson in ten innings, 2–1. The deciding tally came when Brock, the object of Bleacher Bum scorn earlier in the season, launched a long home run to right field. It was Brock's first homer in nearly two months, but it made the difference as the Cubs had now scored a grand total of four runs in four Holtzman starts against the Cardinals for the year. "It was a high curve inside, and I just wanted to show it to him," Holtzman said of his fateful pitch to Brock, perhaps his only mistake of the game. "I was going to come back and challenge him with a fastball on the next pitch." Meanwhile, the Pirates had finally cooled off the Mets with a 5–3 win in Pittsburgh, as Blass beat Nolan Ryan. But with another Cub defeat in St. Louis, the Mets now led by three and a half games.

The Chicago collapse appeared complete, and Hodges stood with the hammer ready over the final nail. On September 15 even 19 strikeouts from Steve Carlton—the most ever by a pitcher in a National League game to that time—was not enough to stop the Mets, as the marauding New Yorkers got back on track with a 4–3 win over the Cardinals behind two home runs by Ron Swoboda. That night in Montreal, after the Expos had already lost their one-hundredth game of season, the Cubs sagged to another defeat, 8–2, their eleventh setback in twelve games. They were stymied on three hits by Mike Wegener, the rookie pitcher who had not won a game in almost nine weeks. The Montreal batters deposited the ball in all corners of Jarry Park off of Selma, Aguirre, Abernathy, and Nye, opening a 7–1 lead before the fifth inning was complete. For the first time since the recent plunge began, Langford noticed, there were no "We'll get 'em tomorrows" in the locker room afterward. Confidence was gone, nerves were frayed, and hope had sunk.

Pure logic might have suggested that lightning could not have struck more quickly, for in the thirteen days from September 3 to 15, the Cubs went from having a five-game lead to a four-and-a-half-game deficit.

Perhaps the most telling sign of wear was on the tired body of Kessinger, who amazingly by the middle of September had played in every inning of every game on the year—all while also performing his military obligations, usually in far-off cities, on each off day that the rest of the team was enjoying. His weight was down to 155 pounds—20 pounds less than where he had started the season—and his uniform hung on him like drapes as the final weeks approached.

§

"It was like the old days yesterday in Wrigley Field," Langford commented upon the team's return to the home park on September 17 to play the Phillies. "Not necessarily the good days—just the old days." He was referring to the sad emptiness of the beautiful yard, occupied by only 6,062 fans in a clear statement of disappointment and loss of faith in the team.

"In the old days, the Cubs always struggled," Langford continued. "They're supposed to be above that sort of thing now, but for the past two weeks everything has demanded a maximum effort of them, yesterday's nine to seven victory over the Philadelphia Phillies being no exception. . . . You could stretch out over two or three empty chairs because—like in the old days—there were plenty of them." Jenkins finally got his 20th win, Banks got his 100th RBI, and Nye his 3rd save, but the Mets also got their 12th win in their last thirteen outings and maintained a four-game advantage. After treading water for a day, Chicago slipped to five games behind New York, as another shutout for Seaver was combined with a 5-3 Cub loss to the Phillies. The Mets were loose and carefree and confident, evidenced by their other young right-hander Nolan Ryan. Ryan was found walking around the clubhouse that day with a big cigar in his mouth, looking for a light. When a teammate offered one, Ryan bit down on the rubber toy and shot a stream of water into the unwitting helper's face. Adding to the fun, Seaver—upon returning from the shower—had his street clothes vanish from his locker courtesy of Swoboda as a sarcastic "thanks" for pitching the Mets to victory.

Willing to try anything to reverse the fortunes of his own club, Durocher gave the ball to George Decker—a young Californian who insisted that everyone call him "Joe"—as the pitcher started in his Major League debut. Even fewer paying customers (5,796) wandered in on this day, but the total inched past the previous day's mark as 2,500 women admitted at no cost provided a little boost (not surprisingly, it was the smallest Ladies' Day attendance for the year). Decker provided a solid effort, allowing only two runs over six innings of work, as Popovich finally gave Kessinger a day off at shortstop. The bullpen failed the young hurler, however—a circumstance that had become more and more common in the past couple of months for the Cubs. Regan entered in the eighth in relief of Nye, after the left-hander had surrendered the go-ahead home run to Cookie Rojas. It was another flat performance for the Chicagoans in a crucial game against a less-than-average club—everyone knew that merely trading a win for a loss every other day would leave the team in the Mets' wake.

It was now New York that was the following the magic number to the title—their number was now in single figures, down to eight. In their past nine games the overwhelming New York pitching staff had given up a total of 11 runs and had a streak of nineteen straight games of not surrendering a home run. "They've hauled out all the old clichés and exhausted the supply of adjectives describing the derring-do of the Miracle Mets this year," wrote Jack Lang of *The Sporting News*, "but they may have to come up with some new ones before the frenzied National League East race is over." As incredible as the turn of events had been, an even more compelling sprint to the finish was being maintained in the West, with the Giants ahead of both the Dodgers and the Braves by half a game, and the Reds a mere two games back. San Francisco was relying on its cast of veterans, led by the great one, Mays, who was taking it one day at a time with his painful, injured, thirty-eight-year-old body. "There are only a few games left," he said, doing his best to ignore the discomfort that he endured daily. "We have a chance to win this race. I want to help as much as possible." Less than a week later Mays would strike the 600th home run of his career, second only to Babe Ruth at the time.

Rumors were circulating that Durocher—currently under contract through the 1970 season—would resign if the Cubs didn't overtake the Mets. "That doesn't sound like Leo to me,"

Phil Wrigley answered, in a strong show of support for his field manager. "He's done a great job however we finish, and you can bet he'll be back next season." It was announced that Pete Reiser was retiring from coaching and going back to his home in California (and by the end of the regular season, Rod Carew of the Twins would tie Reiser's Major League record of stealing home seven times in one year). Becker was next, wishing to submit a letter of resignation, but Leo did not accept it. Walker, Franks, Amalfitano, and Gene Oliver, meanwhile, planned to return as assistants for Durocher in 1970.

As he spoke to reporters Durocher was surprisingly cool and to the point. "We've just got to challenge them tomorrow," he said as he previewed the motivational strategy that he and his coaching staff would take. "Go like hell. It's far from over. It won't be over until somebody wins it. We're not going to give up, I'll tell you that. . . . Billy Williams has been playing a month with a bad back, Randy Hundley has been catching with a bruised hand, and Ron Santo's been playing even though he's banged up. Not a one of them has been complaining. We'll come out of it." For the first time in what seemed like months, the news reporters— sensing the stress that the man was enduring—gave Leo a genuine "thank you" for his time as they left his office.

Disappointment and disinterest on the part of Cub fans turned into rage and fury the next day, September 19, as the Cardinals came to Wrigley for a doubleheader. "Spectators showed the fight which they feel, perhaps, the Cubs no longer have," opined Dozer. In the opener Holtzman had exacted revenge on Gibson for the loss of five days earlier, as once again the two pitchers battled to a 2–1 outcome in ten innings, with the Cubs left-hander the victor this time around. Lou Brock was once again involved in controversy with the Bleacher Bums in left field while Hickman batted with two out in the tenth. Williams stood at second with the winning run, as Hickman drove a ball high to the wall in left. When a fan reached down to grab the ball, it bounced back into the field of play as third base umpire Steve Landes called the play a ground-rule double, which permitted Williams to score and end the game. Once again Brock was furious with the fans. "There is no doubt I would have caught the ball," he later claimed. Gibson had been incredibly wild on the day, walking eight men. All of a sudden, momentum seemed to have shifted back to the North Siders, who also celebrated Banks's career hit number 2,500, which came in the fifth inning.

But in the nightcap, a 2–2 tie that Selma had carried into the sixth inning could not be held by the bullpen. It was the seventh straight start that Selma had not been able to complete, while Colborn, Aguirre, Nye, and Abernathy each permitted runs that resulted in a 7–2 St. Louis decision that provided a split on the day. The Mets got swept in a twin bill by the Pirates, so only a negligible half-game advance was achieved by Chicago on a day that could otherwise have reversed the direction of the Cubs.

Though an improvement from the previous days' crowds, the park that day was not quite half-full (15,376). Nonetheless, a portion of the Wrigley gathering turned into an angry mob. Projectiles were launched onto the field, a Bleacher Bum sprinted out to second base after scaling down the ivy in right field, and even fistfights were breaking out in isolated sections of the stands. "The wind was sour with the smell of spilled beer and a highly-vocal minority of patrons in the box seats [who] were venting their stored anger and frustrations built over the last three weeks on a down and beaten team," Langford wrote, describing the ugly events unfolding below his view in the press box. Severe name-calling had erupted as the most frequent choice of protest, fired in the direction of the Cubs dugout in a barrage full of highly personal, vulgar remarks that were also within earshot of the players' families nearby.

"It was hard to accept the argument that a fan pays for his seat and can utter anything he wished," an obviously disturbed Langford continued in reflecting on the previous day's events. "If he had shouted those epithets anywhere but in Wrigley Field, he would be arrested this morning in either a jail or a hospital."

The Mets, appearing vulnerable, were beaten for the third time in a row by the Pirates as Pittsburgh's twenty-one-year-old Bob Moose threw a no-hitter. The feat—the first no-hit game for a Pirate pitcher in ten years—was saved by Roberto Clemente, who made a leaping grab at the wall off the bat of Garrett in the sixth inning. The recent reeling of the New York club issued some flickering, last-minute hope to the Cubs, presenting a Battle-of-the-Bulge mentality for Chicago with the opportunity for one last fight. But whereas the Cubs had been finding ways to win in May and June, they were now finding ways to lose. Carrying a 1–0 lead into the eighth on Hickman's 21st homer and the superb pitching of Hands, a pair of errors by Santo (his 27th on the year) and Beckert (his 24th) opened the door for the Cardinals to score four runs. Mudcat Grant finished things off for the starter Carlton, and the Cubs, mired in their own inability to seize the opportunity, lost again to remain four games behind the Mets. New York had ten games left to play, and the Cubs had eight.

The Cubs officially prevented the Cardinals from repeating as National League Champions in the series finale, with Jenkins winning his 21st game, 4–3, over Chuck Taylor on September 21. Still looking for answers, Durocher had switched the batting order, moving Santo from fourth to sixth for the first time in Leo's tenure. Hickman, without question the team's best hitter for the previous six weeks, was rewarded with the clean-up spot. Leo had wanted the services of Qualls in center field, as Young was fading; Qualls, however, was done for the year with a dislocated shoulder. Another change to the lineup had been Popovich at shortstop, as Kessinger had rested for the past few games since his remarkable consecutive-innings streak from the start of the year. "Kessinger still doesn't admit he is out of gas," wrote Dozer, "but he says it with his eyes. And what he does make clear is the fact that he's in Popovich's corner all the way, crediting him with a 'Great job' these last few games. How does it feel to be a witness instead of a participant? 'It's all right with me as long as we win,' answered Kessinger."

The whole team, though still physically and mentally fatigued, hadn't lost its spirit. "We ain't dead yet," Durocher proclaimed. "I still remember the '51 Giants [whom Durocher managed], who were five games behind the Dodgers with eight to play. We won the last eight for tie, and won the pennant in the playoff. . . . It's not over. Somebody's got to come in here and tell me it's over be-fore I'll accept it." After their recent bout with anger, the crowds had now come back to Wrigley, with the 28,287 in attendance on September 21 setting a Chicago baseball record for a season. A total of 1,649,612 spectators had seen them play at Clark and Addison during the summer of '69, snapping the city mark set by the White Sox at Comiskey Park in 1959. Good news had to be salvaged where it could, for the Mets had righted themselves and swept a doubleheader from the Pirates behind Koosman and Cardwell, pushing the team to a four-and-a-half game lead at the end of the day despite the Cub win.

The Cardinals were now going to New York, and the Montreal Expos were headed to Wrigley Field—two series that had the po-tential of ending the National League East race.

Before Montreal arrived the Cubs had an off day on the 22nd, a refreshment desperately needed because no open date had ap-peared in the schedule for almost three weeks. However, Duro-cher revealed that a practice would have been scheduled for the open date if the team had lost the day before.

As the Cubs napped and nursed injuries in Chicago, the Mets reduced their magic number to three with Seaver's 24th triumph (and 9th in a row for him), a 3–1 cruise past the Cardinals.

It is quite evident in sports when the defining moment suggests that a team is beaten—beaten in a game or in a season. It can be argued that it occurred for the 1969 Chicago Cubs in the late afternoon of September 23, as the Expos—losers of 104 games on the year, their first in existence—handed the powerful Cubs a 7–3 loss at the Friendly Confines of Wrigley Field. Holtzman had started the game, and in all probability it would be his final start of the season; he was seeking to join Jenkins in the ranks of 20-game winners on the club. But even with a personal stake in the issue, he was uninspired. The left-hander, who had charmed the home crowds for most of the season culminating with the no-hitter in August, left to the scant "boos" of the slightly more than three thousand fans who bothered to show up at the park, the smallest collection of the season. It was certainly ironic that, while these few folks were at the park, season-ticket holders for the Cubs were simultaneously receiving applications for playoff tickets in their mailboxes that afternoon.

Even fewer appeared the next day—2,217—with Hands going the distance for a 6–3 win over the Expos. It was all the team could do—for all the Mets needed was one more win and the division crown would be theirs. The final score from the East Coast arrived a few hours later, at 8:07 p.m. Chicago time. The Cubs, with their victory, were at least able to spare themselves the shame of being run out of the race in front of their home fans; the team would be hitting the road for three games in Pittsburgh before concluding the season with two contests against Hodges's club at Wrigley Field. The Mets were also leaving town after the day's game and, conversely, would be able to claim the prize in front of *their* supporters. In the final regular-season game at Shea Stadium on the year, Gentry induced Torre to ground into a double play in the ninth and shut out Carlton and the Cardinals on four hits by a 6-0 score. The offense was powered by two home runs off the bat of Clendenon for New York—a club obviously undaunted by the strikeout performance Carlton had placed on them a week prior.

Like a pack of scalded dogs, loads of Mets fans darted past security and onto the field to meet their heroes, champions of the East.

For the Chicago faithful, it was the end of the "flood of oppression in the 40 days and 40 nights that followed that happy day last month [August 14]," as Dozer scribbled, in reference to the date when the Cubs held their double-digit lead on the New York club. Those sunny June days seemed so long ago, Langford added, when Santo would jump and kick his heels to the delight of a throng of forty thousand at Wrigley, celebrating another Cub win. Now there was nothing, except another "next year" for the North Siders.

In the home locker room at Shea, shaving cream and champagne were being sprayed everywhere in joyous celebration, turning the room "into a combination revolving cocktail lounge, bath house, and barber shop."

Was Hodges surprised? "Yes, in a way," the Mets manager admitted. "I did think we'd have an improved ball club and perhaps win 85 games to put us a little over the .500 mark. But they've done more than I expected. We jelled sooner than I thought we would. I know that we have some fellows playing regularly that few people know. But these 'newcomers' have filled in."

Hodges continued: "Much has been said in sports—other than baseball—about team effort. I'll have to buy that within our Mets. This has been a great cooperative job." He then scooted out of his office, went home to Brooklyn, and took the phone off the hook to catch up on his rest.

And way out on the other side of the country, in Glendale, California, the vice president of the Mets couldn't hide his approval either. "They can play!" exclaimed Mr. Casey Stengel. "If they can still stay hot, they might win the whole thing."

When the sun rose on the East Coast the next morning, it revealed a mess at the Flushing Meadows ballpark that made it look as if a rock concert had taken place the preceding evening. "In one of the most incredible souvenir-snatching safaris in baseball history," the Associated Press reported, "Shea Stadium was stripped of everything that wasn't tacked down—and a number of things that were." No usually sacred spot was spared, as graffiti covered the center-field wall and even the American flag was stolen from atop its pole. It was estimated that as much as 1,500 square feet of sod was unearthed as take-home material as well. "They celebrated by breaking three wheels off the batting cage and stripping the netting off it," the unofficial police report in the newspaper continued. "They celebrated by tearing up the all-weather matting in the coaches' boxes behind first and third base. They celebrated by taking pieces of the scoreboard. And they celebrated by stealing home plate." The taking of home plate was particularly disturbing, the Mets' grounds crew had noted, for it would have required someone to vigorously dig it up from its footing.

The last road trip of the year for the Cubs found them playing against the Pirates in Forbes Field in Pittsburgh. It was expected to be the final time the Cubs would play in the old ballpark, with the presumed opening of the shining new downtown structure,

Three Rivers Stadium, set for April 1970 (but would actually be later). The two also-rans were looking for a little last-minute respect before closing up shop for the year, as were their managers. Durocher had decided that he would let Amalfitano run the club for most of the series; on the other side of the field, Alex Grammas had taken over the manager's position for Pittsburgh only a few hours before the first game in replacing the fired Larry Shepard. It turned out to be a spark for the Bucs, as the only Chicago victory in the three-game set was in the finale by Hands. The victory allowed Hands to join Jenkins in the 20-win club, the first time the Cubs had a pair of such pitchers in one year since 1935 (on that day—September 28—the Mets broke a team record with forty-two consecutive scoreless innings pitched, as Gentry, Ryan, and Ron Taylor posted another shutout, 2–0, over Philadelphia, for the team's 8th straight win).

The frustration that Fergie had built over the preceding weeks continued to grow. Little five-foot-five-inch Freddie "The Flea" Patek hit a four-hundred-foot, two-run homer in the opener (on what Becker frankly called "strictly a careless pitch"), the only runs of the game, as Jenkins finished the year with nearly as many losses as wins, 21-15—as did Holtzman, who in dropping the middle contest finished with a personal mark of 17-13. In that game Durocher relieved all of the regulars except for Kessinger. Spangler, who had not seen regular action in months, was placed in right field, alongside Gamble in center and Jimmie Hall in left. Hall, recently acquired from the Yankees, had nailed 33 homers for the Twins in his rookie year of 1963 but had not equaled such heights since. Durocher was hoping that Hall would provide a challenge for one of the outfield spots in 1970. The victory by Hands ended an eleven-game losing streak for Chicago in Forbes Field (dating back to July 1968) and allowed the Cubs one more victory in the old stadium. "I'd a lot rather my twentieth win today would have clinched first place," Hands reasoned, "but when you're out of the race, you do think of personal achievements."

The historic ballfield near Schenley Park would actually survive until June 1970, when it would be demolished to make more room for buildings on the University of Pittsburgh campus. Ironically, in over four thousand Major League games that were played at the site, Forbes Field never hosted a no-hit game. Part of the outfield wall would be left in place, and home plate would remain in its position, under glass, in the lobby of the new Posvar Hall. The wrecking of Forbes Field would not begin until midsummer of 1971, although a Christmas Eve fire in 1970 would prematurely raze part of the structure (and another fire would damage the park on July 17, 1971, just eleven days before its demolition).

With two days off before the Mets came to Chicago for the final two regular-season contests on October 1 and 2, there was plenty of time for the previously bold predictors to hide their faces, as Condon figured that the Mets would arrive in town with a menu for him of "crowburger, crow fricassee, crow pizza, crow stew, crow a la Gekas, and just plain crow for breakfast, lunch, and dinner." There was also plenty of time to watch the race in the National League's other division. On September 30 the Atlanta Braves brought postseason big league baseball to the South for the first time as they clinched the Western Division with a 3–2 win behind Phil Niekro—their tenth in a row—over Cincinnati in Fulton County Stadium. It was Niekro's 23rd win, which was second in the league to Seaver's 25 in a game that was saved by another knuckleballer, forty-six-year-old Hoyt Wilhelm, who had just been acquired from the California Angels. In an amazing new record, Niekro did not permit a lone sacrifice fly over the course of the season in his 284 innings pitched. "Have a cigar," Braves pitcher Cecil Upshaw blurted around the joyous locker room. "We just had a baby—it's called a pennant." Someone reminded Upshaw that, with the new divisional format, the pennant had yet to be won, as his Braves still needed to get past the new national darlings, the New York Mets, to get to the World Series. In the American League the Baltimore Orioles would face the Minnesota Twins for the same privilege.

The Mets wanted to leave Chicago proving in no uncertain terms who was the best team in the division. To that end Hodges employed six of his pitchers and twenty-one total players in a twelve-inning affair on October 1 that ended in another New York triumph—their 9th in a row, and 100th on the season—by a 6–5 score. Durocher himself used five pitchers, starting Holtzman, who went nine innings to bring a tie game into the extra frames. The Cubs were able to jump ahead in the first inning with two runs, which put an end to the shutout streak of the imposing New York moundsmen.

As the regular season came to a close the following day, anger raced through the seats at Wrigley Field. The hoodlums from New York, those seen as responsible for ripping away from the Cubs what was rightfully theirs, were leaving town to enjoy the playoffs. It was a constant, all-afternoon reminder of what could have been. "This is just like the last day of school," an unnamed Cub mentioned, ready for it to be over. "I can hardly wait for it to end."

Before it did end, the Bleacher Bums wanted their voices to be heard, have their presence felt, or—as the headline in the *Tribune* sports section the next day offered—"earn their nickname." With the Cubs batting in the bottom of the second inning, one of the bleacher inhabitants flung a smoke bomb toward Cleon Jones in left field, which smoldered a red disturbance into the short sky and momentarily caused a delay of the game. When the trouble seemed to subside, play continued. Santo put the Cubs on the board in the fourth as he walloped home run number 29 for the season. Banks also rose above all the mischief occurring in the ballpark and responded with his leadership. With the Cubs trailing in the sixth inning by a score of 5–3, he took a mighty swing and drove a long home run to left with two teammates aboard, the 497th of his glorious career, to give his team an instant 6–5 lead. One of the runners on base was Williams, who had reached on account of a batted ball that was misplayed by Garrett; moments earlier, a presumed "curse" was put on the New York third baseman, as a woman ran onto the field and gave the unsuspecting player a long hug and kiss.

Hands had started the game and was removed after the fifth, allowing him to reach another personal goal—300 innings pitched for the season. He was replaced by the promising rookie Decker, who held on to the lead provided by Banks through the seventh and eighth. By then, over one hundred of the official core of the left-field Bleacher Bums had abandoned their normal positions behind the outfield, marched defiantly through the right-field stands, scooted across the catwalk that connected the bleachers to the grandstand, and finally seeped their way into the many open box seats in the lower deck. With some carrying their own children, they belligerently pushed aside the few Andy Frain ushers who were doing their best, all the way to the bitter end, to keep order. When congregated behind the plate, the mob then divided into two attacking legions; one stormed on top of the visitors' dugout on the first base side, and the other did the same on top of the Cubs' hideaway. They marveled at each other from across the field, seeking attention from the other patrons who were disgusted with the display. When they felt that their sideshow had reached maximum appeal, they retreated toward their original seats in left field, trying to lap the entire ballpark. Amid all the distraction Banks popped up to end the eighth inning.

Minutes later, Chicago's 1969 baseball campaign ended with Boswell tapping a grounder to Banks at first as Decker covered the bag on the play, capping four scoreless innings he had pitched in gaining his first big league victory by a 6–5 margin. Immediately, the left-field bleachers poured forth, as a wave of Bums hung precariously for a moment from the top of the wall and then tumbled to the warning track. Edward Prell described the embarrassing scene: "One girl was taken by the nearby fire department ambulance to a hospital. It was feared she suffered a broken back. Another girl required attention for an ankle injury. . . . They [others from the bleachers] raced around the infield, sliding into bases ahead of an imaginary tag. There were self-appointed coaches at third and first, waving home phantom runners. . . . They were there a full hour before suddenly realizing that the season was over, at least for the Cubs." Either in mockery or complicity, the organist at Wrigley Field hummed out the tune "Happy Days Are Here Again" while the ugliness continued.

As Mets outfielder Swoboda witnessed the disgrace from the steps of the New York dugout, he philosophized under his breath: "Frustration and envy manifest themselves in strange ways." And as a few of the rabble-rousers were pointing angrily at Swoboda, he responded as politely as he could. "It's hard to admit you were not good enough, isn't it? You were good, but not good enough." Among the saddest witnesses was the Cubs' loyal broadcaster, Brickhouse, who had seen his share of baseball heartbreaks over the years. When the announcer's career finished at the outset of the 1980s, Steve Daley of the *Tribune* suggested that "Jack Brickhouse has seen more bad baseball than any person, living or dead."

The last ugly act by the group of fans at Wrigley Field most certainly affected the national view, for *Sports Illustrated* writer Robert Jones wrote: "Chicago appears in its true colors. A loser. Not even the Second City anymore, but the one city that has to blow it. For the stale smell of defeat lingers in every dark corner of Chicago, and not even the coarse, cold wind off Lake Michigan can scour it clean."

Posing as the more understanding father figure, Phil Wrigley had another perspective. "Naturally, I'm disappointed that the Cubs didn't win," he said in conclusion. "But by this time, I'm used to disappointments. I've had a lot of disappointments in forty or so years with the Cubs. I just don't let them get me down anymore." In considering the talented young players on his team, Mr. Wrigley added, "Nothing takes the place of experience, and sometimes it's costly to get."

§

The Mets' frantic charge to the Eastern Division title can be traced very easily on the calendar. On Wednesday, August 13, the team had just finished losing three straight games in embarrassing and bumbling fashion to the Astros in Houston. At that point they had fallen behind the Cardinals to third place, a full ten games behind the front-running Cubs. Beginning that following weekend, after a travel day and a rain day—and as the first guitar strums were being heard up the road from the hills of Woodstock—the New York club went 38-11 for the rest of the season. The Mets, who at the start of the season were 35-to-1 odds just to win the Eastern Division, finished up the final month of the schedule with a record of 24-8; the Cubs were 10-18 over the same stretch, the worst in baseball. Even more startling, the Cubs were in first place 155 days in 1969 (including 149 days by themselves), the longest hold on the top spot ever for a team not to win the championship.

"I admit we played horribly in the last few weeks," confessed Durocher. "We played some of the worst baseball I've seen in years. But that doesn't discount the fact that the Mets played like hell. If they had played like the Pirates or Cardinals, we would have been all right. But they got in a streak, and couldn't lose." In any event, Chicago would have to wait yet another year for a chance at a World Series birth.

"I honestly hope Ernie Banks gets in one," Al Kaline had said back in spring training before the 1969 season, after his Tigers had won the '68 series against the Cardinals. Kaline knew the feeling better than perhaps anyone, having spent sixteen years with Detroit before getting to play for a World Championship. "It tops everything. I know how it feels to keep waiting and hoping year after year that maybe you'll get into a World Series someday. All I can say is it's worth waiting for. You appreciate it more."

Fittingly, Banks responded with his optimistic smile: "Good things come to those who wait . . . and wait . . . and wait."

EPILOGUE

The Mets disposed of the Braves in a three-game sweep in the inaugural National League Championship Series, as did Baltimore with Minnesota in the American League (after leading the Twins to the AL West title, Billy Martin was fired by the club). Hodges had been to seven World Series as a player, and now he would battle for honors for the first time as a manager in his second year with the New York club. Despite their flourish at the end of the season, the Mets were still considered by many to be underdogs in the 1969 World Series against the powerful Orioles, winners of 109 games in the regular season, a figure that tied the Orioles with the 1961 Yankees for the most wins ever in a 162-game schedule. When the series was finished, however, the Mets had precisely equaled their final six weeks of the season by continuing to play .800 ball—they beat the Orioles in four out of five games, with Clendenon being named MVP in hitting .357 with three home runs. Swoboda and Al Weis chipped in with averages above .400, while Seaver, Koosman, and Gentry dominated off the hill. It was Agee who singlehandedly took over game three, however. He homered off Palmer in leading off the bottom of the first inning and later in the game robbed Paul Blair and Elrod Hendricks of extra-base hits with runners on base by making two spectacular catches in center field.

With the rule changes that entered the game in 1969 designed to benefit the hitters, those in the big league front offices got the cause and effect that they wanted: more of an offensive game, and a subsequent increase in attendance. And coupled with expansion, the more attractive product did in fact help attendance in the National League swell to a record 15,094,946. The Major Leagues saw nearly a tripling of the number of .300 hitters over 1968, but some pitchers benefited from the offensive deluge as well, for the fifteen pitchers who won 20 or more games in '69 were the most in one season for almost four decades.

Four days before the start of the World Series between the Mets and the Orioles, a trade was arranged that would change baseball forever—even though the trade would never be completed. Flood, McCarver, Joe Hoerner, and Byron Browne were sent from the Cardinals to the Phillies for Allen, Cookie Rojas, and Jerry Johnson. Three months later, however, Flood would sue Major League Baseball in federal court, claiming that the reserve clause—which held players legally bound to the club that signed them—violated national antitrust laws. Flood lost his case in August 1970, and the decision was upheld by the U.S. Circuit Court of Appeals in April 1971, but its discussion made enough of an impression for the players' union to take up the issue in the next round of contract negotiations with the owners. Flood sat out all of the 1970 season as a result of the case and would appear in only thirteen games for the Washington Senators in 1971 as his career came to an abrupt end. In 1972 the U.S. Supreme Court upheld the two lower courts' decisions; by 1976, however, Major League Baseball's exemption from federal antitrust laws would end, and the era of free agency and multimillion-dollar salaries soon followed.

The Cubs were represented in postseason accolades for 1969. Kessinger picked up his first Gold Glove at shortstop and finished second in the league in doubles with 38, while Jenkins edged Gibson by four in the strikeout chase with a final total of 273. Seaver won the Cy Young Award with his 25-7 record and 2.21 ERA. Santo fell three short in the RBI list to McCovey (126), as the Giants first baseman took home the National League's Most Valuable Player award with near-Triple Crown numbers (McCovey nipped Aaron by one for the home run lead with 45, while batting .320). In addition, McCovey's .656 slugging percentage was the highest ever for a National League first baseman. Pete Rose had beaten out a bunt for a base hit in his final at-bat in Atlanta, which also allowed him to beat out Clemente for the National League batting title by .006 of a point, with Rose finishing at .3477 and Clemente at .3471. Rose also won his first Gold Glove in the outfield, breaking up the Mays-Flood-Clemente triumvirate that had dominated the award since 1962 (Rose took Mays's spot for 1969). In other notable feats, Bobby Bonds of the Giants struck out a record 187 times, Jimmy Wynn of the Astros tied the National League record for walks (148), Wayne Granger of the Reds became the first pitcher to appear in 90 games in a season, and the Astros' pitchers struck out a record 1,221 batters.

What caused the Cubs' collapse? Dozer claimed it was a lack of depth, in addition to the strong charge of the Mets. "Expansion cut into everyone's bench this season," he reflected. "But in retrospect, something was needed to compensate, and the Mets had the most of the one commodity that is best able to cover up for the rest: a starting mound staff that was four and five deep." He also pointed out that Hundley, a leader on the field, was hurt on August 12 and didn't return until August 23—the period when the Mets began their fantastic run.

Gene Mauch, whose lowly Expos even applied some critical blows to the Cubs down the stretch, was asked to compare the Chicago club to his Phillies team that dropped the ball in the pennant chase of 1964. In noting similarities between the teams, he said that "there was a concentrated effort on the part of everybody on the team to relax." He was pointing out that the talented Cubs were tired and had simply been trying too hard. Along these lines, historian David Claerbaut noted some of the stark drop-offs in batting averages that occurred throughout September from some of the Cubs' more productive offensive sources:

	To 9/2	From 9/5 to 9/23
Beckert	.293	.203
Kessinger	.287	.148
Banks	.262	.156
Hundley	.273	.188

Some of the more revealing remarks about the fatigue factor came from Kessinger: "What I remember most is that we were a tired ball club. A lot of it had to do with playing day baseball in Wrigley Field. It's the sun that does it. I just feel when you play eight guys in the hot sun most everyday, you had to be a lot better than everyone else to win. We may have been better, but unfortunately we weren't a lot better. I just can't blame Leo; if he had come to me in August and asked, 'Do you want a day off?' I would have said no. I was playing great and felt good." Hundley agreed with him. "It's real easy to have hindsight, retrospect, and all that stuff," the catcher noted. "But if Leo had taken me out of that lineup in those days, he would have heard from me. You do what you have to do as a manager—you put your best guys out there."

Hands, however, disagreed. "I don't want to hear all the stuff about day games and the guys being tired," he asserted. "I don't buy that. I thought it was such an advantage to play in Chicago. We had so much pressure on us that we folded. It's that simple— we folded."

In consensus, most Cub players—past and present—have viewed playing day games at Wrigley as a general advantage, allowing them to have a normal dinner, a normal night's sleep, and breakfast with the family before heading to work, similar to a nine-to-five job—for, as Ernie Banks said, "By the time a player gets home after a night game, the dog is asleep. There is no relationship."

For the most part the Cub players appreciated the efforts that Durocher gave. "That man has shown me more class in the last three weeks than most managers show in an entire season," Hickman said as the season came to a close. "Leo kept an even keel, even during the stretch drive when the Mets overtook us." While not all of the players agreed with Leo's tactics, they knew that his heart was just as broken as anyone's. "We were an enthusiastic team going into the 1969 season," Fergie Jenkins once was quoted as writing. "We were a team with absolute faith in Durocher's leadership." Jenkins went on to be the Cubs' Opening Day starter for the next four years through 1973. When Jenkins achieved the 20-win plateau in 1969, he became the first Cub to do it three years in a row since Hippo Vaughn, who did likewise from 1917 to 1919. Furthermore, the 42 starts he made on the year was a Cub record, and the most by one man in the National League since 1903. "It wasn't managerial tactics that lost that pennant," added Holtzman. "Nobody can blame Leo."

"I think we were emotionally drained," Beckert offered. "None of us were accustomed to the crowds and the intensity. An awful lot of what happened was mental. The whole thing was a sobering experience, but we were young. I still believe that if we had won in 1969, we would have won again and again." And Santo said: "It has also become fashionable to say we were tired down the stretch. That isn't true. The adrenaline alone of being in a pennant race kept us going; I know it did for me."

On the bright side, attendance at Wrigley Field for the season totaled 1,674,993—the most ever, and a Wrigley record that would stand until the Cubs finally reached the playoffs in 1984, when the ballpark would see two million customers for the first time. So despite no postseason appearance, there was some extra money to go around in the front office. As thanks to Childers for "keeping the books" on their public appearances and endorsements down the stretch, the Cub players dug up home plate at Wrigley Field, autographed it, and gave it to him as a gift. Yes, things could have certainly been worse—such as in Cleveland, where the Indians finished in last place for the first time in over fifty years, surpassed in winning percentage even by the expansion Royals and Pilots.

Banks hit his 500th career homer at Wrigley Field on May 12, 1970, off Pat Jarvis of the Braves. Carty, the Braves' left-fielder, had been able to retrieve the ball after it had bounced back into the outfield, and he presented it to Ernie. Banks retired a year later as the Cubs' all-time leader in games played (2,528), at-bats (9,421), home runs (512), total bases (4,706), and extra-base hits (1,009). He would never get to play in a World Series, and as one of the greatest players of the 1950s and '60s, he would miss out on the big money enjoyed by even mediocre players in the decades to follow. Nothing, however, could put "Mr. Cub" in a bad mood. "The riches of the game are in the thrills," he said simply, "not the money."

Kessinger spent six more seasons with the Cubs, with All-Star appearances in '70, '71, '72, and '74; in 1976 he was traded to the Cardinals. Even though he was then playing three hundred miles to the south in a warmer climate, he noticed that the game-time temperature seemed milder in St. Louis. "If anything, I noticed that St. Louis was hotter than Chicago in the summertime, so playing night games there made a difference for me, a difference I really noticed," Kessinger recalled. In 1977 he returned to Chicago with the White Sox, and in 1979 he became their player-manager. The 664 at-bats that he recorded with the '69 Cubs is two shy of the all-time team record, set by Billy Herman in 1935.

Beckert's appearance in the 1969 All-Star Game would the first of four straight for the second baseman, who would join his keystone partner Kessinger for three more years with the honor. In 1971 Beckert wound up third in the National League batting race with a .342 average; in 1974 he was traded to San Diego for outfielder Jerry Morales.

With his 151 games caught, Hundley became the first man in Major League history to catch 150-plus games in three straight seasons. In all, Hundley had caught over 90 percent of the Cubs' games from 1966 to 1969—a feat matched in the twentieth century by only Gary Carter, Jim Sundberg, and Yogi Berra for their own teams.

Between 1961 and 1971 Santo had played an average of 159 games per season, continuing on as a steadying influence for the Cubs at third base. Back in 1958, at age eighteen, he had learned that he had diabetes, but he would not admit it publicly until making an announcement at "Ron Santo Day" at Wrigley Field on August 11, 1971. "I was always careful not to give myself a shot of insulin in the locker room in front of anybody," Santo said, discreet about his self-treatment all those years. "I always did it in private." Early in his career he tried to conquer the disease without insulin by using a strict diet; after losing twenty pounds in the months following his rookie year, however, he knew that regular injections would become a part of his life.

Santo's destination would soon change and would be an unseemly match. Sportswriters in Boston still comment on how unfitting Bruins hockey star Bobby Orr looked in a Blackhawks uniform at the end of his career, finally playing six games with the 'Hawks in the 1978–79 season. Much the same had been said by Chicago scribes about Santo, as five years earlier he had been dealt to the South Side for the 1974 season. The White Sox delivered pitcher Steve Stone and three Minor Leaguers to the Cubs in exchange for Santo, as the trade was consummated shortly before Christmas 1973. Just a few days earlier Santo had successfully vetoed a trade that would have sent him to the California Angels, as pressure for players' rights had increased since Flood made his statement four years earlier. "I felt that Chicago was Chicago, and that's why I chose the White Sox," Santo revealed years later about his regretted decision to go to the South Side. "But in all honesty, I wish I had just shut it down right then."

Williams' consecutive-games streak would end on September 4, 1970. In 1971 he became the first Cub player to ever make $100,000 in a season; in 1972 he led all of baseball with a .333 average. "I can't imagine where the Chicago Cubs would have been in the 1960s, particularly 1969, without Billy Williams," Santo once wrote. Williams would be sent to the Oakland A's in 1975. Williams said, "I'd like to close out my career playing for a winner, and I figure my best chance is with the Athletics."

Hickman had a breakout year in 1970, highlighted by driving in Pete Rose in the twelfth inning for the spectacular winning run for the National League in the All-Star Game. The ensuing play, in which Rose upended American League catcher Ray Fosse at home plate, became famous. After retiring in 1974 Hickman returned to his farm in Tennessee. He rose above the pressure of the pennant race and became the Cubs' best hitter in the stretch drive of 1969. In part because of Hickman's newfound consistency, the Cubs organization had all but given up on the promising young outfielders from the spring of 1969—Dunegan would get only one hit in ten at-bats in the Major Leagues (all ten coming in 1970), and McMath would get only two hits in fourteen trips in his career (all in '68).

Willie Smith played one more year with the Cubs in 1970 and then finished his career in Cincinnati the following season, still laughing and provided left-handed hits off the bench. Smith is believed by some historians to be the only black player in Major League history to appear in at least twenty games as a position player and twenty games as a pitcher.

Don Young came to bat only sixty-nine times after the "fly ball incident" in New York in July 1969. Nonetheless, after hitting .357 in spring training in 1970, he got ready to get on a bus to head north and meet the Cubs in Philadelphia, where the team would be starting the regular season. He was stopped by a coach, however, and told instead that he had been sold to Tacoma. "I never saw Leo Durocher," Young said of his release. "He never said a word to me about being cut." Fifteen months later Young was out of baseball, and he took a job cleaning golf clubs at Camelback Country Club in Scottsdale—a club that many of the Cubs players frequented.

"People should understand this about Don," said Rich Nye, when asked about Young's current whereabouts. "He has always been a loner. When he lived in an apartment in Chicago, over near Lake Shore Drive and Irving Park, he would go out at night alone wearing dark glasses and a wig. He would go down Division Street wearing that wig and sit in the corner of a bar so nobody would recognize him.

Nye continued: "So what if he screwed up one game for the Cubs? So what? So who cares? How many games did other guys blow that season?"

By 1976 Nye would be a graduate of the Veterinary School at the University of Illinois—and today, living in the western suburbs of Chicago, he is considered one of the foremost experts on exotic bird diseases in the world.

The trade for Popovich (which sent Dolf Phillips and Jack La-mabe to the Expos) proved valuable into the future, as he continued to be a steady role player—particularly on defense—for the Cubs through the 1973 season. Phillips played sparingly for the next three seasons with the Expos, and later for the Indians in Cleveland. After the trade was completed, Lamabe, who had already been with eight different clubs in his career, would never pitch in the Major Leagues again.

Even though Phil Wrigley wished to keep most of the team intact, he and Holland executed several moves aimed at putting the Cubs back in pennant contention in 1970. Gamble and Selma were traded to the Phillies after the season for Johnny Callison. Selma had fallen out of favor in Chicago with his late-season troubles, and Callison was seen as an immediate contributor in the outfield despite the potential that Gamble held. Hank Aguirre was released in 1970 but would be brought back in 1971—primarily to ease tensions that were growing between the players and Durocher, as Aguirre had always been viewed as a "calming influence" by Mr. Wrigley.

In the early seventies Jenkins was quoted as saying that he "belongs in his own class" in terms of quality pitching in the National League. "The players on the Cubs—Ron Santo, Billy Williams, Randy Hundley, and the rest—have put me in that class by scoring runs for me." Unfortunately, Jenkins's life would take a wrong turn on August 25, 1980. While he was reentering Canada, customs officers discovered a small amount of cocaine on Jenkins's person. Four months later a Canadian judge dismissed the charges, but Kuhn decided that Jenkins should pay $10,000 toward antidrug education programs and make public appearances about the dangers of drug abuse. Jenkins was traded to the Texas Rangers in 1974 for infielders Bill Madlock and Vic Harris, where he would pick up 115 wins in the American League with the Rangers and the Boston Red Sox before returning to the Cubs for two final years in 1982. Most ironically, he would retire one year short of the Cubs' playoff march in 1984.

Holtzman soon came at odds with Durocher and wished to be dealt to another team. "A lot of players talked about being traded, but none of them went to John Holland's office to make the request as I did. When I talked to John, that's exactly what I said. I went out and found happiness." Heading to Oakland (three years before Williams in 1972), Holtzman would go on to post the highest slugging average in the 1973 World Series (1.333) for any player—hitter or pitcher—as his A's defeated the Mets for the second of their three straight World Championships. He also won another World Series ring as a member of the Yankees in 1977. But he called 1969 his "most exciting season," even more than the pennant and World Championship years he had later.

Hands was traded with Decker to Minnesota after the 1972 season for fellow pitcher Dave LaRoche. Decker's departure schedule went into overdrive after a "defiant" (according to Leo) confrontation on the mound with Durocher in St. Louis.

The fury of the Bleacher Bums didn't end with the last game of 1969. After some of the group had leaped onto the field after the Cubs' home opener in 1970, the team installed a "basket" atop the wall, a piece of fencing that extended out forty-five degrees and was nearly three feet long. The basket caught balls for home runs but also kept fans off the field. It was reported later that the individuals who rushed the field that day in 1970 were not even baseball fans; rather, they were part of a group that had been making an antiwar demonstration downtown, had drank too much, and had carried their emotion over to the ballpark.

To include a friendly face, Herman Franks—the man who had recommended Durocher for the Cubs' managerial job to Phil Wrigley—rejoined Leo on the bench in 1970, replacing the ill Joe Becker. By the end of the 1971 season, however, things had grown bitter between Durocher and the team. On August 23— with the Cubs five games behind the front-running Pirates in the standings, and only eleven days after Santo was honored and had publicly revealed his diabetic condition—Durocher lit into the club in the locker room. His main target at first was pitcher Milt Pappas, who the previous day had given up a game-losing hit to the Astros on a bad pitch. According to Talley, what happened next was an escalation of frustrations, beginning with first baseman Joe Pepitone, who had been acquired from the Yankees the year before.

"Why are you always blaming people?" Pepitone shot at Durocher. "Pappas didn't mean to throw that pitch. Santo didn't want to be in a slump. All you ever do is criticize players. When I played for Ralph Houk, he stuck up for his players. That's why we won pennants. The players came first. But all you do is criticize."

After Leo waited, patiently but angrily sitting on a stool, he answered, "Are you through?" Santo recalled that Durocher's face was starting to get purple with rage.

Leo then stood up and hollered right in Pepitone's face. "What are you, a f_____ clubhouse lawyer???"

"I knew I should've kept my mouth shut," Pepitone responded.

"You had your say," Durocher went on, shaking with fury. "Now, I'll have mine." He started talking about the great team players that Williams and Beckert were, and then he sauntered over to Santo and looked him right in the face.

"Does Beckert ever miss batting practice?" he snapped at Ron.

"What are you trying to say, Leo? That I don't practice hitting?"

"Well, did you take hitting today?"

"No, and the reason is that I'm out of my slump and I want to keep the feeling I've got. That doesn't mean I don't want to improve myself. If I was hitting .300, Leo, you wouldn't give a s_____. But I'm hitting .260, so you're on my ass, and you use my roommate, who's hitting .300, as an example. That's a great example, Leo."

Then Durocher—uttering something he would regret for the rest of his life—said to Santo, "I didn't want to bring this up, Ronnie, but I'm going to say it. The only f_____ reason that you're having a 'Ron Santo Day' is that Billy and Ernie had one and you asked John Holland for one."

It was at that point when Santo forgot himself. He lunged for Durocher, but after a moment the other players were able to keep them apart. According to Holtzman, Santo had grabbed Durocher by the throat, "and Leo's tongue was sticking out six inches before we pulled Santo off him." After Durocher broke loose he went up to his office and Santo followed him—for he thought that Leo was seeking out Holland to falsely corroborate the story. Holland and Durocher made their way back downstairs to the dressing room, and Santo—standing there in front of the two men, with the whole team watching—demanded that Holland say in front of everyone that Durocher's assertion wasn't true. However, Holland would say that it wasn't directly the case, implying that Santo had indeed subtly asked for a "day" during contract negotiations. Santo once again denied it, believing that Holland was afraid of Durocher because of the favor that Leo held with Phil Wrigley.

Finally, on September 3, 1971, Wrigley attempted to bring closure to the matter by purchasing a page-length advertisement in the Chicago newspapers that displayed the following letter:

> This Is For Cubs Fans, and Anyone Else Who Is Interested
>
> It is no secret that in the closing days of a season that held great possibilities the Cub organization is at sixes and sevens and somebody has to do something. So, as head of the corporation, the responsibility falls on me . . .
>
> Many people seem to have forgotten, but I have not, that after many years of successful seasons, and five league pennants, the Cubs went into the doldrums and for a quarter of a century were perennial dwellers of the second division in spite of everything we could think of to try and do.
>
> We figured out what we thought was needed to make a lot of potential talent into a contending team, and we settled on Leo Durocher, who had the baseball knowledge to build a contender and win pennants, and also knowing he had always been a controversial figure . . . particularly with the press because he just

never was cut out to be a diplomat. He accepted the job at less than he was making because he considered it to be a challenge, and Leo thrives on challenges.

In his first year we ended in the cellar, but from then on came steadily up, knocking on the door for the top.

Each near miss has caused more and more criticism, and this year there has been a constant campaign to "Dump Durocher" that has even affected the players, but just as there has to be someone to make final decisions for the corporation, there has to be someone in charge on the field to make the final decisions on the spur of the moment, and right or wrong, that's it.

All this preamble is to say that after consultation with my baseball people, Leo is the team manager and the "Dump Durocher Clique" might as well give up. He is running the team, and if some of the players do not like it and lie down on the job, during the off-season we will see what we can do to find them happier homes.

Phil Wrigley, President
Chicago National League Ball Club, Inc.

P.S.—If only we could find more team players like Ernie Banks

"No matter how smoothly things were sailing, life with Leo Durocher was always an adventure," Beckert told writer Peter Golenbock. "Leo was the sort of man who didn't play by the rules. The players didn't mind, but his unconventional activities gave the newspaper men reams of paper to fill." But by 1972 Leo's act was getting old for many in Chicago, and Whitey Lockman replaced him as manager in the second half of the season. "You can't manage players today," Durocher said in later years. "They know it all. If you try to give them some advice, they'll show you that $300,000 paycheck and tell you to shove it."

Brickhouse wrapped up Durocher's tenure with the Cubs quite succinctly. "In those early days, he was a son of a bitch, but he was a sharp son of a bitch. But by the time he was finished in Chicago, he was just an old son of a bitch." Talley pointed out that "from their high point of 1969, a record of 84-52 on September 2, Durocher's immensely talented teams played exactly .500 ball (221-221) until he was fired in mid-1972." One reason theorized for their inability to compete into the 1970s was the appearance of Astroturf in many National League parks; it was argued that the Cubs did not have the youth or team speed to compete with other teams in the league that were being developed around the art of base running. The great Cub teams from the 1960s, for sure, were aging. "You lose your quickness," Banks said about the growing-old process for a ballplayer. "And you hear whispers, rumors. 'He used to make that play.' 'He used to hit that pitch.' Or maybe they don't say anything, but you can see it when they look at you. You can see it in their eyes."

Many of the personal shortcomings of some Major League baseball players were candidly addressed for the first time in 1970 with the release of the book *Ball Four*, written by pitcher Jim Bouton, which provided an exposé of the off-field vices of members of the New York Yankees, with whom Bouton had spent most of his career. Durocher, despite his disdain for the modern player and the Astrodome, accepted an offer by the Houston Astros to manage the team for the final thirty-one games of 1972 and for all of 1973. He finished '73 with yet another winning record—82-80—thus retiring with only five sub-.500 seasons in his lifetime, capping a managing career that stretched back to 1939.

§

At a reunion banquet for the 1969 Cubs in 1983, many of the players were present. The seventy-eight-year-old Durocher also attended, and it was obvious that he wanted to mend some fences. "Leo was at the microphone saying a lot of nice things about people," Hundley recalled, "and it was like he wanted to 'get things right' because he'd had a pretty good scare [after having open-heart surgery]. Then, out of the blue, he says, 'And, I want to apologize to Ron Santo. . . . I made a mistake, and I've been wanting to say so to Ronnie and his family for the longest time.'" The moving speech by Leo had most of the room in tears.

Beckert was one of the many players moved not only by Durocher's comments but by the sentiment of Cub followers in general. "Wrigley Field fans are extremely loyal, not only when a player wore the uniform but after we retired. It was like if you played for the Cubs you were all right in their minds forever."

Indeed, perpetual forgiveness and love are at the heart of a true Cub fan, and 1969, a year that closed one of the most tumultuous decades in the history of the United States, was one of the most heartbreaking seasons of all. The decade ended violently in December, when the Rolling Stones attempted to duplicate the Woodstock gala at their ill-fated concert at the Altamont Speedway in northern California. A riot broke out, and as fatal violence reigned over the stage and in the audience, the people of the nation were ready to leave the turmoil of the past ten years behind. For many Cub fans, 1969 was a season to forget as well.

But Gene Oliver asserted that it wasn't the loss of a pennant for which he would remember that strange year; rather, it would be marked in his mind by the joy of personal camaraderie among teammates that playing a long baseball season together brings forth.

"All of us have had setbacks in our lives. We were there for Fergie. We were there for Randy when he had his knee problems. He has an artificial hip. We stay in touch, we love each other, we're concerned for each other, and they are always there for you.

"*That* is the lasting legacy of the '69 Cubs."

Final 1969 Standings

National League

Eastern Division	W	L	Pct.	GB
New York	100	62	.617	—
Chicago	92	70	.568	8
Pittsburgh	88	74	.543	12
St. Louis	87	75	.537	13
Philadelphia	63	99	.389	37
Montreal	52	110	.321	48

Western Division	W	L	Pct.	GB
Atlanta	93	69	.574	—
San Francisco	90	72	.556	3
Cincinnati	89	73	.549	4
Los Angeles	85	77	.525	8
Houston	81	81	.500	12
San Diego	52	110	.321	41

American League

Eastern Division	W	L	Pct.	GB
Baltimore	109	53	.673	—
Detroit	90	72	.556	19
Boston	87	75	.537	22
Washington	86	76	.531	23
New York	80	81	.497	28.5
Cleveland	62	99	.385	46.5

Western Division	W	L	Pct.	GB
Minnesota	97	65	.599	—
Oakland	88	74	.543	9
California	71	91	.438	26
Kansas City	69	93	.426	28
Chicago	68	94	.420	29
Seattle	64	98	.395	33

Chicago Cubs' Final 1969 Batting Statistics

Player	AB	R	H	2B	3B	HR	RBI	BB	SO	Avg
Popovich	154	26	48	6	0	1	14	18	14	*.312*
Williams	642	103	*188*	33	*10*	21	95	59	70	.293
Beckert	543	69	158	22	1	1	37	24	24	.291
Santo	575	97	166	18	4	*29*	*123*	*96*	97	.289
Kessinger	*664*	*109*	181	*38*	6	4	53	61	70	.273
Hundley	522	67	133	15	1	18	64	61	90	.255
Banks	565	60	143	19	2	23	106	42	*101*	.253
Qualls	120	12	30	5	3	0	9	2	14	.250
Hairston	4	0	1	0	0	0	0	0	2	.250
Smith	195	21	48	9	1	9	25	25	49	.246
Young	272	36	65	12	3	6	27	38	74	.239
Hickman	338	38	80	11	2	21	54	47	74	.237
Gamble	71	6	16	1	1	1	5	10	12	.225
Phillips	49	5	11	3	1	0	1	16	15	.224
G. Oliver	27	0	6	3	0	0	0	1	9	.222
Spangler	213	23	45	8	1	4	23	21	16	.211
Hall	24	1	5	1	0	0	1	1	5	.208
Rudolph	34	7	7	1	0	1	6	6	11	.206
Jimenez	6	0	1	0	0	0	0	0	2	.167

Player	AB	R	H	2B	3B	HR	RBI	BB	SO	Avg
N. Oliver	44	15	7	3	0	1	4	1	10	.159
Heath	32	1	5	0	1	0	1	12	4	.156
Bladt	13	1	2	0	0	0	1	0	5	.154
Bobb	2	0	0	0	0	0	0	0	1	.000
C. Smith	2	0	0	0	0	0	0	0	0	.000

Note: Team leader is shown in italics.

Stolen bases: Kessinger, 11; Beckert, 6; Williams, 3; Hickman, 2; Hundley, 2; Qualls, 2; Santo, Young, Smith, and Phillips, 1

Miscellaneous Leaders

Hit by pitch—Banks, 7

Sacrifice hits—Hands, 11

Sacrifice flies—Santo, 14

Intentional walks—Williams, 15

Total bases—Williams, 304

On-base percentage—Santo, .384

Slugging percentage—Santo, .485

Grounded into double plays—Santo, 21

Chicago Cubs' Final 1969 Pitching Statistics

Player	W-L	ERA	Sv	G	GS	IP	H	BB	SO	HRA
Reynolds	0-1	2.45	0	2	2	7	11	7	4	1
Hands	20-14	*2.49*	0	41	41	300	268	73	181	21
Aguirre	1-0	2.60	1	41	0	45	45	12	19	2
Johnson	1-2	2.84	1	9	1	19	17	13	18	2
Decker	1-0	2.92	0	4	1	12	10	6	13	0
Colborn	1-0	3.07	0	6	2	15	15	9	4	2
Abernathy	4-3	3.16	3	56	0	85	75	42	55	8
Jenkins	*21-15*	3.21	1	43	*42*	*311*	*284*	71	*273*	27
Holtzman	17-13	3.58	0	39	39	261	248	*93*	176	18
Selma	10-8	3.63	1	36	25	169	137	72	161	13
Regan	12-6	3.70	*17*	*71*	0	112	120	35	56	6
Niekro	0-1	3.72	0	4	3	19	24	6	7	3
Lemonds	0-1	3.86	0	2	1	5	5	5	0	0
Distaso	0-0	3.86	0	2	0	5	6	1	1	0
Nye	3-5	5.11	3	34	5	69	72	21	39	13
Nottebart	1-1	7.00	0	16	0	18	28	7	8	2
Ross	0-0	13.50	0	2	1	2	1	2	2	0

Note: Team leader is shown in italic type.

Miscellaneous Leaders

Complete games—Jenkins, 23

Shutouts—Jenkins, 7

Games finished—Regan, 49

Intentional walks issued—Jenkins, 15

Wild pitches—Selma, 8

Balks—Jenkins, Selma, Abernathy, and Colborn, 1

Hit batsmen—Jenkins, 8

Batters faced—Jenkins, 1,275

BIBLIOGRAPHY

Bjarkman, P. (1991). *The baseball scrapbook.* New York: Dorset Press.

Buck, J. (1997). *That's a winner!* Champaign IL: Sagamore.

Chadwick, A. (1995). *Illustrated history of baseball.* Edison NJ: Chartwell.

Chieger, B. (1987). *The Cubbies.* New York: Atheneum.

Claerbaut, D. (2000). *Durocher's Cubs.* Dallas: Taylor.

Enright, J. (1975). *Baseball's great teams: Chicago Cubs.* New York: Macmillan.

Gentile, D. (2002). *The complete Chicago Cubs.* New York: Leventhal.

Gifford, B. (1981). *The neighborhood of baseball.* New York: E. P. Dutton.

Golenbeck, P. (1996). *Wrigleyville.* New York: St. Martin's.

Langford, J. (1980). *The game is never over.* South Bend IN: Icarus.

Muskat, C. (2001). *Banks to Sandberg to Grace.* Lincolnwood IL: Contemporary Books.

Myers, D. (1999). *Essential Cubs.* Lincolnwood IL: Contemporary Books.

Neft, D., & Cohen, D. (1995). *The sports encyclopedia: Baseball.* New York: St. Martin's.

Nemec, D. (1992). *Twentieth century baseball chronicle.* Montreal: Tormont.

Skipper, J. (2000). *Take me out to the Cubs game.* Jefferson NC: McFarland.

Talley, R. (1989). *The Cubs of '69.* New York: Contemporary Books.

Theodore, J. (2002). *Baseball's natural.* Carbondale: Southern Illinois University Press.

Wilbert, W., & Hageman, W. (1997). *Chicago Cubs: Seasons at the summit.* Champaign IL: Sagamore.

INDEX

Page numbers in italics refer to the illustrations following page 122.

University of Nebraska Press

Baseball from a different era:

STREAK
Joe DiMaggio and the Summer of '41
By Michael Seidel

"This book chronicles the intricate factual events of DiMaggio's achievement, and pays the best kind of proper respect, while providing the right sort of description. . . . [It] succeeds with a simple and honorable premise. The streak itself is such a good story, such an important event in our cultural history, that the day-by-day chronicle will shape a bare sequence into a wonderful drama with beginning, middle and end."—*The New York Review of Books.*

ISBN: 0-8032-9293-7; 978-0-8032-9293-2 (paper)

BASEBALL AND OTHER MATTERS IN 1941
By Robert W. Creamer

"[Creamer] recalls this momentous year in baseball and world history. He reprises Joe DiMaggio's 56-game hitting streak, Ted Williams's .406 batting average, Hank Greenberg and the draft, the furious Dodgers-Cardinals pennant fight, and the ensuing World Series. All this is portrayed against the looming U.S. entry into World War II."—*Library Journal.*

ISBN: 0-8032-6406-2; 978-0-8032-6406-9 (paper)

Order online at www.nebraskapress.unl.edu or call 1-800-755-1105.
Mention the code "BOFOX" to receive a 20% discount.